Tap 10 D

C000269800

PUBLISHED

Jane Austen: *Emma*   DAVID LODGE
Jane Austen: *'Northanger Abbey' & 'Persuasio[...]*
Jane Austen: *'Sense and Sensibility', 'Pride an[...]
Park'*   B.C. SOUTHAM
William Blake: *Songs of Innocence and Experie[...]*
Charlotte Brontë: *'Jane Eyre' & 'Villette'*   M[...]
Emily Brontë: *Wuthering Heights*   MIRIAM ALLOTT
Browning: *'Men and Women' & Other Poems*   J.R. WATSON
Bunyan: *The Pilgrim's Progress*   ROGER SHARROCK
Chaucer: *Canterbury Tales*   J.J. ANDERSON
Coleridge: *'The Ancient Mariner' & Other Poems*   ALUN R. JONES & WILLIAM
TYDEMAN
Congreve: *Comedies*   PATRICK LYONS
Conrad: *'Heart of Darkness', 'Nostromo' & 'Under Western Eyes'*   C.B. COX
Conrad: *The Secret Agent*   IAN WATT
Dickens: *Bleak House*   A.E. DYSON
Dickens: *'Hard Times', 'Great Expectations' & 'Our Mutual Friend'*   NORMAN
PAGE
Dickens: *'Dombey and Son' & 'Little Dorrit'*   ALAN SHELSTON
Donne: *Songs and Sonets*   JULIAN LOVELOCK
George Eliot: *Middlemarch*   PATRICK SWINDEN
George Eliot: *'The Mill on the Floss' & 'Silas Marner'*   R.P. DRAPER
T.S. Eliot: *Four Quartets*   BERNARD BERGONZI
T.S. Eliot: *'Prufrock', 'Gerontion', 'Ash Wednesday' & Other Shorter Poems*
B.C. SOUTHAM
T.S. Eliot: *The Waste Land*   C.B. COX & ARNOLD P. HINCHLIFFE
T.S. Eliot: *Plays*   ARNOLD P. HINCHLIFFE
Henry Fielding: *Tom Jones*   NEIL COMPTON
E.M. Forster: *A Passage to India*   MALCOLM BRADBURY
William Golding: *Novels 1954-64*   NORMAN PAGE
Hardy: *The Tragic Novels*   R.P. DRAPER
Hardy: *Poems*   JAMES GIBSON & TREVOR JOHNSON
Gerard Manley Hopkins:   MARGARET BOTTRALL
Henry James: *'Washington Square' & 'The Portrait of a Lady'*   ALAN SHELSTON
Jonson: *Volpone*   JONAS A. BARISH
Jonson: *'Every Man in his Humour' & 'The Alchemist'*   R.V. HOLDSWORTH
James Joyce: *'Dubliners' & 'A Portrait of the Artist as a Young Man'*   MORRIS
BEJA
Keats: *Odes*   G.S. FRASER
Keats: *Narrative Poems*   JOHN SPENCER HILL
D.H. Lawrence: *Sons and Lovers*   GAMINI SALGADO
D.H. Lawrence: *'The Rainbow' & 'Women in Love'*   COLIN CLARKE
Marlowe: *Doctor Faustus*   JOHN JUMP
Marlowe: *'Tamburlaine the Great', 'Edward the Second' & 'The Jew of
Malta'*   JOHN RUSSELL BROWN
Marvell: *Poems*   ARTHUR POLLARD
Milton: *Paradise Lost*   A.E. DYSON & JULIAN LOVELOCK
O'Casey: *'Juno and the Paycock', 'The Plough and the Stars' & 'The Shadow of a
Gunman'*   RONALD AYLING
John Osborne: *Look Back in Anger*   JOHN RUSSELL TAYLOR
Pinter: *'The Caretaker' & Other Plays*   MICHAEL SCOTT
Pope: *The Rape of the Lock*   JOHN DIXON HUNT

Shakespeare: *A Midsummer Night's Dream*  ANTONY PRICE
Shakespeare: *Antony and Cleopatra*  JOHN RUSSELL BROWN
Shakespeare: *Coriolanus*  B.A. BROCKMAN
Shakespeare: *Hamlet*  JOHN JUMP
Shakespeare: *Henry IV Parts I and II*  G.K. HUNTER
Shakespeare: *Henry V*  MICHAEL QUINN
Shakespeare: *Julius Caesar*  PETER URE
Shakespeare: *King Lear*  FRANK KERMODE
Shakespeare: *Macbeth*  JOHN WAIN
Shakespeare: *Measure for Measure*  G.K. STEAD
Shakespeare: *The Merchant of Venice*  JOHN WILDERS
Shakespeare: *'Much Ado About Nothing' & 'As You Like It'*  JOHN RUSSELL BROWN
Shakespeare: *Othello*  JOHN WAIN
Shakespeare: *Richard II*  NICHOLAS BROOKE
Shakespeare: *The Sonnets*  PETER JONES
Shakespeare: *The Tempest*  D.J. PALMER
Shakespeare: *Troilus and Cressida*  PRISCILLA MARTIN
Shakespeare: *Twelfth Night*  D.J. PALMER
Shakespeare: *The Winter's Tale*  KENNETH MUIR
Shelley: *Shorter Poems & Lyrics*  PATRICK SWINDEN
Spenser: *The Faerie Queene*  PETER BAYLEY
Sheridan: *Comedies*  PETER DAVISON
Swift: *Gulliver's Travels*  RICHARD GRAVIL
Tennyson: *In Memoriam*  JOHN DIXON HUNT
Thackeray: *Vanity Fair*  ARTHUR POLLARD
Trollope: *The Barsetshire Novels*  T. BAREHAM
Webster: *'The White Devil' & 'The Duchess of Malfi'*  R.V. HOLDSWORTH
Wilde: *Comedies*  WILLIAM TYDEMAN
Virginia Woolf: *To the Lighthouse*  MORIS BEJA
Wordsworth: *Lyrical Ballads*  ALUN R. JONES & WILLIAM TYDEMAN
Wordsworth: *The Prelude*  W.J. HARVEY & RICHARD GRAVIL
Yeats: *Poems 1919-35*  ELIZABETH CULLINGFORD
Yeats: *Last Poems*  JON STALLWORTHY

*Medieval English Drama*  PETER HAPPÉ
*Elizabethan Poetry: Lyrical & Narrative*  GERALD HAMMOND
*The Metaphysical Poets*  GERALD HAMMOND
*Poetry of the First World War*  DOMINIC HIBBERD
*Poetry Criticism and Practice: Developments since the Symbolists*  A.E. DYSON
*Thirties Poets: 'The Auden Group'*  RONALD CARTER
*Comedy: Developments in Criticism*  D.J. PALMER
*Drama Criticism: Developments since Ibsen*  ARNOLD P. HINCHLIFFE
*Tragedy: Developments in Criticism*  R.P. DRAPER
*The English Novel: Developments in Criticism since Henry James*  STEPHEN HAZELL
*The Language of Literature*  NORMAN PAGE
*The Pastoral Mode*  BRYAN LOUGHREY
*The Romantic Imagination*  JOHN SPENCER HILL

OTHER CASEBOOKS ARE IN PREPARATION

# Webster

## *The White Devil*
and
## *The Duchess of Malfi*

A CASEBOOK

EDITED BY

# R. V. HOLDSWORTH

MACMILLAN
EDUCATION

First published 1975
Third reprint 1987

Published by
MACMILLAN EDUCATION LTD
Houndmills, Basingstoke, Hampshire RG21 2XS
and London
Companies and representatives
throughout the world

Printed in Hong Kong

ISBN 0-333-15483-5

TO MY FRIEND PAUL CROSSLEY

# CONTENTS

*Acknowledgements* 7

*Note on Texts* 8

*General Editor's Preface* 9

*Introduction* 11

Part One: *Comment from 1617 to 1957*

HENRY FITZGEFFREY, p. 30 – ABRAHAM WRIGHT, p. 31 –
LEWIS THEOBALD, p. 31 – CHARLES LAMB, p. 33 – H. M.
(*Blackwood's Magazine*), p. 34 – WILLIAM HAZLITT, p. 35 –
ALEXANDER DYCE, p. 37 – CHARLES KINGSLEY, p. 39 –
A. C. SWINBURNE, p. 41 – JOHN ADDINGTON SYMONDS,
p. 43 – WILLIAM ARCHER, p. 45 – WILLIAM POEL, p. 48
– C. V. BOYER, p. 51 – RUPERT BROOKE, p. 53 – F. L.
LUCAS, p. 57 – UNA ELLIS-FERMOR, p. 58 – FREDSON
BOWERS, p. 62 – DAVID CECIL, p. 66 – TRAVIS BOGARD,
p. 69 – HERBERT J. MULLER, p. 71 – NORTHROP FRYE,
p. 72

Part Two: *Articles and Essays from 1949 to 1972*

IAN JACK: The Case of John Webster (1949) 76

JOHN RUSSELL BROWN: from Introduction to *The White
Devil* (1960) 84

JAMES L. CALDERWOOD: *The Duchess of Malfi:* Styles
of Ceremony (1962) 103

IRVING RIBNER: from *Jacobean Tragedy: The Quest for
Moral Order* (1962) 118

ROMA GILL: 'Quaintly Done': A Reading of *The White
Devil* (1966) 145

**6**                                              CONTENTS

PETER B. MURRAY: from *A Study of John Webster* (1969)  164

J. W. LEVER: from *The Tragedy of State* (1971)     190

RALPH BERRY: from *The Art of John Webster* (1972)   213

Part Three: *Reviews of Productions from 1919 to 1971*

ANON.: 'A play . . . preposterously incoherent' –
*The Duchess of Malfi* (1919)               224

E. M. FORSTER: *The White Devil* at Cambridge (1920)  226

ANON: 'A stylised masque of rhythmic movement' –
*The Duchess of Malfi* (1935)               229

ANON: 'A classic which time has tamed' – *The Duchess of
Malfi* (1945)                    230

STEPHEN POTTER: *The White Devil* at the Duchess
Theatre (1947)                  232

JACK LANDAU: Elizabethan Art in a Mickey Spillane
Setting (1955)                  233

KENNETH TYNAN: A Sea of Cold Sweat (1960)   235

BENEDICT NIGHTINGALE: Gaudy Monster (1969)   237

RONALD BRYDEN: Malfi as Madhouse (1971)   239

RONALD BRYDEN: Blood Soaked Circus (1971)   241

*Select Bibliography*                  245

*Notes on Contributors*            247

*Index*                      251

# ACKNOWLEDGEMENTS

The author and publishers wish to thank the following, who have given permission for the use of copyright material: The Clarendon Press, Oxford, for selection from Ralph Berry, *The Art of John Webster* © 1972 Oxford University Press; the author as controller of all the rights, for Travis Bogard, *The Tragic Satire of John Webster* (University of California Press, 1955); Routledge & Kegan Paul Ltd, for extract from C. V. Boyer, *The Villain as Hero in Elizabethan Tragedy* (1914); Princeton University Press, for selection from Fredson Thayer Bowers, *Elizabethan Revenge Tragedy 1587–1642*, pp. 177–80, 183, copyright 1940, 1968 Princeton University Press; John Russell Brown and Methuen & Co. Ltd, for extract from Introduction to *The White Devil* (1960); the *Observer*, for reviews by Ronald Bryden, 'Malfi as Madhouse' (24 January 1971) and 'Blood Soaked Circus' (18 July 1971); James L. Calderwood, for '*The Duchess of Malfi*: Styles of Ceremony', from *Essays in Criticism*, XII (1962); David Higham Associates Ltd, for extract from David Cecil, *Poets and Storytellers* (1949); Methuen & Co. Ltd, for extract from Una Ellis-Fermor, *The Jacobean Drama* (1936); the *New Statesman*, for E. M. Forster, review of *The White Devil* (20 March 1920); Princeton University Press, for selection from Northrop Frye, *Anatomy of Criticism*, pp. 219–20, © Princeton University Press 1957, 1971; Roma Gill, for 'Quaintly Done: A Reading of *The White Devil*', from *Essays and Studies*, XIX (1966); Ian Jack and Cambridge University Press, for extract from 'The Case of John Webster', *Scrutiny*, XVI (1949); J. W. Lever and Methuen & Co. Ltd, for extract from *The Tragedy of State* (1971); the Literary Estate of the late F. L. Lucas and Chatto & Windus, for extracts from Introduction to *The Complete Works of John Webster* (1927); Alfred A. Knopf Inc., for excerpt from Herbert J. Muller, *The Spirit of Tragedy* (1956); Peter B. Murray and Edicom, Netherlands, for excerpt from *A Study of John Webster* (Mouton & Cie, The Hague, 1969); the

*New Statesman*, for unsigned review of *The Duchess of Malfi* (19 January 1935), for Benedict Nightingale's review, 'Gaudy Monster' (21 November 1969), and for Stephen Potter's review of *The White Devil* (15 March 1947); Irving Ribner and Methuen & Co. Ltd, for excerpt from *Jacobean Tragedy: The Quest for Moral Order* (1962); the *Spectator*, for unsigned review of *The Duchess of Malfi* (29 November 1919); *The Times*, for unsigned review of *The Duchess of Malfi* (19 April 1945); the *Observer*, for Kenneth Tynan, 'A Sea of Cold Sweat' (18 December 1960).

The publishers have made every effort to trace the copyright-holders. If they have inadvertently overlooked any, they will be pleased to make appropriate arrangement at the first opportunity.

The editor is especially grateful to Miss Clare Colvin, Miss Linda Webley and Mr Grevel Lindop for their assistance and advice.

# NOTE ON TEXTS

Throughout this volume all quotations from and references to *The White Devil* and *The Duchess of Malfi* have been standardised in accordance with the editions by John Russell Brown in the 'Revels Plays' series (Methuen).

# GENERAL EDITOR'S PREFACE

Each of this series of Casebooks concerns either one well-known and influential work of literature or two or three closely linked works. The main section consists of critical readings, mostly modern, brought together from journals and books. A selection of reviews and comments by the author's contemporaries is also included, and sometimes comments from the author himself. The Editor's Introduction charts the reputation of the work from its first appearance until the present time.

The critical forum is a place of vigorous conflict and disagreement, but there is nothing in this to cause dismay. What is attested is the complexity of human experience and the richness of literature, not any chaos or relativity of taste. A critic is better seen, no doubt, as an explorer than as an 'authority', but explorers ought to be, and usually are, well equipped. The effect of good criticism is to convince us of what C. S. Lewis called 'the enormous extension of our being which we owe to authors'. A Casebook will be justified if it helps to promote the same end.

A single volume can represent no more than a small selection of critical opinions. Some critics have been excluded for reasons of space, and it is hoped that readers will follow up the further suggestions in the Select Bibliography. Other contributions have been severed from their original context, to which some readers may wish to return. Indeed, if they take a hint from the critics represented here, they certainly will.

A. E. DYSON

# INTRODUCTION

Of all the major English dramatists, John Webster has probably provoked the sharpest and most persistent controversy. Critics have not only differed in their interpretation of his plays; many have doubted his right to be treated as a serious artist at all. The following judgements, all expressed in terms of a comparison with Shakespeare, show how fundamental disagreement has been :

[Webster] tells the reader [in his preface to *The White Devil*] that he writes very slowly, which, from the extreme inaccuracy and poverty of a vast number of his lines, might not have been suspected. . . . It is somewhat curious to remark the manner in which Webster classes the dramatic writers of his age. It seems never to have occurred to him, that Shakespeare was quite of a different order of beings from them all. ('H. M.', 1818)

His White Devil and Duchess of Malfy, upon the whole perhaps, come the nearest to Shakespear of any thing we have upon record. (William Hazlitt, 1820)

Cynicism, disgust, and despair, were brief and casual refuges of his [Shakespeare's] spirit. These moods are the permanent and congenial dwelling-places of minds like Webster's . . . a type of mind so defective in sanity of vision, so poor in humour, so remote from healthful nature, so out of touch with genial reality. (William Watson, 1893)[1]

*The Duchess of Malfi* . . . the finest tragedy in the English language outside the works of Shakespeare. (Edmund Gosse, 1894)[2]

There are too many inconsistencies in Webster's plays; and whereas inconsistencies are readily passed over when – as in Shakespeare – they are subservient to some important dramatic purpose, in Webster there is no deeper purpose than to make our flesh creep. (Ian Jack, 1949)

Webster has created an integrated, important world through his
tragic action which makes his plays a profound comment on life.
Second only to Shakespeare . . . (Travis Bogard, 1955)

'Major dramatist' would be a risky assumption if opinion were
still in the state of ferment these contradictions imply, but during
the last twenty years or so a new phase in the history of Webster's
critical reception has begun, marked by general agreement on the
fact, if not on the qualities, of his greatness. The last full-blooded
attack was in 1955.[3] Since then, the staple charges of tawdry
showman and rickety plotter, specious moraliser and shameless
plagiarist, have been paraded more often to display their in-
adequacy than to damn the defendant, and critics have been
less concerned to sit in final judgement than to offer fresh evidence
of the complex artistry of Webster's two tragedies by close attention to their themes, structure, imagery, and presentation of
character. Even the once fashionable compromise verdict, that
the plays are poetical masterpieces but so lurid in their effects
and crude in construction as to be all but unactable, has – in
light of the succession of stimulating stage productions since the
war – been thrown out of court. 'After Shakespeare's plays,
Webster's tragedies, *The White Devil* and *The Duchess of Malfi*,
are more often produced today than the work of any other
Jacobean dramatist.'[4]

Webster's reception in his own century scarcely anticipates the
battleground he was to become in the nineteenth. Contemporary
comments are few but mostly favourable, and to judge from
the details of their publication and performance both *The White
Devil* and *The Duchess of Malfi* enjoyed reasonable if un-
remarkable literary and theatrical success. The former, acted and
published in 1612, had been reprinted three times by 1672 and
was revived several times on the stage between 1661 and 1671.
(Webster would have been gratified to learn that a sophisticated
Restoration audience and an intimate indoor playhouse would
thus replace the 'ignorant asses' and the theatre 'so open and
black' which he complains in his preface marred the play's first
production). *The Duchess* was acted in 1613 or 1614 and
published in 1623, 'with diuerse things Printed, that the length
of the Play would not beare in the Presentment'. As it achieved a

longer run of revivals (1661–1707) and four reprints (1661–
1708), during the second half of the century it was probably the
more popular play of the two.

Early comment is too brief and desultory to permit one to
generalise about contemporary interpretation of the plays.
Various remarks remain useful, though chiefly as pointers to
areas of controversy which were to attract later critics. Thus, the
disturbing moral ambiguity of the characters in *The White
Devil*, much discussed in the present century, is noticed by Samuel
Sheppard in a tribute to Webster in 1651 :

> *Brachianos* Ill,
> Murthering his Dutchesse, hath by thy rare skill
> Made him renown'd, *Flamineo* such another,
> The Devils darling, Murtherer of his brother :
> His part most strange, (given him to Act by thee)
> Doth gaine him Credit, and not Calumnie :
> *Vittoria Corombona*, that fam'd Whore,
> Desp'rate *Lodovico* weltring in his gore,
> Subtile *Francisco*, all of them shall bee
> Gaz'd at as Comets by Posteritie.[5]

Similarly, Abraham Wright's indictment of *The White Devil*, 'y<sup>e</sup>
lines are to much riming', which suggests a dissatisfaction with
Webster's fondness for moralising couplets or *sententiae*, has
been frequently re-echoed, as has his objection to the time-
scheme of *The Duchess*, 'y<sup>e</sup> buisinesse was 2 yeares a doeing',
pointing to the break between Acts II and III. (It should be
noted, however, that with Wright the cause of complaint is a
violation of the unity of time – 'y<sup>e</sup> lawes of y<sup>e</sup> scene' – whereas
with modern critics it is the strain on probability which results
from the delay imposed on Ferdinand's revenge.) One other
early set of remarks which anticipate a modern viewpoint is
Henry Fitzgeffrey's satirical cameo of Webster in the section of
his *Satyres* entitled 'Notes from Blackfriars'. 'Crabbed
*Websterio*/The *Play-wright, Cart-wright*', sour in temper,
clumsy, laborious, and obscurely learned in style, invites comparison with the rather less disparaging image of the dramatist
composed three centuries later by Rupert Brooke : an essentially

literary Webster, a great railer against man's moral deformities, not fully at home in the theatre, who 'worried his plays out with a grunting pertinacity', and whose dramaturgy is 'slow', 'old-fashioned', and even, at times, 'uncouth'.

During the eighteenth century Webster was largely ignored. This is not surprising : in an age whose art was characterised by a civilised restraint in the handling of emotion and a preoccupation with decorum – the subordination of every detail to the whole – in matters of style, a dramatist who favoured an apparently piecemeal method of writing and excelled in scenes of stark mental and physical anguish was not likely to please. The century is, indeed, noteworthy only for two attempts to adapt the plays in accordance with prevailing taste. In 1707 Nahum Tate, now chiefly remembered as the hack who revamped *King Lear* and gave it a happy ending, published a much simplified and sentimentalised version of *The White Devil* entitled *Injur'd Love: or, The Cruel Husband*. Tate's title indicates the effect of his revisions : the play becomes a trite domestic melodrama of type characters. Isabella's role as 'The injur'd Wife' is greatly expanded, Bracciano reduced to a lustful tyrant, Vittoria transformed to a paragon of virtue, faithful to Camillo and innocent to the end. The edifying purpose of the play Tate discloses in an epilogue; it is 'To fright Ill-natur'd Husbands to their Wits'. *Injur'd Love* was never performed, but Lewis Theobald's adaptation of *The Duchess, The Fatal Secret*, was staged twice at Covent Garden in 1733. Theobald's redaction is even more drastic than Tate's. He regularises the plot, beginning the action after the marriage (which entails the omission of the wooing scene), fixing the locale in Malfi throughout, removing the delay between Acts II and III (no children are born to Antonio and the Duchess), and omitting Julia. He also regularises the verse, so that, for example, the famous line –

Cover her face : mine eyes dazzle : she died young

– admired by a modern critic as 'a miniature three-act play',[6] becomes

Cover her Face; my Eyes begin to dazzle.

The painfulness of the play is relieved wherever possible. Thus, in the Duchess's lines of farewell —

> Go tell my brothers, when I am laid out,
> They then may feed in quiet

— the metaphor vividly condemns the predatory ferocity of her murderers, while the tone juxtaposes the qualities of submissiveness and pride which inform her own character. This is too near the bone for Theobald; he prefers something more innocuous and anaemic :

> When I am dead,
> My vengeful Brothers then may sleep in Quiet.

So, too, with the action : the dead man's hand (IV i 43) is replaced with Antonio's ring, the Duchess dies off-stage. This last change enables Theobald to draw the sting from Webster's conclusion, and indeed to transform the whole play. The Duchess is not, in fact, dead; the corpse Ferdinand saw was a wax effigy cleverly substituted by Bosola. She and Cariola are resurrected in the final scene, and reunited with Antonio, the young Duke of Malfi (a problematic figure in the original, mentioned at III iii 69–70 and thereafter ignored), and Delio. Some moralising sentiments from the Duchess round everything off :

> Some Tears are due
> T'appease th' offended Pow'rs. Had I not breath'd
> A guilty Vow, my Brothers had not bled
> Till Penitence shall erase that Debt of Sorrow,
> I must not yield to Joy

— though in case we should take this too seriously, Theobald adds an epilogue which expatiates on the theme that it is shameful for widows not to remarry. It is interesting to relate all these changes to Theobald's criticisms of Webster in his preface (extracted below).

The real point of departure for Webster criticism, however, is the early nineteenth century, and more precisely the year 1808, when Charles Lamb's highly popular and influential *Specimens of English Dramatic Poets Who Lived about the Time of Shakespeare* was first published (there were numerous reprints). Lamb's approach to the drama – and the same is true of other Romantic critics, for example Hazlitt, Dyce, and to some extent Swinburne – is easily faulted. The plays are treated as poems, not as theatrical documents shaped by the demands of an actual stage; characters are tacitly assumed to be 'real people', independent, abstractable personages with a history and a future, rather than interdependent elements in a larger, unified thematic design; scenes and passages ('beauties', 'gems') are singled out for praise, as if each play were a repository of separate 'specimens' and not appreciable or significant as an organised whole. This said, it is indisputable that students of Webster are heavily indebted to the pioneering work of Lamb and his successors. They strove to come to terms with the horror in the tragedies, refusing to set it down, as various later critics were to do, to the supposed barbarity of Elizabethan taste; and their portrait of Webster as a metaphysical searcher, darkly pondering the mysteries of identity, free-will, evil and death, is still – if with rather less Romantic colouring – widely accepted. Further, their interest in character occasions some stimulating insights : compare, for example, the different views of Lamb, Hazlitt and Dyce on Vittoria's behaviour in the trial scene. These contributions, aided, no doubt, by the eloquence and enthusiasm with which they were offered (often ecstatic, occasionally, in the case of Swinburne, hysterical) generated a renewed and lively interest in the plays.

Lively, but often far from benign. Writing in *Blackwood's Magazine* for 1818, 'H. M.' struck the opening blows in a campaign which was to mount in intensity as the century progressed. This critic seems at first to take his cue from Lamb, praising the 'strange and fantastic horrors' of the tragedies and finding 'some single scenes' of great power and 'much fine poetry'; but here the disjunctive approach serves only to increase the plays' vulnerability to attack. 'H. M.' is really concerned to take an overall view, and what he sees prompts him to damn the plays for structural incoherence and lack of moral purpose. *The Duchess* contains 'much low and worthless matter' (though somewhat redeemed by the Duchess's 'purity of feeling' and by 'the delineation of the mutual affection and attachment of the Duchess and her husband'); its final act is redundant. *The White Devil* fares worse: 'scene follows scene of shameless profligacy'; the action is 'disjointed', 'irregular, confused', and the characterisation correspondingly fitful. In neither play, in fact, 'is there a single character that clearly and boldly stands out before us, like a picture'.

These two (ultimately inseparable) issues, morality and structure, provide the main rallying points for Webster's detractors for the rest of the century. In 1856 Canon Charles Kingsley declared himself especially outraged by the plays' moral decadence, and indeed by that of virtually the entire Jacobean drama:

as the staple interest of the comedies is dirt, so the staple interest of the tragedies is crime. Revenge, hatred, villainy, incest, and murder upon murder are their constant themes, and (with the exception of Shakespeare, Ben Jonson in his earlier plays, and perhaps Massinger) they handle these horrors with little or no moral purpose, save that of exciting and amusing the audience.

Kingsley's bullying rhetoric does not work in his favour ('Are plays objectionable, the staple subject of which is adultery?') and his tone betrays all the pompous bluster of scandalised Victorian prudishness ('We should call him a madman who allowed his daughters or his servants to see such representations'); but the main fault of his argument is logical – the familiar one of identifying the descriptive facts of a story with a prescriptive effect. To assert that 'the whole story of *Vittoria Corrombona* is one of sin and horror', for example, and that the play is therefore 'disgusting *and injurious*' (my italics) is not good reasoning. The same confusion is evident, even more blatantly, in a similar announcement of moral outrage by William Watson later in the century. In this case, however, the view of the dramatist on which the outrage is based – a nihilist expressing a nightmare vision – is interesting in itself:

Life seems a chance medley, a rendezvous of bewildered phantoms; virtue in this disordered world is merely wasted, honour bears not issue, nobleness dies unto itself. . . . In reading him we lose for the time all sensation of an ordered governance of things. Life seems a treacherous phantasm or lawless dream, in which human shapes chase one another like fortuitous shadows across an insubstantial arena.[7]

Watson is unable to come to terms with his response to the plays : his next remark, 'The ethical infertility of such a presentation of the world is manifest enough', is an obvious escape-hatch. Surprisingly, neither 'H. M.' nor Kingsley nor Watson pauses to reflect that his extreme moral indignation might itself be proof of Webster's moral seriousness, and the soundness of his technique.

'H. M.' 's second charge, structural bungling, is elaborated by various critics after *The Duchess of Malfi*'s return to the stage in 1850. Reviewing this production, based on a much cut down and rearranged text prepared by R. H. Horne, G. H. Lewes declares the play 'a terrific melodrama, it delights the pit', but as a work of art 'feeble and foolish'. Horne has made the best of a bad job :

He has made it less tedious and less childish in its horrors, but the irredeemable mediocrity of its *dramatic* evolution of human passion is unmistakeable. . . . Instead of 'holding the mirror up to nature', this drama holds the mirror up to Madame Tussaud's and emulates her 'chamber of horrors'; but the 'worst remains behind', and that is the motiveless and false exhibition of human nature.

Lewes's test-case is the character of Ferdinand :

How ludicrously absurd is this Ferdinand – who has never given a hint of any love for his sister, any sorrow for her shame, any reluctance in perpetrating these cruelties – to be suddenly lachrymose and repentant as soon as she is dead ! This is not the work of a *dramatist*; it is clumsy ignorance. *The Duchess of Malfi* is a nightmare, not a tragedy.[8]

A further charge of lack of planning in *The Duchess* was brought by George Saintsbury in 1887 ('the fifth act is a kind of gratuitous appendix of horrors stuck on without art or reason'[9]), but the century's most sweeping indictment of Webster's powers of

organisation appeared five years later, in response to William
Poel's production of the play at the Opera Comique. Poel boldly
stressed the horror (he had luminous skeletons painted on the
backs of his madmen) and it was this aspect of *The Duchess* that
the dramatic critic William Archer, a vigorous supporter of the
realistic 'new drama' of Ibsen and Shaw, found most deeply
offensive. Accordingly, Archer takes issue with 'what may be
called the Lamb tradition with respect to the Elizabethan
dramatists', since it was this tradition which had enthused so
eloquently over Webster's mastery of the horrible. Lamb, Archer
claims, was blinded by Webster's poetic skills. The plays are
'robed in the regal purple of pure poetry', but the robes cover
some very ramshackle scaffolding. There are too many excrescences, motivation is muddled (Ferdinand is again the main
offender), and the horrors are '*un*skilfully moved . . . frigid,
mechanical, brutal', slipped in perfunctorily for immediate effect
to gratify the vulgar taste of 'a semi-barbarous public'. 'They
are not constructed plays, but loose-strung, go-as-you-please
romances in dialogue.'

Towards the end of the century these attacks begin to produce reactions from less hostile critics, who either come to
Webster's defence or seek to reconcile the growing conflict of
judgements. Some lines of defence are stronger than others.
Edmund Gosse, for example, merely side-steps the issue of the
theatrical viability of *The Duchess* by labelling the play 'pre-
eminently a tragic poem to be enjoyed in the study'.[10] J. A.
Symond's diametrically opposite argument concerning both
plays is more suggestive : 'it is probable that able representation
upon the public stage of an Elizabethan theatre gave them the
coherence, the animation, and the movement which a chamber-
student misses'. More successful than either view, as a rebuttal
of Archer's strictures, is William Poel's assertion that 'Webster's
poetry, of all others, cannot be separated from its dramatic
interest'. (Archer's approach, Poel is aware, dissociated poetry
from drama, language from action, far more damagingly than
Lamb's had done.)

Poel's argument has a surprisingly modern ring, but this is less
true of his second defensive tactic – his appeal to history to justify
the apparent sensationalism of Webster's plots and characters.

In his view, the plays testify to an ever-present 'desire for truth to Italian life'. The Cardinal is a 'typical Cardinal of the Italian Renaissance, a man experienced in simony, poisoning, and lust'; Bosola (whose character according to Archer has merely 'an appearance of subtlety . . . because it is full of contradictions') is 'a masterly study of the Italian "familiar", who is at the same time a humanist. . . . A man forced by his position to know all the inward resources of his own nature, passing or permanent, and conscious of the possibility of a very brief period of power and influence'. It is not easy to reconcile this approach with that favoured by modern critics, guided by Eliot's emphasis on the crucial value of convention to the Jacobean drama; namely, that Webster's characters are 'not, of course, real Italians',[11] that the world of his plays is 'the Inghilterra Italianata of the Elizabethan imagination',[12] a 'hot-house setting – a northerner's view of Italy',[13] 'little more than convenient shorthand to express a symbolic world where the individual is lost in the mazes of political activity'.[14] But it is possible to see both views as relevant, and even complementary. Recently J. W. Lever has combined them in some persuasive remarks:

It is usual to dismiss the Italian setting of the typical revenge play as a never-never-land of the northern imagination . . . but the choice of country and the political manners depicted have more solid foundations than the fancies of the English playwright. . . . The annals of the Italian age of despots describe tyrannies and atrocities, plots and revolts, which make the inventions of the Jacobeans rather pedestrian. . . . Nevertheless, the writers of revenge tragedy should not be judged by standards of historical realism. Their aim was not to recreate history, but to express contemporary anxieties by transposing them into a period and setting which had become the type and pattern of naked despotism. Had the Italy of the revenge play been pure fantasy, their serious concerns might have been swamped in the sensationalism of their fictions. Actually, the basis of truth underlying a stylized approach added to the play's validity.[15]

It is worth remembering that both plays dramatise actual events, and that in the case of *The White Devil* these had occurred as recently as the 1580s.

Poel excepted, most of Webster's critics around the turn of

the century prefer to assimilate earlier adverse comment into
their accounts of the dramatist than to reject it. Thus, J. A.
Symonds, while stressing Webster's 'acute sense for dramatic
situations' and his incisiveness as a psychologist of the criminal
mind – 'his firm grasp upon the essential qualities of diseased
and guilty human nature', displayed in 'brief lightning flashes of
acute self-revelation' – feels obliged to concede also that his
plots 'do not rightly hang together'; 'each part is etched with
equal effort after luminous effect upon a murky background;
and the whole play is a mosaic of these parts. It lacks the breadth
which comes from concentration on a master-motive.' Symonds's
comments represent the standard view of Webster until the
1930s. Not only the same ideas, but the same vocabulary and
metaphors regularly recur. Compare Barrett Wendell's estimate
of 1904:

His work is full of isolated situations, and phrases, and touches of
character which seem almost ultimate in their combined power and
truth to life. What makes the total effect of them bewildering is
that he could never quite fuse them into organic unity. His fragments of tragedy are like some unfinished mosaic needing a flash
of electric fire to melt their outlines into the intelligible unity of
painting.[16]

The conclusions of Rupert Brooke (1916) and F. L. Lucas
(1927) are substantially similar.

If opinions of Webster were in danger of ossifying, this
was averted by the appearance of T. S. Eliot's essays on Elizabethan and Jacobean literature during the twenties and thirties.
Eliot introduces a new approach, a set of fresh ideas, and draws
into the debate aspects of the plays hitherto neglected. Two essays
are of central importance: 'The Metaphysical Poets' (1921) and
'Four Elizabethan Dramatists' (1924). In the first, Eliot describes the unified sensibility of Donne and his fellow poets,
signalled by their 'recreation of thought into feeling', their habit
of 'amalgamating disparate experience', and their linguistic in-
ventiveness and energy. This last feature Eliot detects also in
certain playwrights:

This telescoping of images and multiplied associations is characteristic of the phrase of some of the dramatists of the period which Donne knew : not to mention Shakespeare, it is frequent in Middleton, Webster, and Tourneur, and is one of the sources of the vitality of their language.

Soon after Donne, 'a dissociation of sensibility set in, from which we have never recovered'. In the second essay, Eliot quarrels with both the Lamb–Swinburne approach to the drama and that adopted by Archer. Though superficially opposed, 'their assumptions are fundamentally the same'; 'each rests on the admission that poetry and drama are two separate things'. Archer is guilty of a further error. He 'confuses faults with conventions', whereas 'the Elizabethans committed faults and muddled their conventions' :

The great vice of English drama from Kyd to Galsworthy has been that its aim of realism was unlimited. . . . The weakness of Elizabethan drama is not its defect of realism, but its attempt at realism; not its conventions, but its lack of conventions. . . . The aim of the Elizabethans was to attain complete realism without surrendering any of the advantages which as artists they observed in unrealistic conventions.

Unfortunately, Eliot failed to apply these ideas to Webster in an extended study, possibly because for all his differences with Archer he shared some of his objections. In a radio talk on *The Duchess* in 1941 (permission to reprint this important piece has been refused) he points to the play's 'loosely constructed' plot and 'the inconsistency of people's behaviour', and declares that 'romance and sensation come first, truth to human nature only second'. Nevertheless, many of Eliot's comments, in this talk and elsewhere, are full of interest. Reviewing the Phoenix Society's production of *The Duchess* in 1919, for example, a disaster much ridiculed by the press, he offers a provocative − if not entirely convincing − argument against the standard view of the horror as decadent or absurd. The play will only succeed when actors and audience alike abandon a realistic approach for one which embraces the conventions which Webster was exploiting :

It was self-evident that the scene of the severed hand and the torture of the Duchess are extraordinarily fine on the stage . . . here, one felt, the actors were held in check by violent situations which nothing in their previous repertory could teach them to distort. Here the play itself got through, magnificently, unique. And the 'tragedy of blood' was vindicated. I mean that the horrors were vindicated; and as for the general assassination – that is merely a convention (as much a convention as the Nuntius or the Confidente). It is a convention which even a modern audience could be brought to accept, if the modern actor understood that a violent death need not invariably be represented as an important event. The only deaths which are essential to the tragedy are those of the Duchess and Cariola; the rest are a form of Exit. They no more indicate an appetite for blood than the Nuntius and the Confidente indicate a strong interest in the servant class.[17]

One might object here that Act v seems once again in danger of being declared redundant, but Eliot would have countered this with the assertion that *The Duchess* contains deeper sources of unity than the mechanics of its plot; a 'pattern below the level of "plot" and "character" '.[18] He returns to this idea several times in commenting on the plays :

Webster, in his greatest tragedies, has a kind of pity for *all* of his characters, an attitude towards good and bad alike which helps to unify the Webster pattern.[19]

Beaumont and Fletcher could also write single impressive scenes, but there is this difference, that there is throughout Webster's finest plays a consistency of tone, if not of plot and character, which indicates, I believe, a profounder moral and artistic seriousness.[20]

I have not yet spoken of one very important reason why Webster's plays, in spite of their loose construction and incoherences, give a greater effect of unity than those of his contemporaries, and that is his greater gift of language. . . . Webster has a natural overflowing gift for language, conspicuous in a time of rich and surprising phrase . . . the poet of whom he most reminds us, in this gift of startling phrase, is John Donne. In comparing Webster to a poet who was not a dramatist, I do not mean to suggest that the value of his writing lies in the poetry and *not* in the drama. His verse is essentially dramatic verse, written for the theatre by a man with

a very acute sense of the theatre. The later Elizabethan and the
Jacobean poetry is forever brooding upon the more terrifying aspect
of death, of the death of evil-doers, and of physical mortification
and corruption . . . but in Donne, and to a less degree in the plays
of Webster, there is a spiritual terror as well.[21]

One traces, in this last passage, the Webster of Eliot's poem
*Whispers of Immortality*, 'much possessed by death' and finding like Donne 'no substitute for sense,/To seize and clutch and
penetrate'; and also the Webster of 'Four Elizabethan Dramatists': 'a very great literary and dramatic genius directed toward
chaos'.

Eliot's ideas on the drama were immediately influential, but
many of the critics who applied them to Webster during the
thirties and forties were far from sharing his assessment of 'very
great'. Webster is repeatedly condemned as narrow, shallow, dis-
honest, confused. For M. C. Bradbrook the basic weakness is
the unhappy marriage of realism and convention to which
Eliot had drawn attention. Webster's characters are deliberately
'blurred', and though this makes for greater naturalism, it means
that 'there is no pattern of characters, nor . . . any structure of
themes'. This fault is compounded with another: Webster is
'concerned with perfection of detail rather than general design'.
One finds unity of a sort, but it is '*only* a unity of tone
and temper . . . dependent upon continuity of mood alone'.[22]
L. G. Salingar detects the same ruinous trend towards 'semi- or
pseudo-naturalism' ('Webster, unable to come to rest on any
attitude, from which to value his people, more stable or more
penetrating than a pose of stoical bravado, could not write
coherent drama at all'), and W. A. Edwards finds Webster's obsession with death 'too much an obsession to be made the basis of
any comprehensive vision of life'. Equally, Webster's concern with
chaos is less a theme than a symptom of his own moral sterility:
'events are not within control, nor are our human desires; let's
snatch what comes and clutch it, fight our way out of tight
corners, and meet the end without squealing'.[23] These various
lines of attack receive their most cogent expression in Ian Jack's
'The Case of John Webster', printed below. Jack's title is a
quotation from Eliot's 'Four Elizabethan Dramatists', but

instead of 'profound moral and artistic seriousness' this critic can discern only a 'peculiarly limited and deformed notion of ethics' and 'flagrant artistic insincerity'. The basic trouble was that 'no moral order represented itself to [Webster's] imagination as real'. In consequence, one finds 'no convincing statement of the *positive* aspect of Degree', merely an attempt 'to shore up chaos with a sentencious philosophy' irrelevant to the action of the plays. The dissociation of sensibility, in other words, has set in with a vengeance.

Since the forties Webster criticism has been concerned to rescue the plays from these charges by means of close analysis and comment, and this has led inevitably to questions of interpretation. For Lord David Cecil Webster is 'a stern moral teacher', whose characters are neatly ranged in moral divisions; 'there are the good and there are the bad'. The plays embody a Calvinistic theology, in which 'Divine justice' operates inexorably, linking sin with punishment and damnation. Travis Bogard stands at the opposite extreme. In his view the plays present life as a moral chaos, where there is 'no justice, no law, either of God or man'. Good and evil thus have no meaning, and the sole value which the plays assert is 'integrity of life', consistency to self, which transcends traditional moral categories. Both views seem excessively simplifying in the light of later criticism. Particularly that of Bogard, whose 'integrity of life' is hard to defend as 'a standard of positive *ethical* judgement'. (Bogard anyway misunderstands the phrase: in its context – *The Duchess*, v v 120 – it clearly means probity, moral truth.) Other commentators provide more persuasive replies to Jack's strictures. Both Ribner and Murray find firm moral coherence in the plays, the former in human, ethical terms, since Webster 'creates a world which is incompatible with any system of religious belief', while the latter points to the wealth of biblical allusions in *The Duchess* in support of a Christian interpretation. Both critics see *The White Devil* and *The Duchess* as offering respectively a negative and a positive statement of Webster's moral vision, and both locate in various patterns of imagery a deeper level on which this statement is made. Two other interpreters stress the plays' political and social concerns. Discussing *The Duchess*, J. L. Calderwood rebuts Jack's charge that the doctrine of Degree is not con-

vincingly endorsed (though few critics would accept the censure
of the Duchess's conduct to which this leads him), and J. W.
Lever, in one of the best essays on Webster yet produced,
identifies the plays' overriding theme as the corruption and
tyranny of political power and 'state'. The plays were thus
sharply topical to the Jacobeans, and remain so today. 'The
White Devil is not Vittoria Corombona but Renaissance Europe',
and the court of Amalfi offers an instructive parallel to the
scheming, factious, sycophantic, and sexually bizarre court of
James I.

One feature which the above studies share, to a greater or
lesser degree, is a tendency to regard Webster's characters as
types, vehicles of ideas, rather than psychologically complex and
developing individuals. (Calderwood's sensitive analysis of
Ferdinand is an exception.) Several critics show that this is less
than adequate. Webster's characters are often not 'all black or
all white but . . . grey' (Bowers), and in *The White Devil* this has
the effect of manipulating the audience into 'uncomfortable
moral positions' and 'setting our moral natures at variance with
our instinctive sympathies' (Roma Gill). Rather than inconsistent or blurred, Webster's characterisation is 'impressionistic', a
series of 'flashlight moments' (Brown); it is misguided to go in
search of 'a final "character" ' (Berry). This approach discloses
further themes in the plays : identity, role-playing, mixed
motives, and self-delusion. And these, in turn, suggest that
Webster the psychologist and Webster the moral thinker should
not be viewed apart.

Webster is no clumsy sensationalist, no mere deviser, to borrow
a jibe once made against Poe's tales, of complicated machines for
saying 'boo'. It is true that various theatre producers have been
eager to condescend to him in these terms. In 1919 Ferdinand died
standing on his head; in 1935 the scenes of horror in *The Duchess*
were softened so as to appear almost decorously charming, and
the masque of madmen was made *rhythmic* (precisely what it
should not be); in 1969 *The White Devil* was converted to something very close to a 'lewd, camp pantomime' (p. 238); in 1971
the Royal Court *Duchess* was set throughout in a lunatic asylum.
But this is a comment on the modern staging of Elizabethan plays
– reminiscent, at times, of the mutilations of Tate and Theobald

– not on Webster; and it is significant that the most successful productions in this century, those described by E. M. Forster, *The Times* (1945), Stephen Potter and Jack Landau, have also been the most responsibly conservative, at least in the sense of being the most reluctant to browbeat the audience with an 'interpretation'. ('At least' because the length of both plays makes cutting inevitable : in 1955, for example, the papal election was omitted from *The White Devil*, in 1947 the final appearance of Giovanni.) The last word might well be with Webster. At the end of *The White Devil* he appended a short tribute to the actors of his play, saluting them for their 'true imitation of life, without striving to make nature a monster'.

NOTES

1. *Excursions in Criticism* (London, 1893) pp. 13–18.
2. *The Jacobean Poets* (London, 1894) p. 166.
3. L. G. Salingar, 'Tourneur and the Tragedy of Revenge', in *The Age of Shakespeare, The Pelican Guide to English Literature,* ed. B. Ford, vol. 2 (Harmondsworth, 1955).
4. J. R. Mulryne, '*The White Devil* and *The Duchess of Malfi*', *Stratford-upon-Avon Studies I: Jacobean Theatre* (London, 1960) p. 201.
5. 'On Mr Webster's Most Excellent Tragedy Called the White Devil', *Epigrams Theological, Philosophical, and Romantick* (London, 1651) pp. 132–3.
6. F. W. Bateson, *A Guide to English Literature* (London, 1965) p. 62.
7. *Excursions in Criticism*, pp. 17–18.
8. '*The Duchess of Malfi*', *The Leader* (30 November 1850); reprinted in *Dramatic Essays*, ed. W. Archer and R. W. Lowe (London, 1896) pp. 119–20. Comparison with Madame Tussaud's occurred also to George Bernard Shaw, who jeered at 'the opacity that prevented Webster, the Tussaud laureate, from appreciating his own stupidity' (*Our Theatres in the Nineties*, 3 vols, London, 1932, III, 317), and see Ronald Bryden below, p. 243.
9. *A History of Elizabethan Literature* (London, 1887) p. 278.
10. *The Jacobean Poets*, p. 167.
11. T. S. Eliot, '*The Duchess of Malfy*', *The Listener*, XXVI (18 December 1941) 825.

12. E. M. Forster, below p. 226.

13. John Russell Brown, below p. 84.

14. G. K. Hunter, 'English Folly and Italian Vice : John Webster', in *John Webster: A Critical Anthology*, ed. G. K. and S. K. Hunter (Harmondsworth, 1969) p. 262.

15. *The Tragedy of State* (London, 1971) pp. 19–20. Poel is not alone in his call for 'historical imagination' (below, p. 51) : in 1877 Hippolyte Taine praised Webster for 'depicting the shameless depravity and refined ferocity of Italian manners' (*A History of English Literature*, trans. H. Van Laune, 3 vols, Edinburgh, 1871, 1, 252) and fifty years later F. L. Lucas remarked : 'Again and again critics have cried out at characters like Flamineo or Francisco or Ferdinand with the refrain of Judge Brack – "But people do not do such things". And to that the only answer is "They did"; and the only remedy, to read the history of the time' (*The Complete Works of John Webster*, 4 vols, London, 1927, 1, 92).

16. *The Temper of the Seventeenth Century in England* (New York, 1904) p. 88. It is interesting to note that Wendell taught T. S. Eliot at Harvard.

17. 'The Duchess of Malfi* at the Lyric : and Poetic Drama', *Art and Letters*, III (1920) 37–8.

18. Eliot's preface to G. Wilson Knight, *The Wheel of Fire* (London, 1930) p. xviii.

19. 'Cyril Tourneur' (1930), in *Selected Essays*, 3rd ed. (London, 1951) p. 184.

20. 'The Duchess of Malfy', 826.

21. Ibid.

22. M. C. Bradbrook, *Themes and Conventions of Elizabethan Tragedy* (Cambridge, 1935) pp. 186–212.

23. L. G. Salingar, 'The Revenger's Tragedy and the Morality Tradition', *Scrutiny*, VI (1937–8) 421–2; W. A. Edwards, 'John Webster', *Scrutiny*, II (1933–4) 21–3.

# PART ONE

# Comment from
# 1617 to 1957

## Henry Fitzgeffrey

But h'st ! with him[1] Crabbed *Websterio*
The *Play-wright, Cart-wright* : whether? either ! *ho* –
No further. Looke as yee'd bee look't into :
Sit as ye woo'd be *Read* : *Lord* ! who woo'd know him?
Was euer man so mangl'd with a *Poem*?
See how he drawes his mouth awry of late,
How he scrubs : wrings his wrists : scratches his Pate.
A *Midwife* ! helpe ! By his *Braines coitus,*
Some *Centaure* strange : some huge *Bucephalus,*
Or *Pallas* (sure) ingendred in his *Braine,*
Strike *Vulcan* with thy hammer once againe.

This is the *Crittick* that (of all the rest)
I'de not haue view mee, yet I feare him least,
Heer's not a word *cursiuely* I haue *Writ,*
But hee'l *Industriously* examine it,
And in some 12. monthes hence (or there *about*)
Set in a shamefull sheete, my errors *out.*
But what care I, it *will* be so obscure,
That none shall vnderstand him (I am sure).

SOURCE : *Satyres: and Satyricall Epigrams: with Certaine
Obseruations at Black-Fryers* (1617).

### NOTE

1. [An affected singing-man.]

# Abraham Wright

## Vittoria Corombona

But an indifferent play to reade, but for y^e presentments I beeleeue good. y^e lines are to much riming. in y^e last act y^e scene beetweene Lodouico, Gasparo, and y^e Duke where they come to bee [con]fessors to y^e Duke, and afterward strangling him, threatning to him in his eare just at his departing all hell torments, is good; and soe is all y^e 5 act for y^e maine plot.

## y^e Tragedy of y^e dut: of Malfy

A good play, especially for y^e plot at y^e latter end, otherwaies plaine. in his language hee vses a little too much of scripture, as in y^e first act speaking of a captaine full of wounds hee saies hee lied like y^e children of Israel [sic] among tents. and in y^e same act their liuers are more spotted then Labans sheepe. And w^ch is against y^e lawes of y^e scene y^e buisinesse was 2 yeares a doeing as may bee perceaud by y^e beeginning of y^e 3^d act; where Antonio has 3 children by y^e dutchess, when in y^e first [sic] act hee had but one.

SOURCE: 'Excerpta quaedam per A. W. Adolescentem',
British Museum Add MS. 22608 (*c.* 1640).

# Lewis Theobald

Tho' I call'd it *The Fatal Secret*, I had no Intentions of disguising from the Publick, that, (as my Friend has confess'd for me in the Prologue) *John Webster* had preceded me, above a hundred Years ago, in the same Story. I have retain'd the Names of the Characters in his *Dutchess of* MALFY, adopted as much of his Tale as I conceiv'd for my Purpose, and as much of his Writing

as I could turn to Account without giving into too obsolete a
Diction. If I have borrow'd his Matter freely, I have taken it up
on fair and open Credit; and, hope, I have repaid the Principal
with Interest. I have no where spared my self, out of Indolence;
but have often engrafted his Thoughts and Language, because I
was conscious I could not so well supply them from my own Fund.
When I first read his Scenes, I found something singularly engaging in the Passions, a mixture of the Masculine, and the
Tender, which induced me to think of modernizing them:
Another Motive was, that the Distress of the Tale is not
fictitious, but founded on authentick Record. And, besides the
Historians of *Naples, Goulart* has given this Story a place in his
*Histoires Admirables de notre Temps*; the *Italian, Bandello,* has
work'd it up into one of his Novels; and *Lopez de Vega*
brought it upon the *Spanish* Stage, under the Title of *El Mayor-
domo de la Duquesa de Amalfi....*

As to our Countryman *Webster,* tho' I am to confess Obliga-
tions to him, I am not oblig'd to be blind to all his Faults. He is
not without his Incidents of *Horror,* almost as extravagant as
those of the *Spaniard.* He had a strong and impetuous Genius,
but withal a most wild, and indigested one: He sometimes conceived nobly, but did not always express with Clearness; and
if he now and then soars handsomly, he as often rises into the
Region of Bombast: his Conceptions were so eccentric, that we
are not to wonder why we cannot ever trace him. As for Rules,
he either knew them not, or thought them too servile a Restraint.
Hence it is, that he skips over *Years* and *Kingdoms* with an
equal Liberty. (It must be confess'd, the *Unities* were very
sparingly observ'd at the Time in which he wrote; however, when
any Poet travels so fast, that the Imagination of his Spectators
cannot keep pace with him, Probability is put quite out of
Breath.) Nor has he been less licentious in another Respect: He
makes mention of *Galilæo* and *Tasso,* neither of whom were born
till near half a Century after the Dutchess of *Malfy* was murther'd.

SOURCE: Preface to *The Fatal Secret* (1735).

# Charles Lamb

## I *The White Devil*, III ii

This White Devil of Italy sets off a bad cause so speciously, and pleads with such an innocence-resembling boldness, that we seem to see that matchless beauty of her face which inspires such gay confidence into her; and are ready to expect, when she has done her pleadings, that her very judges, her accusers, the grave ambassadors who sit as spectators, and all the court, will rise and make proffer to defend her in spite of the utmost conviction of her guilt.

## II *The Duchess of Malfi*, IV ii

All the several parts of the dreadful apparatus with which the Duchesses death is ushered in are not more remote from the conceptions of ordinary vengeance, than the strange character of suffering which they seem to bring upon their victim, is beyond the imagination of ordinary poets. As they are not like inflictions *of this life*, so her language seems *not of this world*. She has lived among horrors till she is become 'native and endowed unto that element'. She speaks the dialect of despair, her tongue has a smatch of Tartarus and the souls in bale. – What are 'Luke's iron crown', the brazen bull of Perillus, Procrustes' bed, to the waxen images which counterfeit death, to the wild masque of madmen, the tomb-maker, the bell-man, the living person's dirge, the mortification by degrees! To move a horror skilfully, to touch a soul to the quick, to lay upon fear as much as it can bear, to wean and weary a life till it is ready to drop and then step in with mortal instruments to take its last forfeit: this only a Webster can do. Writers of an inferior genius may 'upon horror's head horrors accumulate' but they cannot do this. They mistake quantity for quality, they 'terrify babes with painted devils' but they know not how a soul is capable of being moved; their terrors want dignity, their affrightments are without decorum.

SOURCE : *Specimens of English Dramatic Poets* (1808).

# H. M. (Blackwood's Magazine)

Some single scenes are to be found in his [Webster's] works inferior in power of passion to nothing in the whole range of the drama. He was a man of a truly original genius, and seems to have felt strong pleasure in the strange and fantastic horrors that rose up from the dark abyss of his imagination. The vices and the crimes which he delights to paint, all partake of an extravagance which, nevertheless, makes them impressive and terrible, and in the retribution and the punishment there is a character of corresponding wildness. But our sympathies, suddenly awakened, are allowed as suddenly to subside. There is nothing of what Wordsworth calls 'a mighty stream of tendency' in the events of his dramas, nor, in our opinion, is there a single character that clearly and boldly stands out before us, like a picture. . . .

## 1 *The White Devil*

This play is so disjointed in its action, – the incidents are so capricious and so involved, – and there is, throughout, such a mixture of the horrible and the absurd – the comic and the tragic – the pathetic and the ludicrous, – that we find it impossible, within our narrow limits, to give any thing like a complete and consistent analysis of it. . . .

There is great power in this drama, and even much fine poetry, – but, on the whole, it shocks rather than agitates, and the passion is rather painful than tragical. There are, in truth, some scenes that altogether revolt and disgust, – and mean, abandoned, and unprincipled characters occupy too much of our attention throughout the action of the play. There is but little imagination breathed over the passions of the prime agents, who exhibit themselves in the bare deformity of evil, – and scene follows scene of shameless profligacy, unredeemed either by great intellectual energy, or occasional burstings of moral sensibilities. The character of Vittoria Corombona, on which the chief interest of the drama depends, is sketched with great spirit and freedom, – but though true enough to nature, and startling by her beauty and her wickedness, we feel that she is not fit to be the chief personage of tragedy, which ought ever to deal only with great passions, and with great events. There is, however, a sort of fascination about this 'White Devil of Venice', which accompanies her to the fatal end of her career, – and something like admiration towards her is awakened by the dauntless intrepidity of her death.

> I will not in my death shed one base tear,
> Or if look pale, for want of blood, not fear.
>
> (v vi 225–6)

## 11 *The Duchess of Malfi*

. . . Hitherto [Acts i–iii] the chief merit of this drama has consisted in the delineation of the mutual affection and attachment of the Duchess and her husband. We have purposely taken no notice of much low and worthless matter in the subordinate conduct of the play. There is something very touching and true to nature in the warmth, yet purity of feeling, that characterises the Duchess; and knowing from the first that fiendish machinations are directed against her peace, we all along consider her as an interesting object, upon whom there is destined to fall some fatal calamity. In the fourth act the tragedy assumes a very different complexion, and the peculiar genius of Webster bursts forth into a strange, wild, fantastic, and terrible grandeur. . . .
The interest of the drama . . . expires with the fourth act.

SOURCE: 'Analytical Essays on the Early English Dramatists', *Blackwood's Edinburgh Magazine* (1818).

# *William Hazlitt*

Webster would, I think, be a greater dramatic genius than Deckar, if he had the same originality; and perhaps is so, even

without it. His White Devil and Duchess of Malfy, upon the
whole perhaps, come the nearest to Shakespear of any thing we
have upon record; the only drawback to them, the only shade of
imputation that can be thrown upon them, 'by which they lose
.some colour', is, that they are too like Shakespear, and often
direct imitations of him, both in general conception and individual expression. So far, there is nobody else whom it would
be either so difficult or so desirable to imitate; but it would have
been still better, if all his characters had been entirely his own,
had stood out as much from others, resting only on their own
naked merits. . . .

## i *The White Devil*

This White Devil (as she is called) is made fair as the leprosy,
dazzling as the lightning. She is dressed like a bride in her wrongs
and her revenge. In the trial-scene in particular, her sudden indignant answers to the questions that are asked her, startle the
hearers. Nothing can be imagined finer than the whole conduct
and conception of this scene, than her scorn of her accusers and
of herself. The sincerity of her sense of guilt triumphs over the
hypocrisy of their affected and official contempt for it. . . .

In the closing scene with her cold-blooded assassins, Lodovico
and Gasparo, she speaks daggers, and might almost be supposed
to exorcise the murdering fiend out of these true devils. Every
word probes to the quick. The whole scene is the sublime of contempt and indifference.

## ii *The Duchess of Malfi*

The Duchess of Malfy is not, in my judgment, quite so spirited
or effectual a performance as the White Devil. But it is distinguished by the same kind of beauties, clad in the same terrors.
I do not know but the occasional strokes of passion are even profounder and more Shakespearian; but the story is more laboured,
and the horror is accumulated to an overpowering and insup-
portable height. However appalling to the imagination and
finely done, the scenes of the madhouse to which the Duchess is
condemned with a view to unsettle her reason, and the interview

between her and her brother, where he gives her the supposed
dead hand of her husband, exceed, to my thinking, the just
bounds of poetry and of tragedy. At least, the merit is of a kind,
which, however great, we wish to be rare. A series of such ex-
hibitions obtruded upon the senses or the imagination must tend
to stupefy and harden, rather than to exalt the fancy or meliorate
the heart.

SOURCE: *Lectures Chiefly on the Dramatic Literature of the
Age of Elizabeth* (1820).

## *Alexander Dyce*

### 1 *The White Devil*, III ii

Brachiano's throwing down his gown for his seat, and then, with
impatient ostentation, leaving it behind him on his departure;
the pleader's Latin exordium; the jesting interruption of the
culprit; the overbearing intemperance of the Cardinal; the
prompt and unconquerable spirit of Vittoria – altogether unite
in impressing the mind with a picture as strong and diversified
as any which could be received from an actual transaction of
real life. Mr. Lamb . . . speaks of the 'innocence-resembling boldness of Vittoria'. For my own part, I admire the dexterity with
which Webster has discriminated between that simple confidence
in their own integrity which characterises the innocent under the
imputation of any great offence, and that forced and practised
presence of mind which the hardened criminal may bring to the
place of accusation. Vittoria stands before her judges, alive to all
the terrors of her situation, relying on the quickness of her wit,
conscious of the influence of her beauty, and not without a certain
sense of protection, in case of extreme need, from the interposi-
tion of Brachiano. She surprises by the readiness of her replies,
but never, in a single instance, has the author ascribed to her one
word which was likely to have fallen from an innocent person
under similar circumstances. Vittoria is undaunted, but it is by
effort. Her intrepidity has none of the calmness which naturally

attends the person who knows that his own plain tale can set
down his adversary; but it is the high-wrought and exaggerated
boldness of a resolute spirit, – a determination to outface facts, to
brave the evidence she cannot refute, and to act the martyr
though convicted as a culprit.

## 11 *The Duchess of Malfi*

The passion of the Dutchess for Antonio, a subject most difficult
to treat, is managed with infinite delicacy; and, in a situation of
great peril for the author, she condescends without being de-
graded, and declares the affection with which her dependant
had inspired her without losing anything of dignity and respect.
Her attachment is justified by the excellence of its object; and
she seems only to exercise the privilege of exalted rank in raising
merit from obscurity. We sympathise from the first moment in
the loves of the Dutchess and Antonio, as we would in a long
standing domestic affection, and we mourn the more over the
misery that attends them because we feel that happiness was the
natural and legitimate fruit of so pure and rational an attachment. It is the wedded friendship of middle life transplanted to
cheer the cold and glittering solitude of a court : it flourishes but
for a short space in that unaccustomed sphere, and is then
violently rooted out. . . .

The sufferings and death of the imprisoned Dutchess haunt
the mind like painful realities. . . . In such scenes Webster was
on his own ground. His imagination had a fond familiarity with
objects of awe and fear. The silence of the sepulchre, the
sculptures of marble monuments, the knolling of church bells,
the cearments of the corpse, the yew that roots itself in dead men's
graves, are the illustrations that most readily present themselves
to his imagination.

Source : Introduction to *The Works of John Webster* (1830).

# Charles Kingsley

The whole story of *Vittoria Corrombona* is one of sin and horror. The subject-matter of the play is altogether made up of the fiercest and the basest passions. But the play is not a study of those passions, from which we may gain a great insight into human nature. There is no trace (nor is there, again, in the *Duchess of Malfi*,) of that development of human souls for good or evil, which is Shakspeare's especial power. . . . [Webster's] characters, be they old or young, come on the stage ready-made, full grown, and stereotyped; and, therefore, in general, they are not characters at all, but mere passions or humours in a human form. Now and then he essays to draw a character; but it is analytically, by description, not dramatically, by letting the man exhibit himself in action; and in the *Duchess of Malfi*, he falls into the great mistake of telling, by Antonio's mouth, more about the Duke and the Cardinal than he afterwards makes them act. . . . But the truth is, that the study of human nature is not Webster's aim. He has to arouse terror and pity, not thought, and he does it in his own way, by blood and fury, madmen and screech-owls, not without a rugged power.

There are scenes of his, certainly, like that of Vittoria's trial, which have been praised for their delineation of character; but it is one thing to solve the problem, which Shakspeare has so handled in *Lear*, and *Othello*, and *Richard the Third*, 'given a mixed character, to shew how he may become criminal', and to solve Webster's 'given a ready-made criminal, to shew what he will say and do on a certain occasion'. To us the knowledge of character shewn in Vittoria's trial-scene, is not an insight into Vittoria's especial heart and brain, but a general acquaintance with the conduct of all bold bad women when brought to bay. . . . Webster's confest master-scene lies simply in intimate acquaintance with vicious nature in general. We will say no more on this matter, save to ask, *cui bono*? – was the art of which this was the highest manifestation likely to be of much use to mankind, much less to excuse its palpably disgusting and injurious accompaniments?

The *Duchess of Malfi* is certainly in a purer and loftier strain;

but in spite of the praise which has been lavished on her, we must take the liberty to doubt whether the poor Duchess is 'a person' at all. General goodness and beauty, intense though pure affection for a man below her in rank, and a will to carry out her purpose at all hazards, are not enough to distinguish her from thousands of other women; but Webster has no such purpose. What he was thinking and writing of was, not truth, but effect; not the Duchess, but her story; not her brothers, but their rage; not Antonio, her major-domo and husband, but his good and bad fortunes; and thus he has made Antonio merely insipid, the brothers merely unnatural, and the Duchess, (in the critical moment of the play,) merely forward. . . .

The prison-scenes between the Duchess and her tormentors are painful enough, if to give pain be a dramatic virtue; and she appears in them really noble, and might have appeared far more so, had Webster taken half as much pains with her as he has with the madmen, ruffians, ghosts, and screech-owls in which his heart really delights. The only character really worked out, so as to live and grow under his hand, is Bosola, who, of course, is the villain of the piece, and being a rough fabric, is easily manu-factured with rough tools. . . .

And so the play ends; as does *Vittoria Corrombona*, with half-a-dozen murders *coram populo*, raving madness, despair, bed-lam and the shambles; putting the reader marvellously in mind of that well-known old book of the same era, Reynolds' *God's Revenge against the Crying Sins of Murther and Adultery*, in which, with all due pious horror, and bombastic sermonizing, the national appetite for abominations is duly fed with some fifty unreadable Spanish histories, French histories, Italian histories, and so forth, one or two of which, of course, are known to have furnished subjects for the play-wrights of the day.

SOURCE: 'Plays and Puritans', *North British Review* (1856).

# A. C. Swinburne

Fate, irreversible and inscrutable, is the only force of which we feel the impact, of which we trace the sign, in the upshot of *Othello* or *King Lear*. The last step into the darkness remained to be taken by 'the most tragic' of all English poets. With Shakespeare . . . righteousness itself seems subject and subordinate to the masterdom of fate : but fate itself, in the tragic world of Webster, seems merely the servant or the synonym of chance. The two chief agents in his two great tragedies pass away – the phrase was perhaps unconsciously repeated – 'in a mist' : perplexed, indomitable, defiant of hope and fear; bitter and sceptical and bloody in penitence or impenitence alike. And the mist which encompasses the departing spirits of these moody and mocking men of blood seems equally to involve the lives of their chastisers and their victims. Blind accident and blundering mishap – 'such a mistake,' says one of the criminals, 'as I have often seen in a play' – are the steersmen of their fortunes and the doomsmen of their deeds. . . .

In all the vast and voluminous records of critical error there can be discovered no falsehood more foolish or more flagrant than the vulgar tradition which represents this high-souled and gentle-hearted poet as one morbidly fascinated by a fantastic attraction towards the 'violent delights' of horror and the nervous or sensational excitements of criminal detail : nor can there be conceived a more perverse or futile misapprehension than that which represents John Webster as one whose instinct led him by some obscure and oblique propensity to darken the darkness of southern crime or vice by an infusion of northern seriousness, of introspective cynicism and reflective intensity in wrongdoing, into the easy levity and infantile simplicity of spontaneous wickedness which distinguished the moral and social corruption of renascent Italy. . . . The great if not incomparable power displayed in Webster's delineation of such criminals as Flamineo and Bosola – Bonapartes in the bud, Napoleons in a nutshell, Cæsars who have missed their Rubicon and collapse into the likeness of a Catiline – is a sign rather of his noble English loathing for the traditions associated with such names as

Cæsar and Medici and Borgia, Catiline and Iscariot and Napoleon, than of any sympathetic interest in such incarnations of historic crime. Flamineo especially, the ardent pimp, the enthusiastic pandar, who prostitutes his sister and assassinates his brother with such earnest and single-hearted devotion to his own straightforward self-interest, has in him a sublime fervour of rascality. . . .

The doctrine or the motive of chance (whichever we may prefer to call it) is seen in its fullest workings and felt in its furthest bearings by the student of Webster's masterpiece. The fifth act of *The Duchess of Malfy* has been assailed on the very ground which it should have been evident to a thoughtful and capable reader that the writer must have intended to take up – on the ground that the whole upshot of the story is dominated by sheer chance, arranged by mere error, and guided by pure accident. No formal scheme or religious principle of retribution would have been so strangely or so thoroughly in keeping with the whole scheme and principle of the tragedy. After the overwhelming terrors and the overpowering beauties of that unique and marvellous fourth act in which the genius of this poet spreads its fullest and its darkest wing for the longest and the strongest of its flights, it could not but be that the subsequent action and passion of the drama should appear by comparison unimpressive or ineffectual; but all the effect or impression possible of attainment under the inevitable burden of this difficulty is achieved by natural and simple and straightforward means. If Webster has not made the part of Antonio dramatically striking and attractive – as he probably found it impossible to do – he has at least bestowed on the fugitive and unconscious widower of his murdered heroine a pensive and manly grace of deliberate resignation which is not without pathetic as well as poetical effect. In the beautiful and well-known scene where the echo from his wife's unknown and new-made grave seems to respond to his meditative mockery and forewarn him of his impending death, Webster has given such reality and seriousness to an old commonplace of contemporary fancy or previous fashion in poetry that we are fain to forget the fantastic side of the conception and see only the tragic aspect of its meaning. A weightier objection than any which can be brought against the conduct of the play might be suggested to the minds of some readers – and these, perhaps, not too exacting or too captious readers – by the sudden vehemence of transformation which in the great preceding act seems to fall like fire from heaven upon the two chief criminals who figure on the stage of murder. It seems rather a miraculous retribution, a judicial violation of the laws of nature, than a reasonably credible consequence or evolution of those laws, which strikes Ferdinand with madness and Bosola with repentance. But the whole atmosphere of the action is so charged with thunder that this double and simultaneous shock of moral electricity rather thrills us with admiration and faith than chills us with repulsion or distrust.

SOURCE: 'John Webster', *Nineteenth Century* (1886).

## *John Addington Symonds*

It is just this power of blending tenderness and pity with the exhibition of acute moral anguish by which Webster is so superior to Tourneur as a dramatist.

Both playwrights have this point in common, that their forte lies not in the construction of plots, or in the creation of characters, so much as in an acute sense for dramatic situations. Their plots are involved and stippled in with slender touches; they lack breadth, and do not rightly hang together. Their characters, though forcibly conceived, tend to monotony, and move mechanically. But when it is needful to develop a poignant, a passionate, or a delicate situation, Tourneur and Webster show themselves to be masters of their art. They find inevitable words, the right utterance, not indeed always for their specific personages, but for generic humanity, under the *peine forte et dure* of intense emotional pressure. Webster, being the larger, nobler, deeper in his touch on nature, offers a greater variety of situations which reveal the struggles of the human soul with sin and fate. He is also better able to sustain these situations at a high dramatic pitch – as in the scene of Vittoria before her judges, and the scene of the Duchess of Malfi's assassination. . . .

Webster, of the two, alone shows lyrical faculty. His three dirges are of exquisite melodic rhythm, in a rich low minor key; much of his blank verse has the ring of music; and even his prose suggests the colour of song by its cadence. . . .

Owing to condensation of thought and compression of language, his plays offer considerable difficulties to readers who approach them for the first time. So many fantastic incidents are crowded into a single action, and the dialogue is burdened with so much profoundly studied matter, that the general impression is apt to be blurred. We rise from the perusal of his Italian tragedies with a deep sense of the poet's power and personality, an ineffaceable recollection of one or two resplendent scenes, and a clear conception of the leading characters. Meanwhile the outlines of the fable, the structure of the drama as a complete work of art, seem to elude our grasp. The persons, who have played their part upon the stage of our imagination, stand apart from one another, like figures in a *tableau vivant*. *Appius and Virginia*, indeed, proves that Webster understood the value of a simple plot, and that he was able to work one out with conscientious firmness. But in *Vittoria Corombona* and *The Duchess of Malfi*, each part is etched with equal effort after luminous effect upon a murky background; and the whole play is a mosaic of these parts. It lacks the breadth which comes from concentration on a master-motive. We feel that the author had a certain depth of tone and intricacy of design in view, combining sensational effect and sententious pregnancy of diction in works of laboured art. . . . Each word and trait of character has been studied for a particular effect. Brief lightning flashes of acute self-revelation illuminate the midnight darkness of the lost souls he has painted. Flowers of the purest and most human pathos, like Giovanni de Medici's dialogue with his uncle in *Vittoria Corombona*, bloom by the charnel-house on which the poet's fancy loved to dwell. . . . [Webster] was drawn to comprehend and reproduce abnormal elements of spiritual anguish. The materials with which he builds are sought for in the ruined places of abandoned lives, in the agonies of madness and despair, in the sarcasms of reckless atheism, in slow tortures, griefs beyond endurance, the tempests of sin-haunted conscience, the spasms of fratricidal bloodshed, the deaths of frantic hope-deserted criminals. He is often melodramatic in the means employed to bring these psychological elements of tragedy home to our imagination. He makes free use of poisoned engines, daggers, pistols, disguised murderers, masques, and nightmares. Yet his firm grasp upon the essential qualities of diseased and guilty human nature, his profound pity for the innocent who suffer shipwreck in the storm of evil passions not their own, save him, even at his gloomiest and wildest, from the unrealities and extravagances into which less potent artists – Tourneur, for example – blundered.

SOURCE: Introduction to *The Best Plays of Webster and Tourneur* (1888).

## William Archer

When we find a playwright, in his two acknowledged master-pieces, drenching the stage with blood even beyond the wont of his contemporaries[1] and searching out every possible circumstance of horror – ghosts, maniacs, severed limbs and all the paraphernalia of the charnel-house and the tomb – with no conceivable purpose except just to make our flesh creep, may we not reasonably, or rather must we not inevitably, conclude that he either revelled in 'violent delights' for their own sake, or wantonly pandered to the popular craving for them? If Mr. Swinburne accepts the latter alternative – if he would have us believe that the Webster of the tragedies is not the real Webster, but is playing an abhorrent part to ingratiate himself with the groundlings – then his position, if essentially unprovable, is also essentially incontrovertible. But I do not understand him to claim any private or peculiar knowledge of Webster's character. What he evidently means is that in these very tragedies we can discover the 'high soul' and 'gentle heart' of the poet, and can *not* discover any morbid predilection for 'violent delights'. High-souled and gentle-hearted he may possibly have been, for these qualities are not incompatible with the vilest perversions of the æsthetic sense. But to argue that Webster's æsthetic sense was refined and unperverted is simply to maintain that black is white and blood is rose-water.

'Webster does not deal in horrors for their own sake,' we shall be told, 'but uses them as means towards the illustration and development of character.' Could he not have made clear to us the resignation and fortitude of the Duchess of Malfi without the ghastly mummery of the dead hand and the waxen corpses? To argue so is simply to deny his competence as a dramatic poet. I have heard it maintained that the strangling of Cariola is designed to contrast with that of the Duchess – the frantic terror of the maid serving to throw into relief the noble courage of the mistress. Who can fail to perceive that if this were the intention, the death of the maid must of necessity precede that of the mistress, not follow it, as in Webster? When an effect of contrast is aimed at, and the things to be contrasted cannot be displayed simultaneously, it is clear that the minor, so to speak, must precede the major, the darkness must precede the light. In other words, the background must be established before the object to be set off against it is presented to our view. And then the children! What effect of contrast is served by the massacre of the innocents? Whose character does it serve to illustrate? Their mother is already dead, or at least unconscious. Had they been strangled before her eyes, the effect would have been one of unparalleled, intolerable brutality, but it would, in a certain sense, have been dramatic. As it is, their death is a mere mechanical piling of horror upon horror. It does not even throw any new light on the character of Bosola; when a man is wading in blood, an inch more or less is no great matter. What it *does* throw light upon is the character, or at least the æsthetic sense, of Webster and his public. It is perfectly evident that Elizabethan audiences found a pleasurable excitement in the crude fact of seeing little children strangled on the stage,[2] and that Webster, to say the least of it, had no insuperable objection to gratifying that taste.

Far be it from me to argue that horror has not its legitimate place in literature and in drama. 'To move a horror skilfully, to touch a soul to the quick' is neither an easy nor an unworthy task. My point is that in *The Duchess of Malfi* (and, to a minor degree, in *The White Devil*) the horrors are *un*skilfully moved – that they are frigid, mechanical, brutal. Literature is literature in virtue of the brain-power implicit in it; and there goes no more brain power to the invention of these massacres and monstrosities than to carving a turnip lantern and sticking it on a pole.

Much might be said, if space permitted, of Webster's construction and characterisation. Of dramatic concentration he did not dream. Though a younger man than Shakespeare (whose 'right happy and copious industry' he bracketted with that of Dekker and Heywood, and postponed to the loftier talents of Chapman and Jonson), he reverted to a stage of literary development which Shakespeare had outgrown. In *The White Devil* and *The Duchess of Malfi* the differentiation between romance and drama is still incomplete. They are not constructed plays, but loose-strung, go-as-you-please romances in dialogue. The motivation of *The Duchess of Malfi* is haphazard even beyond the Elizabethan average. No motive is assigned in the earlier part of the play for the brothers' virulent and almost monomaniac opposition to the very idea of their sister's marrying again. After her death, Ferdinand explains that he hoped to gain 'an infinite mass of treasure' if she died unmarried, and we may presume that the Cardinal would have been his co-heir. But this motive, even when we are tardily informed of it, does not account for his epilepsies of rage and cruelty, which seem sometimes to spring from regard for the family honour, sometimes from a rabid enthusiasm for 'virtue' in the abstract. Perhaps we are to understand that all these motives combine to work up his fundamentally cruel nature to the pitch of madness. This might be a plausible theory enough, but we arrive at it only by conjecture. It is more than doubtful whether Webster himself was at all clear as to his characters' motives. In Ferdinand he provided Burbage with an effective part in which to 'tear a cat', and neither author, actor, nor audience inquired too curiously into the reasons for his frenzies and his cruelties. A similar difficulty confronts us in Bosola. This 'moody and mocking man of blood' is certainly not, like the ordinary melodramatic villain, hewn all of one piece.

There is an appearance of subtlety in his character because it is full of contradictions. But there is no difficulty in making a character inconsistent; the task of the artist is to show an underlying harmony between the apparently conflicting attributes. . . . On the whole, I am inclined to think that Webster came very near to creating in Bosola one of the most complex and most human villains in drama, a living illustration of that age-old but ever new paradox: *Video meliora, proboque; deteriora sequor.*[3] But the fatal lack of clearness ruins everything. . . .

The gist of my argument, so far as it can be summed up in a phrase, is this: that Webster was not, in the special sense of the word, a great dramatist, but was a great poet who wrote haphazard dramatic or melodramatic romances for an eagerly receptive but semi-barbarous public.

SOURCE: 'Webster, Lamb, and Swinburne', *New Review*
(1893).

NOTES

1. There are eight violent deaths in *The White Devil* and ten in *The Duchess of Malfi.*
2. [In fact the children are probably strangled off-stage; cf. J. R. Brown's note to IV ii 239.]
3. ['I see and approve better things, yet follow worse.']

## William Poel

In a recent number of the *New Review* Mr Archer expresses the opinion that Webster was 'a great poet who wrote haphazard dramatic romances for an eagerly receptive but semi-barbarous public'; and adds that Webster excels in verbal felicity, and in writing beautiful language which is full of imagery and literary power. Of Webster's dramatic felicity and dramatic power Mr Archer is apparently incredulous. The play of *The Duchess of Malfi* is 'robed in regal purple of pure poetry', but the dramatic setting in which the poetic jewels are enchased is valueless. In other words, Webster's verse to be admired must be dissociated from the play for which it is written. But Webster's poetry, of all others, cannot be separated from its dramatic interest. The immortal dirge may be, as Mr Archer affirms, true poetry, but coming from the lips of Bosola at a moment when the suffering woman is facing her own grave, the words have an additional force and meaning. They become then convincing. Nor is it reasonable to ignore the dramatic instinct needed to conceive dialogue that gives point to the situation. Later on in the same scene Bosola says to Ferdinand

> You have bloodily approv'd the ancient truth,
> That kindred commonly do worse agree
> Than remote strangers

and these words, in themselves pregnant with knowledge of human nature, are made doubly suggestive by the dramatist's skill in having them spoken at the moment when the action gives reality to them. In fact, Webster's most celebrated passages are not great simply because they are pre-eminent in beauty of idea and felicity of expression, but because they carry with them dramatic force by being appropriate to character and situation. 'The real object of the drama', says Macaulay, 'is the exhibition of human character, and those situations which most signally develop character form the best plot.' Judged by this standard, a well-constructed play may be trifling, dull, and unnatural, while 'a haphazard dramatic romance' that has in it some scenes inferior in power and passion to nothing in the whole range of the drama, may entitle the author to the position of a great dramatist.

A difficulty in appreciating the actions and motives of Webster's characters may arise from that imperfect historical knowledge which we are told is the characteristic of Lamb's criticism. Webster wrote his play not for the purpose of dealing 'in horror for horror's sake', nor 'just to make the flesh creep', but with a desire to give vital embodiment to the manners and morals of the Italian Renaissance, as they appeared to the imagination of Englishmen. As Vernon Lee ably points out, it was the very

strangeness and horror of Italian life, as compared with the dull
decorum of English households, that constituted the attraction
of Italian tragedy for Elizabethan playgoers. They were familiar
with the saying that 'nothing in Italy was cheaper than human
life'. Their own Ascham had written that he found in Italy, during a nine days' stay in one small city, more liberty to sin 'than
ever he heard tell of in our noble citie of London in nine yeare'.
No wonder, then, if the metaphysical judgement of the Puritan
urged Elizabethan dramatists to show, by the action of their
dramas, that there existed a higher power than the mere strength
of those fiercer passions which occurred in Italy, the land of passion in the sixteenth century. Looked at from this point of view,
much in the play that is unintelligible can be explained. Burckhardt, in his *Renaissance of Italy*, tells us that a warm imagination kept ever alive the memory of injuries, real or supposed;
more especially in a country that allowed each man to take the
law into his own hands. Not only a husband, but even a brother,
in order to satisfy the family honour, would take upon himself
the act of vengeance; nor would a father scruple to kill his own
daughter, if the dignity of his house had been compromised by
an unworthy marriage. Besides, an Italian's revenge was never
a half-and-half affair. The Duchess's children are 'massacred'
because the whole name and race of Antonio must be rooted out.
Cariola, too, must die, because she helped to bring about the hated
marriage. It is this desire for truth to Italian life that causes
Webster to introduce Julia, and the pre-eminently Italian dialogue between Julia and Delio. Without Julia we do not get our
typical Cardinal of the Italian Renaissance, a man experienced
in simony, poisoning, and lust. There is even a higher motive
for her appearance in the play. She is designed as a set-off to the
Duchess; as an instance of unholy love in contrast to the chaste
love of the Duchess. Bosola is a masterly study of the Italian
'familiar', who is at the same time a humanist. He is refined,
subtle, indifferent, cynical. A criminal in action but not in con-
stitution. A man forced by his position to know all the inward
resources of his own nature, passing or permanent, and conscious of the possibility of a very brief period of power and influence. It is necessary, moreover, in judging of this play to take
into consideration the restrictions put upon the dramatist by the

novelist. Webster's audience was too familiar with the various incidents of the story to allow of the dramatist ignoring them. In one instance only does Webster depart from a statement of Bandello, and that is in making the Cardinal the younger and not the elder brother – an unaccountable oversight on the part of Bandello – for Italian Cardinals were invariably the younger sons of noble houses.

Mr Robert Louis Stevenson says that to read a play is a knack : the fruit of much knowledge, and some imagination, comparable to that of reading score, 'the reader is apt to miss the proper point of view'. To see dramatic propriety and dramatic power in *The Duchess of Malfi*, there may be needed both critical and historical imagination.

SOURCE : 'A New Criticism of Webster's *Duchess of Malfi*',
*Library Review* (1893).

## C. V. Boyer

From the standpoint of dramatic technique *The Duchess of Malfi* is not properly the tragedy of the Duchess at all, but of her brothers, Ferdinand and the Cardinal, and of Bosola. The fate of the Duchess is profoundly pathetic, and, owing to the dramatic art lavished upon her portraiture in order to make her end pathetic, she stands out more prominently than any other figure during the first four acts; but she is absolutely without tragic guilt, and the play continues for another act after her death to bring about the tragic doom of the three villains who have sought to advance themselves by her destruction. It has been urged[1] that the Duchess pulled her fate upon her own head by her rashness, but such an interpretation of the play does not correspond to our emotional experience. . . .

The fate of her brothers, however, follows from their treatment of her; her murder is their tragic guilt. They employ a villain to torture and kill her, and in the end both are killed by the villain

whom they had employed. They·are not, however, villain-
heroes; they are simply villains. Though they conceive the
wickedness that leads to their sister's death, they hire a tool to
execute it. They themselves are not set forth in high relief; they
are not thoughtfully psychologized; their conflict with moral law
does not interest us, but only the effects of their machinations
upon the Duchess. The art which might have been used to centre
our attention upon them is expended upon Bosola, the tool
whom they employ. It is his activity which constitutes the action
of the play. The Duchess wins our attention and sympathy by her
suffering; Bosola takes an equal share of our attention because
it is he who torments her. After her death our interest centres
upon him exclusively. The author takes pains to make him an
interesting character. And, finally, Bosola's death is in itself tragic.
He therefore becomes the villain-hero. . . .

Bosola's resolution to tear himself from his evil moorings in
order to serve at last the cause of justice restimulates our
exhausted emotions, and points to reconciliation. In the act
which elapses after the death of the Duchess, Bosola displays
resolution, bravery, sympathy, and willingness for self-sacrifice.
. . . And if a play so harrowing and so full of horror can also be
said to please, it is not simply because Ferdinand and the Cardinal
suffer as they deserve, but because, by the development of Bosola,
goodness and bravery are shown to exist even in a soul as
spotted as that of a tool villain. The insufferable strain produced
by the painfully pathetic death of an innocent woman is somewhat relieved, and our confidence in human nature restored by
the fortitude with which Bosola pursues his end and meets his
death. . . .

Nothing could exceed in pathos the death of the Duchess, but
in this scene the tragedy reaches its high-water mark. Pity is present, but without the fear that accompanies tragic guilt, and the
result is simply painful. We are conscious of no such pleasure as
we derive from a Shakespearean tragedy, for that which is simply
painful has no cathartic effect. The Duchess by the very force
of this scene remains the chief figure, but her death, though
dignified, reveals no law of human destiny connecting man's
sufferings with his previous actions. Such a connection between
character and circumstances is attempted with the villains, but

as they are not the really sympathetic figures, the highest tragic effect is lost. The unity of plot is broken; there is the tragedy of the Duchess on one side, and that of her murderers on the other. If her fate is intended for the centre of interest the play should close with her death, though that would be very painful in the absence of tragic guilt; if the fate of villainy is intended for the main issue there should not be so much time and effort expended on the villains' victim, for it puts the villains in a subordinate position. After the fourth act the centre of interest is shifted; the fifth act might not unreasonably be called 'Bosola's Revenge'. Such a change mars the unity of the play.

SOURCE: *The Villain as Hero in Elizabethan Tragedy* (1914).

NOTE

1. E. E. Stoll, *John Webster* (Boston, 1905) p. 130 and note 3.

## Rupert Brooke

The one influence upon Webster that is always noticeable is that of satire. His nature tended to the outlook of satire; and his plays give evidence that he read Elizabethan, and in some form Latin satire with avidity. *Hamlet*, the *Malcontent* and all the heroes of that type of play, 'railed' continually. But with Webster every character and nearly every speech has something of the satirical outlook. They describe each other satirically. They are for ever girding at the conventional objects of satire, certain social follies and crimes. There are several little irrelevant scenes of satire, like the malevolent discussion of Count Malatesti (*The Duchess of Malfi*, III iii). It is incessant. The topics are the ordinary ones, the painting of women, the ingratitude of princes, the swaggering of blusterers, the cowardice of pseudo-soldiers. It gives part of the peculiar atmosphere of these plays.

This rests on a side of Webster's nature, which, in combination with his extraordinary literary gifts, produces another queer characteristic of his – his fondness for, and skill in comment. He is rather more like a literary man trying to write for the theatre than any of his contemporaries. Theatrically, though he is competent and sometimes powerful, he exhibits no vastly unusual ability. It is his comments that bite deep. . . .

Webster's handling of a play, and his style of writing, have something rather slow and old-fashioned about them. He was not like Shakespeare or Beaumont and Fletcher, up-to-date and 'slick'. He worried his plays out with a grunting pertinacity. There are several uncouth characteristics of his that have an effect which halts between archaism and a kind of childish awkwardness, like 'primitive' art of various nations and periods. Sometimes he achieves the same result it can have, of a simplicity and directness refreshingly different from later artifice and accomplishment. Sometimes he only seems, to the most kindly critic, to fail hopelessly for lack of skill. One of these characteristics is the use of couplets, usually to end the scene, and commonly of a generalising nature. This is, of course, old-fashioned. The frequency of such couplets is an often-noticed feature of the early Elizabethan drama. . . .

In three places a different and very queer side of Webster's old-fashionedness or of his occasional dramatic insensibility, is unpleasantly manifest. Here it becomes plainer, perhaps, that it is rather a childish than an old-fashioned tendency which betrays him to these faults. Three times, once in *The White Devil*, and twice in *The Duchess of Malfi*, the current of quick, living, realistic speeches – each character jerking out a hard, biting, dramatic sentence or two – is broken by long-winded, irrelevant, and fantastically unrealistic tales. They are of a sententious, simple kind, such as might appear in Æsop. Generally they seem to be lugged in by their ears into the play. They are introduced with the same bland, startling inconsequence with which some favourite song is brought into a musical comedy, but with immeasurably less justification. . . .

There are still further instances of Webster's occasional extraordinary childishness in drama, namely his shameless use of asides, soliloquies, and other devices for telling his audience the motives of the actors or the state of the plot. . . . The fault, of course, lies in the unnaturalness and the shameless sudden appearance of the dramatist's own person, rather than in the form of a soliloquy. Only, soliloquies are especially liable to this. A legitimate and superb use of soliloquy occurs near the end of *The Duchess of Malfi* . . . where the Cardinal enters, alone, reading a book :

> I am puzzled in a question about hell :
> He says, in hell there's one material fire,
> And yet it shall not burn all men alike.
> Lay him by : – how tedious is a guilty conscience !
> When I look into the fish-ponds, in my garden,
> Methinks I see a thing, arm'd with a rake,
> That seems to strike at me.
>         *Enter* Bosola, *and* Servant *with* Antonio's *body.*

This is an entirely permissible and successful use of soliloquy. The words and thought are mysteriously thrilling. They sharpen the agony of the spectator's mind to a tense expectation; which is broken by the contrast of the swift purpose of Bosola's entry, with the servant and the body, and the violent progression of events ensuing. The whole is in tone together; and the effect bites deep, the feeling of the beginning of sheeting rain, breaking the gloomy pause before a thunderstorm. But there are cases of Webster using the soliloquy badly. In *The White Devil,* when the servant has told Francisco that Bracciano and Vittoria have fled the city together, he goes out. Francisco is left alone, exclaiming, 'Fled – O damnable !' He immediately alters his key :

> How fortunate are my wishes. Why? 'twas this
> I only laboured. I did send the letter
> T'instruct him what to do . . .

One finds the dramatist rather too prominently and audibly there. . . .

All these childishnesses and blunders in Webster's plays, soliloquies, asides, generalisations, couplets, and the rest, are due, no doubt, to carelessness and technical incapacity. His gifts were of a different kind. But the continual generalisations arise also from a particular bent of his mind, and a special need he felt. It is normal in the human mind, it was unusually strong in the Elizabethans, and it found its summit in Webster of all of that time – the desire to discover the general rule your particular instance illustrates, and the delight of enunciating it. . . . Antonio and Vittoria both die uttering warnings against 'the courts of princes'. Other characters alternate human cries at their own distress with great generalisations about life and death. These give to the hearts of the spectators such comfort and such an outlet for their confused pity and grief as music and a chorus afford in other cases. But Webster also felt the need of such broad moralising in the middle of his tragedies. Sometimes he pours through the mouth of such characters as Bosola and Flamineo, generalisation after dull generalisation, without illuminating. Greek choruses have failed in the same way. But when a gnome that *is* successful comes, it is worth the pains. The solidity and immensity of Webster's mind behind the incidents is revealed. Flamineo fills this part at the death of Bracciano. But often he and Bosola are a different, and very Websterian, chorus. Their ceaseless comments of indecency and mockery are used in some scenes to throw up by contrast and enhance by interpretation the passions and sufferings of human beings. They provide a background for Prometheus; but a background of entrails and vultures, not the cliffs of the Caucasus. The horror of suffering is intensified by such means till it is unbearable. The crisis of her travail comes on the tormented body and mind of the Duchess (II i) to the swift accompaniment of Bosola's mockery. Bracciano's wooing, and his later recapture, of Vittoria, take on the sick dreadfulness of figures in a nightmare, whose shadows parody them with obscene caricature; because of the ceaseless ape-like comments of Flamineo, cold, itchy, filthily knowing. . . .

The world called Webster is a peculiar one. It is inhabited by people driven, like animals, and perhaps like men, only by their instincts, but more blindly and ruinously. Life there seems to flow into its forms and shapes with an irregular abnormal and horrible volume. That is ultimately the most sickly, distressing feature of Webster's characters, their foul and indestructible vitality. It fills one with the repulsion one feels at the unending soulless energy that heaves and pulses through the lowest forms of life. They kill, love, torture one another blindly and without ceasing. A play of Webster's is full of the feverish and ghastly turmoil of a nest of maggots. Maggots are what the inhabitants of this universe most suggest and resemble. The sight of their fever is only alleviated by the permanent calm, unfriendly summits and darknesses of the background of death and doom. For that is equally a part of Webster's universe. Human beings are writhing grubs in an immense night. And the night is without stars or moon. But it has sometimes a certain quietude in its darkness; but not very much.

SOURCE : *John Webster and the Elizabethan Drama* (1916).

## F. L. Lucas

The men who crowded The Phoenix or The Red Bull lived, both in the theatre and outside it, far more in the moment for the moment's sake than the cultured classes of today; and accordingly it was a succession of great moments that they wanted on the stage, not a well-made play. They did not at each instant look forward to what was coming or back to what had been. If a dramatist gave them great situations, ablaze with passion and poetry, it would have seemed to them a chilly sort of pedantry that peered too closely into the machinery by which these were produced. They did not want their fireworks analysed. They were, in fact, very like a modern cinema-audience, with the vast difference that they had also an appetite for poetry. And so all their playwrights, Shakespeare included, worked predominantly in scenes. Scenes were the essential units. . . .

The first thing, then, in appreciating an Elizabethan like Webster is to be as cavalier about his plots as he was himself. After all it is not so difficult. *The White Devil*, well acted, can carry an audience breathless with it over all the breaks and rough places in its plot, with the irresistible onrush of a great roller surging up a rocky beach. . . .

It is, I think, quite possible to underrate even his stage-craft until we learn to look at his tragedies as his audience saw them – less as wholes than as a series of great situations. Webster cannot give his plays a close-knit logical unity; he is often childishly irrelevant; and his characters are sometimes wildly inconsistent from scene to scene. That was the fashion of the day. But his work remains more than a mere chaos of dramatic fragments, and he is a highly successful playwright in his own Gothic style. . . .

There is more than mere disgust in Webster. Mere disgust at human littleness, indeed, would never produce tragedy, without a sense of human greatness as well. Yet we may freely admit that, for all the truth in the vision of existence given by *The White Devil* and *The Duchess of Malfi*, it is not the whole truth : and, being one-sided, it is in danger of becoming monotonous. . . . Those who share, then, the contempt of La Rochefoucauld for 'men who have only one kind of genius', may criticize Webster not indeed as a bad dramatist, but as a narrow one, who saw life passionately and intensely, but did not see it whole.

SOURCE : Introduction to *The Complete Works of John Webster* (1927).

## Una Ellis-Fermor

The stress of Webster's two great tragedies is almost unrelieved. And his instinct in this was sound. For so deep is his absorption in the pattern of thought and emotion and in the light he believes this ordered sequence may throw upon the mystery of man's fate, that relief would generally be mere interruption or hindrance. Being a good theatre-man, he leaves his producer free to unbrace the tension of the audience's mood here and there in both plays, but he prefers to do it with a mask or a pas-

sage of grim dialogue capable of comic production, things
which, though they can be used to vary the mood, do not necessarily interfere with the movement of the thought. So that the
two great tragedies are without essentially comic elements.

The variations in mood constitute a kind of relief, akin to that
of the Greek choric odes, but quite distinct from the mingling,
whether close or loose, of the elements of tragic and comic in
much Elizabethan and Jacobean comedy, tragi-comedy and
tragedy. In Webster's plays, the elasticity of the emotions is preserved by variations of mood, tempo and force. Again and again,
after a tempest of rage, the rushing together of two whirlwinds,
there is a sudden pause; the speech that follows seems barely
audible by contrast with the thundering passions that have
passed, but it falls into the silence with incalculable pathos,
solemnity or awe. Sometimes this is no more than a line, a half-
line even, as where Ferdinand, looking on his dead sister,
perceives her truly for the first time since his rage possessed him,
or where later, in the madness that the realization brings, he
moves unnoticing through the crowd of courtiers, his mind
turned inward upon the thought 'Strangling is a very quiet
death', or when Flamineo, wishing he 'were from hence', makes
discovery o fthat 'strange thing', compassion. Sometimes it is the
length of a brief scene, as in that (one of the most moving and
sincere studies of a child in the whole of this drama) where
Giovanni enters to his uncle Francisco with the news of his
mother's death, hard upon the exit of Vittoria, when the violent
tumult of the trial scene has hardly died away : [1]

> *Giov.*        my sweet mother
>          Is –
> *Fran.* How? Where?
> *Giov.* Is there, – no yonder, – indeed sir I'll not tell you,
>          For I shall make you weep.
> *Fran.* Is dead.
> *Giov.* Do not blame me now,
>          I did not tell you so.
> *Lod.*                    She's dead my lord.
> *Fran.* Dead? . . .
> *Giov.* What do the dead do, uncle? do they eat,

> Hear music, go a-hunting, and be merry,
> As we that live?
> *Fran.* No coz; they sleep.
> *Giov.*                    Lord, Lord, that I were dead, –
> I have not slept these six nights. . . .
> *Fran.* O, all of my poor sister that remains !
> Take him away for God's sake.
>
> (*The White Devil*, III ii 312–40)

The only contemporary who makes so subtle a use of such contrasts is Shakespeare. He also in tragedy gives these intervals of gentle, low-toned speech in the midst of tempest, he alone can at once suspend and emphasize the tragic tension by the half-heard murmurs of a mind moving absorbed upon the path of self-discovery that may lead to madness. 'I did her wrong', says Lear in the midst of the Fool's babble when the gates of the castle have been closed against him.[2] Ferdinand echoes it; 'She died young'.

Side by side with this varying of emotional mood and tempo, intimately akin to it, in fact, is the imaginative relief of the poetic imagery, the momentary escape into the world called up by the images, a world like that in which the events and characters move, but, by its very wealth of imaginative concentration, less actual – a hidden country which, though full of macabre and hideous, sometimes obscene, forms, is yet a land of escape, into which we wander, are absorbed for a moment, immersed in its fantasy, and from which we return, as from a dream, to the hurry and clash of events. This world of imagery, which is as different from the world of thought and reflection as that is in its turn from the world of event and action, holds the third place in Webster's dramas, a reality shadowed behind the other realities. Here Webster calls up by a few phrases and their juxtaposition trains of thought which, for a man of an easier habit of mind, would have made a whole dialogue. His is a style that, when the emotion grows intense and the tragic issues approach their climax, passes into that lucidity, those inevitable phrases that distinguish the great poetry of the Greek drama, or, in English, the closing scenes of *Hamlet* and *Macbeth*. It is characteristic, too, of the bitter force of Webster that some of the finest of these are found in his jests, concentrated flashes that illuminate the gloom with devastating revelation; the laughter in these plays is like Duke Ferdinand's, 'A deadly cannon that lightens ere it smokes'.

So deeply is this imagery inwoven with the concept of the play, so essentially is its function part of the function of the whole drama, that in the great closing scenes of *The White Devil* and *The Duchess of Malfi* it is impossible to isolate passages without losing that essential part of their effect which they draw from their dependence upon the whole preceding drama. It is thus the range and interplay of mood, thought and imagery which gives them their richness and their variety, arriving at last at that impression of width and universality of implication which is an essential of great tragedy. For in these scenes Webster gathers together the streams of thought and purpose, bringing up to the surface undercurrents of action and relation hitherto unknown to the characters themselves. On the threshold of death they pause, like Shakespeare's people, to throw a last look back over the course of their lives, and delusion falls from them. In the strange illumination of those moments they see life also as something strange and new. Their last thoughts are cast back upon it, elucidating suddenly what had before been dark.

SOURCE: *The Jacobean Drama* (1936).

NOTES

1. Giovanni is perhaps one of the best child studies in a drama not noticeably successful in its children; in Shakespeare, only young Marcus of *Coriolanus* and Mamillius of *The Winter's Tale* seem as natural as he. He says little that a prematurely old, Elizabethan child might not easily have said. He is not (as so many children of Jacobean drama) the mouthpiece merely of pathetic or shrewdly significant sayings beyond his intention, nor yet (as so many more) a mere portrait of that precocity which was all too common a result of sixteenth-century educational ideals.

2. See *Lear*, I v 8–45, a scene which, in the use of this particular process, surpasses Webster himself.

# Fredson Bowers

*The Duchess of Malfi* did not, as sometimes asserted, bring to a close the tradition of revenge tragedy. It did, however, provide in its plot structure the artistic climax to the particular type of drama which had been in the direct line of descent from Kyd and Marlowe, Marston and Tourneur, and marked the temporary discard of the much modified Kydian plot formula. Webster, together with Fletcher, is the bridge between the older Elizabethans and the so-called decadent drama of Massinger and Ford.

Webster's debt to Kydian tragedy in *The Duchess of Malfi* has been noted in detail – the wanton bloodshed, torture, use of the tool villain, omens, and the like.[1] Only the structure of the plot and the position of the tool villain will occupy us here. The play is peculiar in that the protagonist (the duchess herself) is the victim of the villains' revenge. This much and no more Webster found in his source. The problem, how to bring the guilty persons to justice, remained. If the death of the duchess were delayed until the dénouement, the villains in some inexplicable manner must become so involved as to bring disaster on their own heads or else be disposed of hugger-mugger by Antonio. The Kydian formula would suggest the murder of the duchess to be followed by the revenge of the distraught Antonio, but this would involve not only a decided wandering from the source but also a certain loss in the more pitiful and ironic aspects of the story. Webster clung to his source and accordingly was forced to create original machinery for his catastrophe, a task complicated by the loss of his major hero and the necessity for the early loss of his minor.

The solution came through the extension of the action of the tool villain. Bosola is no mechanical villain of the Lorrique type. He is, instead, a misfit, a man of worthier talents forced into a degrading position and, with a brutal philosophy, making the most of it by the thoroughgoing manner in which he plays his part. If he must be a villain, one senses, he has decided to be an efficient one. Enough flashes of his independent better self are shown to stir the interest of the audience and the more to horrify them by the cynical brutality that follows. Indeed, Bosola has an almost surgical interest in torturing the human spirit to see how much it can endure before the veniality he seeks as the excuse for his existence is forced to the surface.

The unworldly bravery of the duchess proves to Bosola that his theories are false; but his character is so well conceived that his sympathies are not fully enrolled until he is made aware of the fate that awaits him at the hands of an ungrateful master. Already shaken by his experience with the duchess, he is cast completely adrift from his convictions by this second shock, and takes to himself the office of revenger for the duchess upon the men who have ruined him. With dramatic irony the first step in his new rôle is the unwitting murder of Antonio, the man whose life he had resolved to save. Bosola knows then that his life, tainted by years of evil, is doomed, and with that knowledge he becomes the impersonal agent of Death. In the mortal scuffle with his enemies that follows he meets his end, but not before he has seen one of his foes ironically slain and has with his own hand stabbed the second. The fatal retribution begun with the murder of the duchess has at last descended on the guilty parties.

This retribution is the keynote of the play, but it does not come from a Kydian revenger, for in a sense the villains bring it directly upon themselves. Ferdinand goes mad, the cardinal is no longer able to control his accomplice Bosola, and the resultant internecine strife works the havoc. The accomplice had always been the weak link in the Kydian villain's schemes. Webster followed the tradition of the weak link, but exalted the irony of the catastrophe and provided a more fitting doom for his villains by removing the element of accident from the accomplice's betrayal and founding such betrayal on a psychological change in character.

*The White Devil* (1609–12), which immediately preceded *The Duchess of Malfi*, is, however, Webster's real masterpiece in the villain play. In a sense it may be said to complete the merging of the Kyd and Marlowe revenge play. . . . Just as Shakespeare by his emphasis on character had in *Hamlet* created the apotheosis of pure Kydian tragedy, so Webster, to a lesser degree and in a lesser medium, by the same artistic means rather than by any important tinkering with the construction of plot, achieved in *The White Devil* a welding of the most popular features of Kyd and Marlowe. The result is a complete synthesis and the finest villain play of the period.

Superficially the plot seems somewhat old-fashioned. A villain, in order to marry a villainess, has her husband and his own wife secretly murdered. The fact is suspected, and the wife's brother and lover join forces as revengers. They set a trap by which they kill the villains and their accomplices although one of the revengers also falls. The vital change from Kyd, unrevealed by such a bald outline, comes in the position of importance these two sets of opponents occupy in the plot, but more especially in their characterization. The title indicates whose play it is. The victim of the revenger is the protagonist, as in the usual villain play, yet, as with Kyd, the balance of conflict is maintained since the revenge is conceived early and the revengers' intrigue occupies an important part of the play. Definitely it is not the Marlovian *deus ex machina* suddenly raised to bring about a quick catastrophe.

It is chiefly in the characterization, however, that Webster differs. Here is a villain play in which, contrary to Swinburne's opinion, the characters are not all black or all white but all – even to the possible 'good' characters – are gray. The provincialism combined with the intense moral loathing which led Elizabethan tragic writers to portray their Italian villains as impossible pieces of living evil has been replaced by a calmer and more realistic point of view. Webster's villains are not the grinning, self-conscious puppets of the Machiavellian tradition, glorying in evil and at war with religion and good. The Elizabethan Machiavellian villain provoked interest only by the fascinated horror of the audience, but it is evident that Webster's Vittoria, by every means possible to his hand, is intended to appeal to a fascinated sympathy. Therein lay the great change Webster introduced to revenge tragedy. . . .

Webster's leavening has extended even to the highly conventional character of the tool villain. Flamineo is no gulled Pedringano or comic relief Lorrique. In a halting and imperfect way Webster has tried to dignify his essentially undignified rôle by raising the quality of the man within it. Malcontent, pander, murderer, the force of his vitality and depraved cynicism yet makes him a far more important figure in the play than his actual position warrants.

Webster has humanized his villains by substituting for the religious tradition of 'the devil incarnate' real persons with more than their share of vice yet treated so poetically as to arouse the sympathetic as opposed to the antagonistic interest of the audience; moreover, he has strengthened that sympathy by this treatment of the revengers. Like his villains, they are gray. Their revenge is actuated neither by the pure religious frenzy of the Kydian hero revenger nor by the malicious self-interest of the Marlovian villain. They occupy a halfway ground between the two extremes, and Webster, in order not to overthrow the balance of sympathy, is at some pains to taint slightly the purity of their motives and consequently the justice of their action. . . .

The close of *The White Devil* when Lodovico is led forth to be tortured and executed and the young Giovanni uncompromisingly declares Francisco a villainous murderer, represents an hostility to the revenge which is more in keeping with the end of *The Revenger's Tragedy* than with *Hamlet*. There is no doubt that Vittoria and Bracciano are guilty and have pulled their doom on their own heads. Yet Webster balances the scales so nicely that the means of their doom – the revenge of Lodovico and Francisco – has no religious sanction and is conducted in as blameworthy a manner as the deeds which raised it. This realistic rather than melodramatic treatment of a revenge story marks Webster's *White Devil* as almost unique. Not only has he successfully amalgamated the interest of an audience in a Kydian revenge and a Marlovian villain protagonist, but he has also added a new type of treatment which is realistic without becoming bourgeois and thrilling without the introduction of caricature.

SOURCE : *Elizabethan Revenge Tragedy 1587–1642* (1940).

NOTE

1. E. E. Stoll, *John Webster* (Boston, 1905) pp. 93, 118–45.

# David Cecil

His vision is a moral one. Webster sees life as a struggle between right and wrong. Or rather between good and evil. Here we come to one of the key facts about him. He was a child of his age; the age of the Reformation : and he conceived morality in religious terms. An act to him was wrong, not because it interfered with the happiness of man in this world, but because it was a sin; a breach of the eternal laws established by the God who created man. Moreover it was a voluntary breach. Here again he reveals himself the child of a Christian society. Men to him are not the helpless sport of an indifferent fate as they were to the Greeks. Possessed of free will, his villains sin deliberately. These evil voluntary acts are the cause of human tragedy. Indeed his subject matter may be summed up as a study of the working of sin in the world. Each play presents us with a picture of an act of sin and its consequences.

A very sombre picture too! Webster seems to agree with the view of life expressed in the dirge sung over his victim by the murderer of the Duchess of Malfi :

> Of what is't fools make such vain keeping?
> Sin their conception, their birth weeping;
> Their life a general mist of error,
> Their death a hideous storm of terror.

Webster envisages evil in its most extreme form : and he presents it – so far as this life is concerned – as far more powerful than good. His theology is Calvinistic. The world as seen by him is, of its nature incurably corrupt. To be involved in it is to be inescapably involved in evil : all its apparent beauties are a snare and a delusion. There is a couplet of his, expressing what to him must have been a very important truth : for it occurs in both his plays,

> Glories, like glow-worms, afar off shine bright,
> But look'd to near, have neither heat, nor light.

Ambition, pleasure, beauty, passion, the lust of the eyes and the pride of life – to look to these for happiness is to be certain of disappointment and disillusionment. In monarchical seventeenth century England, the Court was the chief home of these specious mortal splendours. Webster makes it his symbol for them. Again and again, and with passion, he makes his characters warn mankind against the lure of the Court. 'Let my son fly the courts of princes' cries the virtuous Antonio with his last breath. And the sinner Vittoria echoes him,

> Oh happy they that never saw the court
> Nor ever knew great man but by report.

Nor are the glories of this world merely a source of disillusionment: they are also dangerous to the soul. They seduce, they corrupt; to obtain them, man is led into sin. That breach of the Divine Law which for Webster is the cause of tragedy comes always from too violent a desire to win this world's prizes. The wicked commit their crimes because their treasure is not laid up in heaven, because their hearts are set on those glories of our blood and state, which are shadows, not substantial things.

Webster's melancholy view of life is reflected in the order he imposes upon human nature. His characters are ranged in moral divisions; there are the good and there are the bad. But, since to act strongly one must believe in the value of worldly activities, only the bad are active and dynamic. They are of two types. The first – Vittoria, Bracciano, Ferdinand, the Cardinal – are the creatures of some ruling passion; lust or ambition or avarice or hatred. Possessed by an insatiate desire to satisfy it, they break every law, shut their eyes to every scruple. The second group is actuated less by passion, than by cynicism. Flamineo and Bosola are not blinded by the violence of their desires. On the contrary they are cold and calculating. But they have a Machiavellian disbelief in human virtue. Mankind to them is made up of fools and knaves all equally struggling for their own ends. The only solid goods are material wealth and success: and, deliberately rejecting every moral consideration, they set to work to get them. Opposed to these two types of villain, stand the good characters; Isabella, Marcello, Cornelia, Antonio, the Duchess, noble, pitiful and courageous. In contrast to the bad, however, they are passive : they cannot identify themselves with the activities of the sin-tainted world. Once she has married Antonio, the Duchess initiates no action. The other good characters never do anything at all. Helpless victims, they are swept into the turmoil set up by the furious energy of the wicked. In the end, more often than not, they are destroyed by them.

A pessimistic view? Not exactly : in a sense Webster does believe in the ultimate victory of virtue. The good are only defeated on the material plane. Morally they triumph. No amount of suffering corrupts them or breaks their courage : on the contrary, their virtue shines even brighter for the blood-stained darkness that gathers about them. Furthermore, though they may be destroyed, so also – and far more dreadfully – are their enemies. God is not mocked, the evil-doer is caught in the net he has woven for others. And he realises why. It is in the stress that he lays on this realisation that the religious foundation of Webster's view of life strikingly appears. His wickedest characters are never moral idiots, who do not understand the enormity of their own, crimes. They may profess to disbelieve in virtue and pour contempt on scruple; but it is against the instinctive promptings of their natures. Before they die they are always forced to recognise the supremacy of that Divine Law, against which they have offended. . . .

Webster's horrors – his ghosts and torturers – are not, as with his lesser contemporaries, mere theatrical devices to awake a pleasing shudder. They are symbolic incarnations of that spiritual terror and diabolical delight in suffering, which are, to him, central features of the human drama. Duke Ferdinand and the Cardinal are creatures of hell : the prison in which they confine the Duchess, made hideous by the clamour of lunatics and the ghastly images of murdered children, exhibit to us, in visible form, the hell on earth, which it is their nature to create. Even Webster's irrelevant scenes of pageantry, little though they have to do with the plot, contribute essential features to his picture of human life. Here, moving before us, are those ceremonies of worldly dignity, of whose superficial seductive splendour Webster is acutely aware, and whose fundamental hollowness he is concerned to expose.

SOURCE : *Poets and Story-Tellers* (1949).

# Travis Bogard

It is idle to seek in Websterian tragedy for a pattern based on 'that development of human souls for good or evil, which is Shakespeare's especial power'. The Websterian characters, Bosola included, are in the end what they were at the outset. The naturally evil men and women remain evil; the good remain good. The more heroic are completely, even stubbornly, consistent. It is a matter of pride with them that misfortune does not change them. Their entire struggle – the struggle which makes them alive on the stage – is to keep themselves as they are, essentially.

A phrase that Webster uses will serve to designate the consistency to self which his characters reveal. It is found significantly in the last two lines of *The Duchess of Malfi*. It is the summing-up. Delio says,

> *Integrity of life is fame's best friend,*
> *Which nobly, beyond death, shall crown the end.*

Integrity of life is the *virtù* of Websterian character. In its context the phrase is applied to an action which would traditionally be judged 'good', but it has a more fundamental application. To Webster, integrity of life cuts across the traditional evaluative divisions of good and evil, and proves, in the final synthesis, to be the sole standard of positive ethical judgment in the tragedies.

It is true that Webster makes use of traditional standards of moral evaluation in delineating his characters. But, for him, these standards shift alarmingly; the usual distinctions between good and evil become inadequate for a true picture of life and are finally passed over. Man's world, as Webster sees it, is a 'deep pit of darkness', and mankind is 'womanish and fearful' in the shadow of the pit. The causes of the fear are many, but chief among them are *oppression* and *mortality*. Oppression is the social cause: man's inhumanity to man, the destruction of the individual by society, represented in the tragedies by a corrupt court of law, perhaps, or the vicious social system where able men are forced to sycophancy to obtain rewards from their prince. Mortality is the natural cause. It too means destruction – the

decay of the living body by disease and the destruction of the
dead flesh by worms and the festering rot of the churchyard. . . .

In Webster's world there is no justice, no law, either of God
or man, to mete out punishment for evil and reward for good.
Death itself is not justice but the normal course of events, the
culmination of spiritual and physical decay. Honor and revenge
do not signify in the end, for, whether the death be violent or
natural, it is always a working out through men of forces larger
than man. Evil and good are dragged down together in death,
just as they are meshed together in life. The only triumph comes
when, even in the moment of defeat, an individual is roused to
assert his own integrity of life. This is not a question of virtue
and vice. In Webster's tragic world, characters are significant not
because of their morality but because of their struggle. Some
lose their identities in the forces of evil. Some die in the attempt
to preserve the good. But ultimately it is the struggling ones, the
splendid fighters for self, who matter. . . .

Life, as it appears to Webster, is a moral chaos. Ultimately, no
clarifying philosophy is possible, for man's mortality renders
meaningless the very terms on which such a philosophy must be
based.

Unable to find a solution to the problems he raises, and yet
unable to effect a compromise with the terrifying world of his
vision, Webster tries to present the ugliness beneath the artificial
glory. Every character of importance, every situation, the
noblest ethical statement in both tragedies is attacked by Webster's relentless analysis. His entire energy is directed toward
teaching man 'Wherein he is imperfect'. Yet this was done without any clear hope of making man perfect, for perfection was
meaningless, 'a bare name, and no essential thing'. As exorcisers
of illusion, the plays present to men the falsity and folly of their
lives. Possibly Webster hoped his work would arouse men to a
concern for their world, but beyond the representation of the
truth as he saw it, he could not progress. None of his recom-
mendations for remedial action have ultimate validity in the
tragic action, and, as a result, the plays remain grim object les-
sons in the same sense that Yorick's skull was an object lesson to
Hamlet. They cut through platitude and delusion to the fact of
death. From the facing of the fact in its bareness, Hamlet came

to an acceptance of all that lay ahead. Webster, characteristically, remained by the open grave.

SOURCE : *The Tragic Satire of John Webster* (1955).

# Herbert J. Muller

The qualities of greatness in Webster throw into sharper relief the serious faults that he never outgrew. His crudities make him seem irresponsible in spite of his basic sincerity, even his desperate earnestness. And his qualities of desperation point to his limited command – intellectual or imaginative – of a tragic condition that made him feel so intensely. He was shocked, obsessed, by an evil that he could not transcend in a larger frame or a longer perspective.

Although this sense of evil may be traced to the medieval heritage, the pessimism of Webster does not seem medieval. The many references to heaven and hell sound as conventional as the many to Fortune; they are not tense with religious feeling. The hell that concerned him was here on earth, and heaven was evidently no compensation for it. Ultimately, his pessimism – and that of Tourneur – seems due to disillusionment with Renaissance ideals. It signified a loss of faith rather than a reassertion of the traditional faith, and so took the form of a violent revulsion. Its most apparent source, or symbol, was the growing rule of money, in a society that was shifting from a feudal to a capitalistic economy. Like other Elizabethans, Webster and Tourneur attacked the Machiavellian politician, but they harped most of all on the theme of greed, the evils of gold.

SOURCE : *The Spirit of Tragedy* (1956).

# Northrop Frye

The first phase of tragedy is the one in which the central character is given the greatest possible dignity in contrast to the other characters, so that we get the perspective of a stag pulled down by wolves. The sources of dignity are courage and innocence, and in this phase the hero or heroine usually is innocent. This phase corresponds to the myth of the birth of the hero in romance, a theme which is occasionally incorporated into a tragic structure, as in Racine's *Athalie*. But owing to the unusual difficulty of making an interesting dramatic character out of an infant, the central and typical figure of this phase is the calumniated woman, often a mother the legitimacy of whose child is suspected. A whole series of tragedies based on a Griselda figure belong here, stretching from the Senecan *Octavia* to Hardy's *Tess*, and including the tragedy of Hermione in *The Winter's Tale*. If we are to read *Alcestis* as a tragedy, we have to see it as a tragedy of this phase in which Alcestis is violated by Death and then has her fidelity vindicated by being restored to life. *Cymbeline* belongs here too : in this play the theme of the birth of the hero appears offstage, for Cymbeline was the king of Britain at the time of the birth of Christ, and the halcyon peace in which the play concludes has a suppressed reference to this.

An even clearer example, and certainly one of the greatest in English literature, is *The Duchess of Malfi*. The Duchess has the innocence of abundant life in a sick and melancholy society, where the fact that she has 'youth and a little beauty' is precisely why she is hated. She reminds us too that one of the essential characteristics of innocence in the martyr is an unwillingness to die. When Bosola comes to murder her he makes elaborate attempts to put her half in love with easeful death and to suggest that death is really a deliverance. The attempt is motivated by a grimly controlled pity, and is roughly the equivalent of the vinegar sponge in the Passion. When the Duchess, her back to the wall, says 'I am Duchess of Malfi still', 'still' having its full weight of 'always', we understand how it is that even after her death her invisible presence continues to be the most vital character in the play. *The White Devil* is an ironic parody-treatment of the same phase.

SOURCE : *Anatomy of Criticism* (1957).

# PART TWO

# Articles and Essays from 1949 to 1972

*Ian Jack*

# THE CASE OF JOHN WEBSTER (1949)

Disintegration characterizes the view of life which inspired Webster's best-known plays. It is perfectly true, as Dr Tillyard remarks,[1] that Webster, like the rest of his age, inherited 'the Elizabethan world-picture'; but in his work we see that world-picture falling in ruins. When Dr Tillyard goes on to say that Webster's characters belong 'to a world of violent crime and violent change, of sin, blood and repentance, yet to a world loyal to a theological scheme', and adds : 'indeed all the violence of Elizabethan drama has nothing to do with a dissolution of moral standards : on the contrary, it can afford to indulge itself just because those standards were so powerful', he is overlooking the highly significant differences between Elizabethan drama and Jacobean drama, and uttering a dangerous half-truth. No doubt there is a definite 'theological scheme' behind Webster, in the sense that it was familiar to his audience and himself, and could therefore be drawn on for imagery; but *The White Devil* and *The Duchess of Malfi* are our best evidence that the Elizabethan theological scheme could no longer hold together.

Henry James pointed out that the ultimate source of a novel's value is the quality of the mind which produced it;[2] and the same is true of drama. Great tragedy can be written only by a man who has achieved – at least for the period of composition – a profound *and balanced* insight into life. Webster – his plays are our evidence – did not achieve such an insight. The imagery, verse-texture, themes, and 'philosophy' of his plays all point to a fundamental flaw, which is ultimately a moral flaw.

If one reads through *The White Devil* and *The Duchess of Malfi*, noting down the *sententiae* and moralizing asides of the various characters, one finds oneself in possession of a definite attempt at a 'philosophy', a moral to the tale :

> *Integrity of life is fame's best friend,*
> *Which nobly, beyond death, shall crown the end.*
> *(The Duchess of Malfi,* v v 120–1)

This philosophy is Stoical and Senecan, with a Roman emphasis
on the responsibilities of Princes :

> The lives of princes should like dials move,
> Whose regular example is so strong,
> They make the times by them go right or wrong.
> *(The White Devil,* I ii 287–9)

But this background of moral doctrine has nothing to do with
the action of the plays : so far from growing out of the action, it
bears all the marks of having been superimposed by the poet in
a cooler, less creative mood, than that in which the Duchess and
Flamineo had their birth.[3] There is no correspondence between
the axioms and the life represented in the drama. This dissociation is the fundamental flaw in Webster.

What was wrong, apparently, was that there was available no
philosophy of life which kindled Webster's imagination as certain
aspects of Hell, or Chaos, kindled it. No moral order represented
itself to his imagination as real. Consequently his plays contain
brilliant passages of poetry – they appear whenever he touches on
the small area which acted as his inspiration – but lack imaginative coherence. They have indeed a unity, the unity for which
the 'mist' is a symbol; but one mood, isolated and out of focus,
cannot be the basis of a profound tragic vision. Webster himself
seems to have understood this better than some of his more enthusiastic critics; but this attempt to shore up chaos with a
sentious philosophy is a flagrant artistic insincerity. Webster
fails to realize his Senecan philosophy as he realizes his glimpses
of Hell.

We might say that Webster suffered from the poverty – the
philosophical poverty – of the tradition in which he worked;
but the fact that he chose to write in the Revenge tradition at all
is itself evidence of a lack of harmony in his own mind. For other
traditions were available, notably the tradition of the Morality,
to which Shakespeare's great tragedies owe more than has even

yet been understood.[4] Webster's choice of the Revenge tradition, his failure to give life to his Senecan moralizings, and (we may add) the fact that his work contains no convincing statement of the *positive* aspect of the doctrine of Degree, are all related : Degree and Order – as we come to see – were not real enough to Webster to stir his imagination. A lower concept of the Universe, and of Man's place in it, was all that he could compass.

This explains the fascination which the 'Machiavellian' had for Webster. To the conservative Elizabethan the Machiavellian doctrine seemed merely the denial of that Order and Degree which held the Universe together : Machiavellianism was anarchism. It is not surprising that a mind as unbalanced as Webster's should have allowed the Machiavellian ideal to usurp the place in his thought which a more conservative poet would have reserved for Degree. As a consequence there are a remarkable number of 'politicians' in his two plays.

Flamineo in *The White Devil* is a good example. He acts as pander to his sister Vittoria, contrives her husband's death, and treats his mother with a cold, sub-human ferocity :

> I pray will you go to bed then,
> Lest you be blasted ?  (1 ii 273–4)

He treacherously murders his brother in his mother's presence, and proclaims that nothing but a limitation of his natural ability prevents him from double-crossing his master, Bracciano : 'I had as good a will to cozen him, as e'er an officer of them all. But I had not cunning enough to do it' (v iii 57–9). He tries to corrupt even Giovanni with cynical advice. It is only when he is listening to the superstitious howling' (v iv 65) of his mother over the brother whom he has killed that Flamineo's Machiavellianism proves imperfect :

> I have a strange thing in me, to th'which
> I cannot give a name, without it be
> Compassion. (v iv 113–15)

Flamineo's philosophy is simply that

Knaves do grow great by being great men's apes.
(IV ii 247)

He explains his own villainy by saying :

I made *a kind of path*
To her [Vittoria's] and mine own preferment.
(III i 36–7; my italics)

Flamineo's attitude to women proves him a 'Courtier' of a very
different cast from Castiglione's ideal :

I visited the court, whence I return'd
More courteous, more lecherous by far. (I ii 325–6)

His attitude to women is that of 'the cynic'. He regards a woman's
modesty as 'but the superficies of lust' (I ii 18), and makes love
to Zanche 'just as a man holds a wolf by the ears' (v i 154) –
to prevent her from turning on him. He looks on women – and
on all humanity – as mere animals : 'women are like curst dogs'
(I ii 198); human love-making he regards as the coupling of mare
and stallion.[5] There is something peculiarly fiendish about his
ironical comment, as he eavesdrops at the love-making of
Vittoria and Bracciano :

*Bracciano.* [*enamoured*] Nay lower, you shall wear my jewel
lower.
*Flamineo.* [*aside*] That's better – *she must wear his jewel lower.*
(I ii 227–8; my italics)

There is an infinite weariness in Flamineo's voice when he says :

O, no oaths for God's sake. (IV ii 147)

The strident courage which Flamineo shows in dying –

Strike thunder, and strike loud to my farewell.
(v vi 276)

– is a quality which he shares with all Webster's Machiavellians; and this, the one admirable quality in so many of his characters, manifests Webster's peculiarly limited and deformed notion of ethics. We find in Webster only the virtue of Hell: the courage of despair. The stridency of this pagan courage is very evident when Bracciano cries :

> . . . Monticelso,
> *Nemo me impune lacessit,* (III ii 178–9)

or when Francisco proclaims :

> *Flectere si nequeo superos, Acheronta movebo.*
>                                              (IV i 139)

Denied insight into any virtue other than Stoical courage, Webster tries to erect unflinching perseverance in evil into the sum of moral goodness. In the process he is disingenuous. As Lamb remarked, 'This White Devil of Italy sets off a bad cause so speciously, and pleads *with such an innocence-resembling boldness*, that we . . . are ready to expect, when she has done her pleadings, that . . . all the court will rise and make proffer to defend her in spite of the utmost conviction of her guilt'.[6] Vittoria is dishonourable : Webster simply makes her behave as if she were honourable. This is an artistic insincerity – a lie in the poet's heart – of which Shakespeare would not have been guilty; but Webster, having no profound hold on any system of moral values, found it easy to write for Vittoria dissembling verse which in its righteous simplicity seems to proclaim her honesty in the face of her accusers.

It is consonant with Webster's unbalanced outlook that the distinguishing mark of his Machiavellian 'heroes' is their individualism. In Shakespeare individualism is an infallible mark of villainy :

> Richard loves Richard; that is, I am I.
>                            (*Richard III*, v iii 236)

Like Richard III, Iago, and Edmund in Shakespeare, Lodovico, the Cardinal, Bosola, and Flamineo are all individualists, and all villains.

The atmosphere in which Webster's characters live is the atmosphere of a corrupt court. The description of 'France' at the beginning of *The Duchess of Malfi* sets off the scene of Webster's play by contrast :

> In seeking to reduce both state and people
> To a fix'd order, their judicious king
> Begins at home ... (1 i 5–7)

To point the contrast, Bosola – who is one of the 'dissolute/And infamous persons' (1 i 8–9) who are banished from any healthy court – enters just as this speech is finished. If Webster were an orthodox Elizabethan, the rest of the play would be an illustration of what happens in a state of which the Prince himself is evil :

> *Death, and diseases through the whole land spread.*
> (1 i 15)

But while the atmosphere of the play is precisely the atmosphere described in these opening lines, there is in Webster, as we have already mentioned, no convincing statement of the positive aspect of Degree; we do not for a moment believe that when the Duke and Cardinal are dead the state of Amalfi will return to a condition of health and normality. While the atmosphere of Webster's plays is as unhealthy as that of 'Vienna' in *Measure for Measure*, there is in Webster no Messianic Duke to return and save the state from chaos. The 'mist' of the two plays is all-embracing : we can form no notion of another world which will be revealed when the rottenness of Amalfi has come to a head and been purged away. Comfortable words spoken at the end of *The White Devil* and *The Duchess of Malfi* carry no conviction; if we take evil away from Webster's world, nothing is left.

This explains the curious futility of all Webster's characters. When Bosola is asked how Antonio was killed, he answers :

> In a mist : I know not how –
> Such a mistake as I have often seen
> In a play. (v v 94–6)

Very similar in tone is the reply of the Duke in *The Duchess of Malfi*, when he is asked why he brought about the death of the Duchess; he replies that he had hoped to gain

An infinite mass of treasure by her death. (IV ii 285)

This explanation is so off-hand and perfunctory that it can only be termed an *excuse* : the Duke is in fact at a loss to find any plausible reason for his actions.

All Webster's characters, indeed, and particularly his most consummate 'politicians', have only the most tenuous hold on reality; they are characterized by the same 'motiveless malignity' that Coleridge noticed in Iago. But whereas Iago is a subordinate character in *Othello*, so that we are prepared to accept the convention by which he is simply 'The Villain', a man who desires evil because it is his nature to do so, Webster's plays are almost entirely peopled by such characters.

Without adopting the attitude of the 'naturalistic' critic, we must maintain that there are too many inconsistencies in Webster's plays; and whereas inconsistencies are readily passed over when – as in Shakespeare – they are subservient to some important dramatic purpose, in Webster there is no deeper purpose than to make our flesh creep, and we feel an inevitable resentment.

There is in fact something a trifle ridiculous about Webster. When we have seen his two plays we have indeed 'supp'd full of horrors', and overheard 'talk fit for a charnel'. An irruption of real humour – humour of the Shakespearean sort – would knock Webster's waxworks into a cocked hat. He is too evidently bent on exploiting the emotions of his audience.

Webster, that is to say, is a decadent. He is decadent in the sense that he is incapable of realizing the whole of life in the form in which it revealed itself to the Elizabethans. By concentrating exclusively on the narrow aspect of life revealed in one mood, he threw the relations of the whole out of harmony. In his work the proper relations between the individual and society, between God and Man, are overthrown. The sensationalism of his plays is the stigma of an outlook on life as narrow as it is intense. Webster sees the human situation as a chaotic struggle, lit indeed by flashes of 'bitter lightning', but fated to sink again into a mist of confusion and sub-human activity.

SOURCE : *Scrutiny*, XVI (1949).

NOTES

1. E. M. W. Tillyard, *The Elizabethan World Picture* (London, 1943) pp. 17–18.

2. *The Art of Fiction* (London, 1884).

3. The fact that Webster used commonplace books supports this diagnosis.

4. *Hamlet* owes more to the Revenge tradition, and less to the tradition of the Morality, than any other of Shakespeare's great tragedies; and while it contains passages of brilliant poetry, *Hamlet* lacks the unity and the tremendous moral force of *King Lear* and *Macbeth*. It is with the Shakespeare of *Hamlet* that Webster has something in common.

5. There is little need to emphasize the remarkable amount of animal-imagery in the two plays. As we should expect, most of the animals mentioned are ravenous or sinister.

6. *Specimens of English Dramatic Poets who Lived about the Time of Shakespeare* (London, 1808). (My italics.)

# John Russell Brown

## FROM INTRODUCTION TO
## *THE WHITE DEVIL* (1960)

In setting his play in Italy, with dukes, cardinals, and mistresses for its characters, with passionate love, ambition, jealousy, and revenge for its motives, and with machiavellian intrigues, poisonings, stabbings, and court ceremonial for its action, Webster was following well-known examples: Shakespeare's Iago and Iachimo are Italian villains in this tradition; Marston's *Insatiate Countess* and Middleton's *Women Beware Women* are set within it. Some dramatists used this hot-house setting – a northerner's view of Italy in the fifteen-seventies and eighties – for its own sake, and to exploit its opportunities for eloquence, passion, and suspense. For others, it was a setting in which to cry aloud for 'Justice', the wild justice of revenge, or the more severe and personal justice of a northern, puritan conscience. For Webster, the Italian setting had both appeals: he rose fully to its eloquence, passion, and suspense, and throughout his play – not always loudly, but persistently – there is the cry for justice and revenge. To the last scene, both dramatic appeals are maintained; we are amazed and awed by the spectacle of Vittoria and Flamineo passionately and ambitiously dying, and we are also caught up in the meting out of justice, not only to them, but also, through Giovanni, to their persecutors. Webster seems to have exploited greedily all possibilities, but, on reflection, we must also own that his amalgam is dexterously consistent.

There are other modes of tragedy which Webster copied, as, for instance, the 'full and heightened style' of Chapman. His was a tragedy which took its form from a considered (if not very deep) view of court society and politics, and of stoical personal behaviour; basically its characters were examples of virtue and vice, and its climaxes were touched with sententious comment

on human life in general. Webster praised Chapman and sometimes imitated him in his dialogue, and an even less 'popular'
writer, William Alexander, he constantly used as a mine of
sententious utterance for his own characters. He followed both,
certainly, in a tendency to generalize : the first 'sentence' is in
the second line of *The White Devil*, and its last scene concludes
with one. Webster's tragedy is not so obviously organized around
a single theme as Chapman's, but its very title suggests that
Vittoria is not only an individual but also a type; there is a
general name which fits her, and which, it may sometimes seem,
she is made to fit.

Webster's tragedy is also akin to various forms of narrative
drama. Chronicle-plays are echoed in its episodes of the papal
election and the wedding festivities, in its exploitation of super-
numeraries such as lawyer, conjurer, courtier, or physician, and
in its presentation of a sequence of events rather than a single
crisis. And like the best history-plays – like Shakespeare's *Richard
II*, *Henry IV*, or *King John* – it presents a series of related and
contrasted figures, not a single hero, and is concerned with
society as well as with individuals – although here it is an exclusively professional and court society. And, like Shakespeare
in *Macbeth* or *Antony and Cleopatra*, Webster combined a
chronicle-play technique with interests and devices derived from
medieval narrative tragedy, and so presented the rise and fall of
Fortune's wheel. Nor is that all, for when Flamineo turns to the
audience and says :

> O men
> That lie upon your death-beds, and are haunted
> With howling wives, ne'er trust them, . . . (v vi 154–6)

Webster may have gone beyond Shakespeare's example and
momentarily borrowed from plays like *Arden of Feversham* or
Heywood's *A Woman Killed with Kindness* – domestic tragedies
of exemplary narrative which were immediately relevant to the
everyday life of their audiences.

By borrowing some structural devices from chronicle-plays,
Webster was bound to lose something of the concentration which
is often considered a hallmark of tragedy; but apparently this

was not a fault in his eyes, for these devices are repeated in *The
Duchess of Malfi*. Moreover, he went outside tragic example
for other features of *The White Devil*. Possibly there is something
of the sophisticated sensationalism of Beaumont and Fletcher's
tragi-comedies in some rapid changes in the attitudes of
Monticelso, Vittoria, and Bracciano, and in Flamineo's feigned
death. Certainly there is much of Marston's satiric mode in the
comments of Flamineo, Lodovico, and Francisco, who are all,
on occasion, satirical observers like the heroes of *The Malcontent*,
*The Fawne*, or Sharpham's *The Fleire*. Tourneur had also
introduced a satirical observer into his tragedies, linking him,
something in the manner of Hamlet, with the more old-fashioned
revenger, and Jonson, while avoiding a single satirical mouthpiece, had chosen subjects for his tragedies which enabled
satirical comments to accompany disaster. Webster may well have
remembered all these examples, for the satire in *The White
Devil* partakes of all these forms. Occasionally, when the relationship of Vittoria and Camillo, or even of Vittoria and Bracciano,
is the object of the satire and Flamineo stands unengaged, manipulating the situation, it might even seem that Webster was
indebted to the citizen comedies of cuckoldry which, earlier in
his career, he had helped Dekker to write, and which – as his
apparent borrowings from Sharpham's *Cupid's Whirligig*
suggest – he was probably still reading with pleasure and
interest.

Webster wrote a mongrel drama – one hesitates to call it
'tragedy' after such a recital – and as far as we know he was only
able to succeed in it twice. That, perhaps, is more than could be
expected, for such cormorant tendencies would normally ensure
a muddled failure. But he was a careful, painstaking writer, as
we have already seen; he worked slowly and his restless mind
was constantly leading him to repeat and modify what he had
written. His compilations were not likely to be thoughtless; even
if they were not perfect wholes, their various parts would be
deeply and minutely considered. And two further points follow :
his plays are highly individual, for, although he borrowed from
others, few borrowed so widely as he; and highly complex, for
few borrowed so repeatedly as he. . . .

Critical opinion cannot speak with certain or united voice

about Webster's purposes; it has proved possible to talk of him as an old-fashioned moralist, as a sensationalist, as a social dramatist, as an imagist or dramatic symphonist, as a man fascinated by death, or a man halting between his inherited and his individual values. Where an artist's purposes are thus uncertain, and where he follows no simple or single tradition, we may proceed towards an understanding of his art by another track, by trying to define more closely the nature of his individual style; for a dramatist this involves a study of his use of language and his dramatic technique – a study of the kind of dramatic experience he communicates to an audience.

For a start we may say that the plot or structure of *The White Devil* is loose and rambling, a gothic aggregation rather than a steady exposition and development towards a single consummation. It has something of the width and range of a history-play. It could be called a revenge tragedy, yet there is no single revenger: Monticelso is at first ready to 'stake a brother's life' for the sake of revenge, but later he says ' 'tis damnable'; Francisco is a revenger who works mostly through other men and escapes scot-free at the end; Lodovico is a revenger who satisfies his own pride while working for Francisco, and finally loses his life, and Giovanni stands for justice in revenge, inexperienced but fully resolved. The play may be also called a tragedy of passion, or of great deeds overthrown, but there is no single disaster: Bracciano, Marcello, and Cornelia take their several exits, and only at the last do Vittoria and Flamineo die together. As a satirical drama, as we have already seen, it has three commentators instead of the more usual single one. (Notice that, when we begin to analyse the nature of Webster's dramatic style, his heterogeneous debts to other dramatists begin to make sense; at least they all seem to serve a consistent technical purpose.) Such multiplicity is not found in any of the contemporary accounts of Vittoria which may have been Webster's sources; it was he who introduced the death of Marcello and the madness of Cornelia in the last act, who developed Flamineo's role, brought Francisco to Padua to act as commentator, gave Lodovico a personal motive for revenge, and added to the importance of Giovanni at the close.

It is popularly supposed that *The White Devil* is contrived to

present the maximum number of deaths and horrors; but this
is true, if at all, of the last act only. In the earlier acts all seems
to be contrived to allow the maximum variety of comment. The
deaths of Isabella and Camillo are carefully presented in dumb
show, so that they forward the narrative without engaging our
interest too closely with their victims. Our interest is chiefly
claimed, at this stage of the play, by arguments and direct
comment : the first scene is an argument, the second and third
present a series of them; when action is called for, Flamineo or
some other is present to describe it and fill out our understanding.
It might be said that Webster indulged an almost literary zeal
for description, to a degree dangerous in a drama. The third
act is chiefly occupied with a trial scene, worked up from the
slightest of hints in his source, and used, as so often in other
plays, for the exciting exploration of a single situation – and in
this play, the situation remains almost the same at the end of it as
it was at the beginning. It is only in the last act of all that action
and horrors press upon us; and even there, a commentary is
maintained throughout. Whatever action takes place, there is
always some one observing and commenting upon it : Francisco
watches Bracciano's helmet being sprinkled with poison, and
Flamineo joins him to watch Bracciano die; Lodovico watches
Zanche make love to Francisco; Francisco and Flamineo observe
Cornelia's madness, and the very assassins are chorus to the
stabbing of Zanche, Vittoria, and Flamineo; Flamineo describes
Vittoria's death and then, uniquely, he alone describes his own.

Our attention has passed from the structure of the play to the
handling of individual scenes; this was perhaps inevitable, for
they show similar techniques. As a commentator is always
provided for the action, so in the course of a scene the speeches
are continually turning from the expression of individual feeling
to the expression of generalities. The poisoning of Bracciano may
be taken as an example : even as he is speaking of his own pain
and helplessness, our attention is drawn aside to the disguised
Francisco ironically commenting 'Sir be of comfort', and to the
despairing Vittoria who cries 'I am lost for ever'; but more
than this, Bracciano himself draws our attention away from himself, towards all physicians, to all soft, natural deaths and to
howling women, and, as soon as he moves off-stage, Flamineo

takes up his theme, speaking of the solitariness of all dying princes. In this play, intimate feeling for a single character is intermittent only: none of its characters draws attention wholly to himself for more than a few consecutive lines;[1] as we tend to identify ourselves with one character, we are forced back, not only to observe the other characters on the stage and their relationships, but also to contemplate the relevance of the action to mankind in general.

It is a restless technique; besides insisting on the general, Webster seems to have aimed at a continual series of shocks, not only large *coups de théâtre* (though the play has its share of them), but brief, stinging changes of direction. One might instance Cornelia trying to explain away the death of Marcello and so defend the life of her remaining son, Flamineo:

> ... and so I know not how,
> For I was out of my wits, he fell with's head
> Just in my bosom.

There is a pause and she looks round for signs of belief, but a page speaks, 'This is not true madam'. 'I pray thee peace', flashes Cornelia, but at once she perceives that all is in vain, and she concludes in tame explanation (a third contrasted reaction):

> One arrow's graz'd already; it were vain
> T'lose this: for that will ne'er be found again.
>
> (v ii 64–9)

More obviously theatrical are the changes of fortune in the last scene, where Webster, risking the serious reception of the play's last moments, introduced a bizarre, almost laughable, mock-suicide: Vittoria and Zanche think they are doomed, but then they see a chance of eliminating the newly dangerous Flamineo, and then are tricked into believing that they have succeeded, and then, finally, are shocked by Flamineo rising to his feet, having merely feigned death. (Webster was not like a photographer who composes a formal portrait or group, and carefully records it with a long exposure; he has recorded the movement of men rather than their composure, the strain as their wills conflict with their impulses, their reasons with their emotions.)

And after so much excitement and movement, Flamineo draws our attention away again, to all men that lie upon their death-beds and to the cunning of all women. *The White Devil* presents its characters in flashlight moments, against a background as wide and general as continual choric comment can establish it.

Webster's use of language is in keeping with such techniques. Two characteristics stand out. First, the dialogue is often knotted and complex : in the more descriptive passages it sharpens towards the epigrammatic; its vocabulary and images are un-expected, various, punning, and sensuously evocative; the pulse of utterance alternately rushes, hesitates, tugs, and reiterates. Secondly, its fine passages – the poetic expressions which remain in the memory and have a winged validity both in and beyond their dramatic context – are for the most part extremely brief, a single image or phrase perhaps, or else are a little more ex-tended, but nervously, almost hesitantly, expressed. There is, in short, little sustained poetic utterance; long speeches are either deliberate description (which is often in prose), or set-pieces like the telling of a dream or tale, or a considered statement in a law-court. The quarrel in Act iv, Scene ii may be taken as an example :

> *Vittoria.* '*Florence*' ! This is some treacherous plot, my lord, –
> To me, he ne'er was lovely I protest,
> So much as in my sleep.
> *Bracciano.*                    Right : they are plots. –
> Your beauty ! O, ten thousand curses on't.
> How long have I beheld the devil in crystal?
> Thou hast led me, like an heathen sacrifice,
> With music, and with fatal yokes of flowers
> To my eternal ruin. – Woman to man
> Is either a god or a wolf. (84–92)

There is an instantaneous change of thought at each dash marked in this passage; and within each train of thought there are progressions or minor changes of emphasis. The most ex-tensive and powerful image is prepared for by another related to it (though more briefly expressed), and is itself presented, as it were, in two stages : 'With music, *and with* fatal yokes . . .'.

And immediately this statement has been attained, the pulse drops and Bracciano continues with a generalized aphorism. There follows, shortly, a more lengthy speech for Vittoria, but this is built up by a number of short questions, giving a breathless rather than a massive indictment. When Vittoria, like Bracciano, reaches a dominant image she expresses it in two, or possibly three, stages, and then changes the tone completely:

> I had a limb corrupted to an ulcer,
> But I have cut it off : and now I'll go
> Weeping to heaven on crutches. – For your gifts,
> I will return them all; and I ... (121–4)

An example of the complex descriptive passages is Flamineo's description of Camillo :

a gilder that hath his brains perish'd with quick-silver is not more cold in the liver. The great barriers moulted not more feathers than he hath shed hairs, by the confession of his doctor. An Irish gamester that will play himself naked, and then wage all downward, at hazard, is not more venturous. So unable to please a woman that like a Dutch doublet all his back is shrunk into his breeches.

(I ii 27–34)

There is a connection between all these details, yet the speaker is never at pains to make it fully explicit; his utterance is staccato and often grammatically incomplete or ironically casual; his images are unexpected and from widely differing sources, and his vocabulary is allusive ('and downward') and punning ('wage ... hazard ... venturous'). The effect of such a style is, as its nature, two-fold. First, it must be followed closely to be fully appreciated; being subtle and complex, it demands detailed attention – and this, of course, is in accordance with the multiplicity of the play's structure, for its audience must be ready to watch and hear many disparate yet related things. Secondly, our appreciation must be nervous, ready to respond to momentary stimulus.

A play's structure, scene-handling, and use of language all affect its characterization. In *The White Devil* this also is impressionistic or momentarily perceived, being repeatedly under the stress of conflict or surprise; and there are contrasts and re-

lationships between many of the characters according to their
roles of mistress, lover, machiavellian, revenger. Vittoria is one
of the dominant characters (if not, as the title proclaims her, *the*
dominant one), yet even she is presented fragmentarily; there
are only four scenes of any length in which she appears and her
mood, or tone, is very different in each of them. For an actress,
this presents a great difficulty, for there is no build-up of
presentation; each of Vittoria's scenes starts on a new note, with
little or no preparation in earlier scenes.[2] Flamineo is the most
consistent and continuously presented character, but his consistency lies in a mercurial nature; Webster made him draw attention to this :

> It may appear to some ridiculous
> Thus to talk knave and madman; and sometimes
> Come in with a dried sentence, stuff'd with sage.
> But this allows my varying of shapes, –
> Knaves do grow great by being great men's apes.[3]
>
>                                        (IV ii 243–7)

So he varies shapes more quickly than other characters vary
moods; the whole is fragmentary, subtle, intricate.

· Such was Webster's dramatic style, the instrument he forged
out of many elements. It is not the instrument to present, with
massive assurance, types of good and evil; if a critic sees that in
*The White Devil*, the assurance must come from him and not
from the play. Nor is it an instrument for presenting a general
society of men, or for varying the presentation of a number of
general themes; if a critic sees only such things in the play, he
must be insensitive to the immediacy of the dialogue which draws
the audience momently towards individual characters. Yet there
must have been some motive for creating so individual an instrument : it is good for variety, for shock and surprise; it is good for
irony and detailed, critical humour; it is good for moments of
poetic utterance and for the subtle, nervous presentation of
human thought and feeling. Its disadvantages would seem to be
– from the point of view of an easy success – its restlessness, its
persistently small scale (in spite of presenting great events), and,
finally, the demand it makes on its audience to pay attention

minutely and unflaggingly. Since Webster created this dramatic
style (and used it only slightly modified in his next play) we may
suppose that he did not rate these disadvantages very highly; he
may even have considered them to be advantages. Let us
examine what is, perhaps, the most dangerous of its shortcomings, the demands it makes on the audience's close attention. If
we can see how this could have appeared as an advantage to
Webster, we may come close to defining the nature of his artistic
purposes, the bias of his dramatic vision.

The very title, *The White Devil,* offers an immediate clue,
suggesting that this play presents some person or persons who
are not what they seem, devils transformed into angels of light.
In the play, this idea is repeated again and again: there are
verbal echoes of it in 'We call the cruel fair' (I ii 213), 'If the
devil/Did ever take good shape' (III ii 216–17), and 'the
devil in crystal' (IV ii 88). And the same idea is expressed in
other images, in passages relating to other characters besides
Vittoria:

> O the art,
> The modest form of greatness! that do sit
> Like brides at wedding dinners, with their looks turn'd
> From the least wanton jests, their puling stomach
> Sick of the modesty, when their thoughts are loose,
> Even acting of those hot and lustful sports
> Are to ensue about midnight ... (IV iii 143–9)

or again:

> O the rare tricks of a Machivillian!
> He doth not come like a gross plodding slave
> And buffet you to death: no, my quaint knave,
> He tickles you to death; makes you die laughing ...
>
> (V iii 193–6)

or more subtly and more comprehensively:

> I have liv'd
> Riotously ill, like some that live in court;
> And sometimes, when my face was full of smiles

Have felt the maze of conscience in my breast.
Oft gay and honour'd robes those tortures try, –
We think cag'd birds sing, when indeed they cry.

(v iv 118–23)

Those that 'live in court' – that is, all the characters of this play –
may be deceitful; as they smile they may be murdering, as they
sing they may be weeping. To recognize their deceit a minute
and determined scrutiny will be necessary. Webster's choice of
images reinforces the same point. He used, for example, an extraordinary number of animal images – on one count, over a
hundred[4] – so that, behind the human activity, sophisticated and
courtly, the audience's attention is constantly drawn to an
activity or habit which is animal. He also used many images
associated with witchcraft, with illusions ('as men at sea think
land and trees and ships go that way they go'), and with poisons
('the canthadries which are scarce seen to stick upon the flesh
when they work to the heart'). And of course conjuring, poison,
disguises and dissimulation are not only images, but recurrent
episodes in the very action of the play.[5] With so much emphasis
on deception in the action, images, and ideas of this play, an
audience must watch closely and subtly if it is to see, hear, and
understand aright; here lies a justification for the demands
Webster's dramatic style makes upon an audience.

As soon as we begin to respond intently, subtleties open up before us: when Bracciano vows to protect Vittoria, we become
aware that he is vowing to execute two murders; when Flamineo
decries women, we become aware that he is encouraging Bracciano to be his sister's lover.[6] Some deceptions are made
abundantly clear by subsequent action – as Francisco's pretence
that he will not revenge[7] – but others are hidden or partly hidden
so that we hardly know how to respond: when Flamineo explains that he has not asked Bracciano for reward, we cannot be
sure that that is not precisely what he has done.[8] Our response
becomes subtle and intricate, and also insecure. The comments
which are so often made upon the action in the course of the play
are no longer straightforward or reliable: all the time we question the true intention of the speaker, asking whether he is
ironic or deceitful, or, for some ulterior purpose, bluntly honest;

the comments do not simplify the play for us, they involve us in
it, and make us question the implications of its action and dialogue. And the more intently we observe individual characters,
the less simple they become : which of Flamineo's many 'shapes'
is his true one? when Bracciano cries on his death-bed 'Vittoria?
Vittoria!', is it in anger, or in love and faith? Isabella has often
been called one of the very few simply 'good' characters in the
play; but such a view can scarcely survive a close scrutiny.
Arriving in Rome, she goes first to her kinsmen and not to her
husband (one might not censure her for this if later she herself
did not hotly deny that she had done, or ever would do, such a
thing), and her thoughts and hopes are all for herself, none for
her husband : the wrongs done to her are pardoned; her arms
shall charm and force him to obey her, and prevent him from
straying from her. All this is said in a quiet, lofty tone, without
any criticism unless it be in Francisco's brisk 'I wish it may. Be
gone'. When Isabella comes, as her kinsmen have arranged, face-
to-face with Bracciano, neither he nor she can speak peacefully :
'You are in health we see,' he tries tentatively, but she answers
with an innuendo, 'And above health / To see my lord well.' At
one and the same time, Isabella presumes the worst of him and
presents herself as selflessly humble. Within half-a-dozen lines,
their incompatibility is manifest; while Bracciano is self-defen-
sively angry, Isabella is always praising herself and reminding
him of his duties and shortcomings. Because she appears as a
defenceless woman speaking in a submissive tone, and because
he is openly angry, scornful, and brutal, the natural tendency is
to side with Isabella. But on a closer, or more sensitive, view, it
is impossible to side with either. There is perhaps a further
subtlety : Isabella suggests laying the blame for their divorce on
her 'supposed jealousy' and promises to deceive the others into
believing this by playing her part with 'a piteous and rent heart',
yet when she does put the blame on herself, she does it with such
abandoned hatred towards Vittoria and in a manner so
calculated to infuriate Bracciano (who must now, of course, say
nothing) that we may be tempted to think she is indeed that
which she seems, 'a foolish, mad, / And jealous woman', perhaps
deceiving herself.

The other supposedly 'good' characters are likewise vulner-

able. Marcello says that his sister's chastity is dearer to him than
her life, but, when Bracciano, by double murder, has made Vittoria his duchess and promised to advance her kindred, he at
once leaves Francisco to follow Bracciano; there is indeed a
touch of smugness and self-pity in Marcello's avowals of honesty
and poverty, and in his question about his brother's misdeed
when a child. Cornelia, so powerful and peremptory in reproof of
vice, also takes advantage of Bracciano's fortunes; and in defeat
she is deceitful, and in madness concerned, not with honour or
virtue,[9] but with the preservation of her son's body; her regard
for virtue has not been, we may suspect, for its own sake. This
may all seem *too* subtle and uncertain; and one must grant that
it would be hard to be conscious of all this during a performance.
Yet the play's title, its imagery and incidental comments, its dis-
simulating action, the complexity of its plot and dialogue, all
invite such a consciousness:

> Know many glorious women that are fam'd
> For masculine virtue, have been vicious . . .
>
>                                        (v vi 244-5)

May not Isabella or Cornelia be of this number?

One aspect of Webster's writing that was noticed earlier is the
manner in which disparate ideas are expressed in a single speech,
both in prose and verse, without any words bridging the gap between them. The only way to deliver such speeches satisfactorily
in the theatre is for the actor to be conscious of the unspoken
connections; if this is not achieved – and a good actor delights
to do it with dialogue so nervously and richly alive as Webster's –
the speeches will remain a sequence of unrelated utterances and
there can be no dramatic development. The essential thing is
for the actor to be aware of the unspoken thoughts and feelings
underneath, sustaining the utterance, and so to find some expression of them. Members of his audience may have very little conscious understanding of such subtleties – they have no time to
ask questions and make explicit judgements – but, nevertheless,
as they respond to the actor's *total* performance, they will, consciously or unconsciously, respond to those elements of it. So
Webster's very manner of writing makes us aware, perhaps un-

consciously, of that which is unspoken – and so why not of the hidden selfishness of Isabella or Cornelia?

Webster's characterization of Vittoria uses a similar 'undertow' of thought and feeling. The dominant impression she gives is of a passionate, courageous woman, and one who suggests that her lover should kill his wife and her husband. But her reaction to Cornelia's rebuke and curse in the first act hints at something else, at a regard for conventional morality underneath; having protested that nothing 'but blood' could have 'allayed' Bracciano's suit to her, she cries 'O me accurst' and rushes from the stage alone, and perhaps frightened. Her attitude here is sharply contrasted to both Flamineo's and Bracciano's. In the trial scene, on the defensive, she gives no sign of a hidden conscience, save only that she counterfeits innocence with alarming exactitude, as if she knew what it might be like. In the scene in the house of convertites, she shows that she can, painfully for Bracciano, give herself over to expressions of repentance; again she may be acting a part, but certainly she acts it to the life. Later when she yields and so regains Bracciano, we can only guess at her thoughts and feelings, for she does not speak at all, perhaps guilefully, knowing this will whet his appetite, or perhaps shamefully, wishing to keep something to herself. At her wedding festivities she is silent also, but when she realizes that Bracciano is poisoned she is horror-struck and, between her cries of grief and attempts to comfort him, we hear only 'I am lost for ever' and 'O me, this place is hell'; then she leaves the stage alone, as she had done after her mother's curse. Such hints that Vittoria feels the 'maze of conscience' (and they include silences as well as words) might escape many people's notice – except, certainly, an actress trying faithfully to perform the part – or if noticed they might be considered of little account. But the intent, involved audience must surely take account of other passages in the last scene, which become, at last, not hints, but bare statement. At the beginning of this scene, Vittoria is 'at her prayers', but when Flamineo enters and threatens her life she is successively scornful, accusing, and pleading; it is Zanche who thinks of a way of escape, and then Vittoria is quickly deceitful, cruel, and exulting – so far, all is unlike her former behaviour. When Flamineo rises from his feigned death, she is at first silent

and then cries for help. At this point her true assassins enter,
masked. Now facing death for the second time, she tries asking
for mercy, but she speaks now with more pride; then she tries
flattery, and then a proud show of courage and womanliness.
As she commands silence and respect, she rises to her part, and,
at first trembling, overcomes her fear at the thought of death :

> I am too true a woman :
> Conceit can never kill me : I'll tell thee what, –
> I will not in my death shed one base tear,
> Or if look pale, for want of blood, not fear.

The stroke itself is felt :

> 'Twas a manly blow –
> The next thou giv'st, murder some sucking infant,
> And then thou wilt be famous.

And then, in the moment of her greatest courage, comes another thought, quite different, but one which has been heard
before :

> O my greatest sin lay in my blood.
> Now my blood pays for't.

This implies no breakdown, for it is at this moment that
Flamineo is drawn to her :

> Th'art a noble sister –
> I love thee now; if woman do breed man
> She ought to teach him manhood : . . .

Vittoria is silent for a time, and when she does speak it is clear
that she has been thinking of life beyond death :

> My soul, like to a ship in a black storm,
> Is driven I know not whither.

And then, finally, her 'greatest sin' reminds her of other lives;
after another long silence her last words are :

> O happy they that never saw the court,
> Nor ever knew great man but by report.

Taken by itself, this might be an expression of momentary weakness; but at such a moment, it may show courage, being the true expression of Vittoria's deepest thoughts. We may think, as Webster suggested at the beginning of this play, that:

> affliction
> Expresseth virtue, fully, whether true,
> Or else adulterate. (1 i 49–51)

Certainly Vittoria's acknowledgement of her 'greatest sin', and of the torment of her soul, expresses thoughts and feelings that have earlier been heard only momentarily; those brief statements and longer silences have all been sustained by a great undertow, and its force she has felt despite her outward committal to a life of passion, ambition, and cunning.

Isabella, Cornelia, and Marcello, hiding self-concern behind an appearance of goodness, Vittoria with a sense of sin behind her courage and passion, Bracciano at once weak and steadfast in his love, perhaps unable to reconcile all he knows within himself ('Where's this good woman? . . . Away, you have abus'd me'[10]) – why was Webster so concerned with such characters, and why did he present them in this manner? Possibly Flamineo is there, at the end, to satisfy such a question. He too has had his moment of truth:

> I have a strange thing in me, to th'which
> I cannot give a name, without it be
> Compassion . . . (v iv 113–15)

and soon afterwards he has admitted that 'sometimes', when his face was 'full of smiles', he has 'felt the maze of conscience' in his breast. But he has put such thoughts behind him, and in the last scene he assumes more 'variety of shapes', to feed his own ambition and his appetite for ceaseless activity. When death comes to him, he tries to have done with all thought; he reiterates that he thinks of nothing:

> I remember nothing.
> There's nothing of so infinite vexation
> As man's own thoughts.

He tries to be concerned only with his immediate existence, for, in his state,

> While we look up to heaven we confound
> Knowledge with knowledge. O I am in a mist.

Yet, as he assumes his last 'shape' of defiant villainy, his denial of conscience is a reality for him, and a pain; he knows :

> This busy trade of life appears most vain,
> Since rest breeds rest, where all seek pain by pain.

In *The White Devil*, Webster has presented a 'busy trade of life', where judgement seems inescapable, not judgement by death merely, but by pain. He shows human beings who are not what they seem : those 'famed for masculine virtue' are not necessarily at peace in their inner consciousness; those who seem careless of consequence may have felt compassion; and the white devil herself may know what sin is, and, in her ultimate access of courage, know what fear and honesty are too. Man lives in a net : if he sins, directly, or by using the outward show of a virtue he has no desire for, or by failing to face the full truth about himself, some retribution must follow; he cannot deceive without bearing the consequence. Man's judgement is within, perhaps unknown to others, perhaps unrecognized as such by himself.

This is the kind of world which Webster has presented in his tragedy, and for which his unique dramatic style seems to have been created; his use of language, the pulse of his verse and prose, his images, the continual choric comment, ironic, humorous, and straightforward, the sensational happenings and sudden changes in action and sentiment, all seem entirely appropriate to this purpose. The multiplicity and looseness of his dramatic structure give a width of presentation; besides the characters that have already been examined here, Monticelso, who veers so suddenly in his attitude towards revenge, and Francisco, who several times so curiously accepts the role of compassionate observer, seem to be caught in the same net, and motivated, on occasion, by some undertow of hidden, and perhaps unconscious, thought and feeling.

There is, possibly, a further purpose in the multiplicity of the play's structure, for the various characters are not merely in apposition and contrast to each other; their stories are inextricably bound together, one event causing others. So Webster showed, it would seem, that man's actions do not influence only himself, but other men also, and that one ill deed brings others with it. For this reason, perhaps, he made Vittoria think in her last moments of those who have not lived where she has lived: in the intensity of her suffering, she may presume that mankind misuses mankind only at the court, that the rest of the world cannot be so dangerous. And when she is dead we are shown the course of hatred and retribution continuing, first in Lodovico's defiant, yet belittling, stoicism, and then in Giovanni's promise that justice shall pursue all the murderers. As his youthful voice points the moral:

> Let guilty men remember their black deeds
> Do lean on crutches, made of slender reeds.

we must surely listen to his words carefully and scrutinize his face; does he really have 'his uncle's villainous look already' as Flamineo has suggested? or is there any hope in his self-reliant, innocent voice that the 'bed of snakes is broke', that will has become purified and that underneath there is now no pride, or greed, passion or selfishness? There is no answer; the play leaves us with a sense of insecurity. The predicament which Webster presented is continual.

In writing such a play Webster took great risks, for he made great demands upon his own craft and imagination, upon the dramatic form, upon his actors and his audience. But as we watch, awed and insecure, we will feel pity in our hearts for those who suffer, for those who by pain seek pain; with its horrors, its deadly laughter and its intricacies, the dramatic experience is humane, and in Vittoria's end ennobling.

SOURCE: Introduction to *The White Devil*
(1960; 2nd edition, 1966).

NOTES

1. It is noteworthy that the only two soliloquies of any length (at the ends of IV i and V iv) are sustained by making the soliloquizer address a vision or ghost of some other person.

2. The actor of Francisco has the same problem in becoming, suddenly, a passive figure in Act V, the actor of Monticelso in the abrupt transition to Paul IV, and the actor of Lodovico on practically every appearance.

3. See also III i 30–1.

4. So Muriel Bradbrook, *Themes and Conventions of Elizabethan Tragedy* (Cambridge, 1935) p. 194.

5. This relation between the play's images and action has been demonstrated in detail by H. T. Price, 'The Function of Imagery in Webster', *P.M.L.A.*, LXX (1955) 717–39; he has claimed that such technique is uniquely elaborate in Webster.

6. These are two of many examples in an admirable discussion of this aspect of Webster's style by J. Smith, 'The Tragedy of Blood', *Scrutiny*, VIII (1939) 265–80.

7. Cf. IV i 3ff.

8. Cf. IV ii 222–42.

9. As Ophelia is in her first mad-scene (the comparison is apposite, for Webster was indebted to *Hamlet* here).

10. V iii 17 and 82.

*James L. Calderwood*

## THE DUCHESS OF MALFI: STYLES OF CEREMONY (1962)

In his review-article, 'Motives in *Malfi*' (*Essays in Criticism*, October 1959), McD. Emslie presents an interesting departure from what has been, until recently, a prevailing fashion in Webster criticism – the careful examination not so much of the plays themselves but of their literary failings. For critics with this sort of aim, Webster has been a fairly easy mark. Admissions are not difficult to make : Webster's plots are replete with the most un-Aristotelian contingencies and blind alleys; his verse, happily suited to the aphorism, is only rarely able to sustain itself well beyond a couple of lines; his action is uncomfortably near to being melodramatic; his characterization is often either vague or else too nearly Theophrastian; and finally – a fault for which some of his critics have been unable to forgive him – his plays were not written by Shakespeare. Underlying much of the specific criticism of Webster is a general distaste for his philosophy, or, more accurately, for his lack of a philosophy, for his failure to supply in his plays a governing moral perspective. For example, W. A. Edwards finds ('John Webster', *Determinations*, ed. F. R. Leavis, London, 1934, p. 176) that 'in Webster's tragedies there is no such internal scale [as that provided in *Hamlet*] to measure depravity'. Ian Jack holds a similar view ('The Case of John Webster', *Scrutiny*, XVI, March 1949, p. 38): 'If one reads through [both plays] noting down the *sententiae* and moralizing asides, one finds oneself in possession of a definite attempt at a "philosophy", a moral to the tale.' However, Jack finds that the tale itself is altogether too discrete from the attempted moral. He concludes (p. 43) that the plays exemplify Webster's 'artistic insincerity' and that Webster himself is a 'decadent in the sense that he is incapable of realizing the whole of life in the form in which it revealed itself to the Elizabethans'.

The argument of Edwards and Jack, however it may apply to *The White Devil*, seems wholly untenable with respect to *The Duchess of Malfi*. Certainly no one, I think, denies that the later play has an abundance of depravity and is embarrassingly rich in unintegrated moral comment, or that there are excrescences of plot and inconsistencies of character. But these faults can be granted without our having to concede either that the play is a dramatic failure or that Webster is morally despicable. On the contrary, the view offered here is that the play is, among other things, a powerful and subtle articulation of a thoroughly Elizabethan theme – the relationship between individual impulse and societal norms, specifically the religious and political doctrine of Degree. And I shall suggest that Webster, far from failing to present an 'internal scale to measure depravity', is entirely willing to test evil against good. His principal dramatic means to this end is his employment of ceremony and ritual for the evaluation of private action. My intention here is to examine several crucial scenes in order to suggest how Webster's use of ceremony helps clarify some of the rather vexing problems of action, motivation, and character.

In a play which focuses so largely upon revenge and violence, motivation is unusually important. In the corruption scene of Act I Ferdinand, referring to the Duchess, says to Bosola: 'she's a young widow – /I would not have her marry again.'

> *Bosola.*                                   No, sir?
> *Ferdinand.* Do not you ask the reason : but be satisfied,
> I say I would not. (I i 255–8)

Bosola, whether satisfied or not, does not ask the reason; but critics have not been so easily put off. What Ferdinand later calls his 'main cause' – his hope to have gained 'An infinite mass of treasure by her death' (IV ii 285) had she died without remarrying – has been unanimously disallowed by critics for having no dramatic confirmation elsewhere. On the other hand, most critics have acknowledged as at least plausible the case made by F. L. Lucas and supported by Clifford Leech that Ferdinand acts from incestuous jealousy. But Leech himself is not very happy with his proposal, for after all, he finds, 'Ferdinand leaves us perplexed, not quite certain of the dramatist's purpose' (*John Webster*, London, 1951, p. 105). However, the perplexity which he complains of is discredited – or at least so I am convinced – by his own findings. A certain haziness of motivation need not result from a corresponding haziness of authorial purpose but may be deliberately built into a character : it is Ferdinand who is unsure of himself, not Webster. From Ferdinand's 'Do not you ask the reason' – certainly an answer that makes us want to ask the reason – we can assume either that he does not understand the grounds of his behaviour or that he prefers not to state them. But a flat refusal to discuss the matter is surely a poor means of concealing information, especially from a man who has been singled out precisely because he is an adept at ferreting facts. Ferdinand's brusqueness here suggests a lack of self-awareness, not so much an irritation at being questioned as a failure ever to have asked himself the same question.

It is in the following exchanges between the Duchess and her brothers that we should expect to find an indication of the motives underlying the demonic punishments of Act IV. There is clearly, even before the offence, a pressure behind Ferdinand's speech that is absent from his brother's. The Cardinal is willing to consider the prospect of remarriage provided it involves 'the addition, honour'; Ferdinand categorically forbids it : 'Marry! they are most luxurious / Will wed twice'. It is Ferdinand who harps upon the sensual temptations of remarriage – 'luxurious' (i.e. lecherous), 'those joys, / Those lustful pleasures', his lamprey metaphor; and he associates sensuality with corruption and disease – 'Their livers are more spotted/Than Laban's sheep' – an association which he dwells upon again, most significantly, later in the play. Taking a cue from the Cardinal, however, Ferdinand does insert one important non-sensual objection to the Duchess's possible remarriage : he likens private marriage to 'the irregular crab, / Which though 't goes backward, thinks that it goes right, / Because it goes its own way'. This is essentially an argument from Degree : the reliance upon private choice, especially when that choice descends upon an inferior, con-

stitutes an infringement of the rigidly established social hierarchy and is, ultimately, an attack upon cosmological order.

There is by no means sufficient evidence here to persuade us
one way or another about the brothers' opposition to a possible
remarriage. However, the Duchess provides us a critical perspective to the scene when she suggests that the brotherly duet has
been a piece of staged ceremony: 'I think this speech between
you both was studied, / It came so roundly off.' The sequence of
mutually supported and elaborated arguments has seemed impressive; but the stylization to which the Duchess calls attention
enables us to observe a schism between the form and the content
of their objections. For in actuality the brothers have offered
only the appearance of an argument, not any logical grounds
for opposition, but merely opposition. What they have said is
simply that they do not want the Duchess to remarry, but their
motives have been left unclarified. Ferdinand's emotional antag-
onism – we cannot at this point give it a more precise title –
has been both partly obfuscated and superficially ennobled by
the ritual formality of a 'studied' presentation. Since the brothers
are wholly unaware that Antonio or anyone else is a potential,
much less a favoured, suitor, their argument from Degree is entirely irrelevant, at best hypothetical. But as we shall see, it is not
irrelevant structurally: the hypothetical attack upon order becomes actual after the brothers' exit, when the Duchess reverses
the courtly tradition in her wooing of Antonio. By comparing
these two brief scenes, as well as others later on, we shall find that
Webster, at times so cavalier in his desregard of dramatic consistency, can at other times unify apparently discrete elements of
action by remarkably subtle nexuses of imagery and structure.

The Duchess conducts her courtship of Antonio as a staged
ceremony which is in effect a casting off of the essential values
represented in ceremony. As a depersonalized, formalized expression of belief and emotion, ceremony is necessarily in the service of
supra-individual interests, and its participants make at least a gesture of endorsing those interests by voluntarily restricting the free
play of private emotion to the symbolic pattern prescribed by the
ceremonial role. Although ceremony and ritual are by no means
prohibitive of individual expression – but merely impose a form
upon the content of private experience – they are confirmations

of order, of an order that exists to some extent regardless of the individual, even if the individual is a Duchess. Indeed, as Antonio's first speech in the play implies, it is precisely because the individual here is a Duchess – the political and moral exemplar who, if corrupt, causes '*Death, and diseases through the whole land*' – that her conduct has serious and even tragic implications. For what the Duchess is engaging in here is not properly ceremony but ceremony-in-reverse, a form of deceremonialization by which she divests herself of the responsibilities of her social role.

The Duchess's defection from Degree is not simply the product of impetuosity; after her brothers' exit her determination to assert herself is couched in convincing terms : 'if all my royal kindred / Lay in my way unto this marriage, / I'd make them my low foot-steps.' Nor, as her last remark to Cariola indicates, is she unaware of the broader implications of her action :

> . . . wish me good speed
> For I am going into a wilderness,
> Where I shall find nor path, nor friendly clew
> To be my guide. (i i 358–61)

This journey beyond the restrictions, but also the safeguards, of Degree into a 'wilderness' where her only guides are the dictates of private impulse cannot help reminding us of Ferdinand's warning about 'the irregular crab, / Which though 't goes backward, thinks that it goes right, / Because it goes its own way'. But the Duchess's 'own way' is not a random one. The 'wilderness' into which she goes may be thoroughly disordered, but her means of getting there are quite systematic.

She first establishes Degree with almost ritual formality. As Antonio enters, at her bidding, her greeting is an expression of superiority : 'I sent for you – sit down.' This is of course ironic, and charmingly so in the light of her intentions; but it is also the initial step towards a moral infraction the gravity of which charm fails to dissipate. It is also significant, particularly in a scene which makes a symbolic point of bodily positions, that at the beginning the audience is presented with a view of Antonio seated and the Duchess standing above him, prepared to dictate her 'will'. She quickly forces an opportunity to use the word *husband*, and then

with considerable psychological subtlety suggests her concern
about 'What's laid up for tomorrow', which, coming hard after
the word 'expense', seems to regard Antonio in his inferior role
as treasurer – and so he interprets it; but then she corrects him by
explaining that she meant 'What's laid up yonder for me', that is,
in heaven, which gently insinuates Antonio into an equality with
her as fellow mortal. Further promptings by the Duchess, the
most important of which are of a ceremonial nature – the transfer
of the ring (415), the symbolic elevation of rank (429–30) –
lead Antonio to realize 'whereto [her] favours tend'; but though
he is tempted by ambition, he remains uncomfortably aware of
his 'unworthiness', of his prescribed station in the hierarchy of
Degree. To the Duchess, for whom Degree is by this time irrelevant, his hesitance is puzzling: 'Sir, be confident, / What is't
distracts you?' Despite his later reminder about her brothers,
it is not fear of violence that is troubling Antonio: it is made
sufficiently clear that he is an excellent soldier, a man of proved
courage and ability. It is also made sufficiently clear that he is
an honourable man, one who would be honest, as he says, 'were
there nor heaven, nor hell'. Indeed, his distraction here could
only be felt by an honourable man, for it stems from a conflict
between private desire and societal values. Part of the irony of
the courtship scene is that the Duchess abandons Degree in
wooing the one man who thoroughly endorses Degree: his
opening lines in Act 1 display his admiration for the French
king who sought 'to reduce both state and people / To a fix'd
order'. It is in the light of Antonio's reluctance to overturn
Degree that Webster, by a kind of literary counterpoint, enables
us to judge the nature of the Duchess's conduct. For the
ceremonial revelation of her feelings to Antonio is necessitated
by the inhibitions of Degree. The 'great', she says,

> Are forc'd to express our violent passions
> In riddles, and in dreams, and leave the path
> Of simple virtue, which was never made
> To seem the thing it is not. (1 i 445–8)

It is surely a perversion of terminology when the 'path of simple
virtue' – which echoes her earlier image of the pathless 'wilderness' – has become representative of uninhibited passion. Having

discarded her own loyalties to 'fix'd order', she had nevertheless been utilizing until now the symbolic forms of order – ceremony and ritual – as psychological weapons designed to overcome Antonio's more entrenched loyalties and to release the passions which those loyalties have so far successfully constrained. Her final resort is to dispense altogether with ceremony and Degree; if he will not rise to her station, she will descend to his: 'I do here put off all vain ceremony, / And only do appear to you a young widow / That claims you for her husband.' It is a telling expedient, and with it Antonio's last resistance breaks. It is characteristic of him that he is unable either to deceive effectively – witness the way he falls apart in II iii, when forced into deceptions – or to cope with deception. But it must be admitted that the Duchess's techniques – first establishing, then suddenly relaxing the formalities of Degree – have been unusually subtle, and, coupled with his own desires, difficult to resist.

Near the conclusion of this movement away from Degree and towards the release of 'violent passions', we have another brief ritual gesture as the Duchess puts her arms around Antonio and then orders him to kneel. It is a fitting end, for the gesture is merely a gesture; far from endorsing ceremony and the values it represents, the Duchess engages in a profane parody, employing the ritual solemnities of Degree to confirm and sanction the autonomy of private impulse, the symbols of order to proclaim the ascendancy of disorder. Of her brothers she says:

> Do not think of them –
> All discord, without this circumference,
> Is only to be pitied, and not fear'd:
> Yet, should they know it, time will easily
> Scatter the tempest. (I i 468–72)

The imagery here, and in the following passages which use musical metaphors (482–4), is strongly reminiscent of Ulysses's famous speech on Degree in *Troilus and Cressida*: 'Take but degree away, untune that string, / And, hark, what discord follows' (I iii 109–10ff.).[1] Degree taken away, discord does indeed follow; but for the moment the lovers seek within the circumference of their own arms to create a private universe, to elevate 'violent passion' to the status of a self-sufficient moral law. The attempt may have its romantic appeal, but the Duchess's speech displays a disrespect for external realities which is, as the remainder of the play demonstrates, dangerously naïve. It is left to Cariola to conclude the scene on a note of ominousness: 'Whether the spirit of greatness or of woman / Reign most in her, I know not, but it shows / A fearful madness; I owe her much of pity.'

If we are correct in assuming that Webster is using ceremony as a dramatic device to explore subtleties of character and action, we should expect it to be used again in other critical scenes. The tragic ironies of the Duchess's speech about 'discord' indicate that Webster was anticipating the dramatic future. The audience is prepared for the next appearance of Ferdinand and the Cardinal, is awaiting with a certain amount of suspense the brothers' reactions to the marriage. In II v, where those reactions are presented, Webster is clearly conscious of the logical and structural claims imposed upon him by Act I. The 'tempest' which the Duchess felt time would scatter has now arisen in the form of Ferdinand's intemperate anger; the association is made exact as the Cardinal says, 'Why do you make yourself / So wild a tempest?' and Ferdinand wishes the metaphor were literal fact: 'Would I could be one . . .'. Ferdinand also embodies the 'discord' of which the Duchess was so disdainful: he produces 'this intemperate noise', and is admonished by the Cardinal, 'Come, put yourself / In tune.' His anger, we may think, is perhaps a vastly amplified echo of Antonio's 'distraction' – that is, that just as Antonio hesitated to overturn Degree, so Ferdinand rages because it has been overturned. But this would hardly explain the Cardinal's relative calmness, his utter inability to comprehend his brother's reactions: 'You fly beyond your reason'; 'Are you stark mad?' Only if we accept the unmistakable suggestions of incestuous jealousy in this scene does Ferdinand's behaviour become more understandable for us than for the Cardinal.

The psychological development here is roughly the reverse of that in Act I. Instead of casting off ceremony to reveal underlying passions, Ferdinand moves from passion to the cloaking of passion in ceremonial robes, from disorder to order. His opening line, 'I have this night digg'd up a mandrake', is meaningfully ambiguous, carrying not only the primary notion of madness but a secondary, sexual implication as well. What is merely implication at this point becomes manifest when Ferdinand's sense of injury shifts to the source of injury :

> Methinks I see her laughing –
> Excellent hyena ! – talk to me somewhat, quickly,
> Or my imagination will carry me
> To see her, in the shameful act of sin. (ii v 38–41)

To this point, and somewhat beyond it, Ferdinand seems wholly lacking in self-awareness; his jealousy receives direct expression in anger, but he is conscious only of anger, and mistakenly assumes that the Cardinal is reacting similarly. But when he tortures himself with images of the Duchess 'in the shameful act' he has clearly gone beyond anything that the Cardinal is feeling. The intensity of his experience is attested by his failure even to hear the Cardinal's 'You fly beyond your reason.' Lost to the immediate situation, he directly addresses his sister from his imaginative station as voyeur (46–8). Dumbfounded by this display, the Cardinal remonstrates with a metaphor that is more accurate than he realises :

> ... this intemperate noise
> Fitly resembles deaf men's shrill discourse,
> Who talk aloud, thinking all other men
> To have their imperfection. (51–4)

Although Ferdinand is unconscious of the nature of his 'imperfection', he has supposed a similar violence of reaction on the part of his brother. It is only now that he senses a difference between them. Immediately he withdraws, knowing that he has somehow exposed himself. His next lines – 'Have not you / My palsy?' – mark an abrupt shift of tone : outwardly directed anger recoils, turns inward, gives way to self-suspicion. The question is wary, the diction ambiguous enough to suggest shaking anger and perhaps also his half-awareness of a deeper motivation springing from bodily disturbance. The Cardinal's reply is significant :

> Yes – I can be angry
> Without this rupture : there is not in nature
> A thing that makes man so deform'd, so beastly,
> As doth intemperate anger . . . (55–8)

The thought moves from the personal to the general, from the admission of private but controlled anger to an explanation of the necessity of control. Disordered passions, whether specifically sexual or not, represent a deviation from the nature of, from what is proper to, man; it is not Ferdinand's impulse to violence that the Cardinal objects to, it is the unrestrained disorder of that impulse. The parallel with the Duchess is obvious : both have become threats to society by departing from communal patterns of ordered behaviour, by representing the chaos of un-inhibited private action. But the parallel ends there. Ferdinand has not deliberately violated Degree in order to release passion; indeed, his very lack of deliberation, the spontaneity of his giving way to emotion, has released to the surface a deformity of man's nature. Although both of them enter a 'wilderness', the Duchess seeks to establish private order amid public disorder, to forge a circumference of harmony in the centre of discord. Secure of self, conscious of her own identity, she conceives of 'wilderness' as being purely external. But Ferdinand blunders into a chaos within himself. Nearly losing complete control of himself, he discovers a self he would prefer to lose. Ultimately he does lose himself all ways, in madness; and ultimately the Duchess retains her self, even triumphantly reasserts her identity despite all Ferdinand can do to destroy her.

Webster's problem now is a delicate one. Unless the prolonged torture and demonic killing of the Duchess have some amount of communal sanction, he will have produced, not tragedy, but only melodrama. Having already suggested the potential tragic justification by presenting the Duchess's marriage as a violation of Degree, he now runs the risk of causing Ferdinand to exact disproportionate retribution as a private agent; the nexus between crime and punishment is in danger of breaking. Webster's solution is to cement that nexus by an inversion of the process which led to the crime.

Throughout II v Ferdinand employs the imagery which will

lead him from private to at least a semblance of public revenge.
From the beginning his mind dwells upon purgation:

> We must not now use balsamum, but fire,
> The smarting cupping-glass, for that's the mean
> To purge infected blood, such blood as hers. (24–6)

If the sin is of the blood, as Vittoria's was in *The White Devil*,
the blood must pay for it. But this medical imagery, which
suggests an impulse towards impersonal action – Ferdinand as
agent of society, the physician–priest who will restore order by
destroying disorder – is unconvincing in light of the private
animus manifest in Ferdinand's outbursts. But there is, as we
noted, a shift of tone following the Cardinal's remonstrance about
'deaf men's shrill discourse', a shift of tone which mirrors
Ferdinand's shift in self-consciousness. After the Cardinal's next
speech, which concludes with an exhortation to order – 'Come,
put yourself / In tune' – Ferdinand, already sobered by self-
doubt, returns a premeditated answer:

> So; I will only study to seem
> The thing I am not. (62–3)

To pause briefly here, we should note the verbal echo from
Act I where the Duchess, lamenting the inhibitions imposed by
greatness, spoke of 'simple virtue, which was never made / To
seem the thing it is not' (447–8), just before she 'put off all vain
ceremony'. Here, however, Ferdinand intends just the reverse –
to submit passion to order, or at least to the appearance of order.
He continues:

> I could kill her now,
> In you, or in my self, for I do think
> It is some sin in us, heaven doth revenge
> By her. (63–6)

This is an entirely new turn of thought, to which the Cardinal
can only react with amazement: 'Are you stark mad?' But this
is a far cry from madness. If we have been correct in gauging
his growth of self-awareness, Ferdinand's acknowledgement of

'some sin in us' which requires expiation employs the plural 'us'
merely as a cover: the sin is within him alone, and he knows it.
More significant, however, is his identification of his with the
Duchess's sin, the linking of his latent desire with her realized
desire; for here is precisely the association needed to justify his
revenge upon her and to expiate his own latent sin: he can now
truly quench his 'wild-fire' with her 'whore's blood'. What would
have been merely a private act of violence now assumes the status
of ritual purgation, with the Duchess as sacrificial scapegoat and
Ferdinand, already her judge, as physician–priest–executioner
who seeks the purgation of his own tainted blood in the purging
of hers. Before the scene closes, Ferdinand reverts to the language
of violence once more, but it is clear that he has found his solution.
His final speech reveals an attitude far more terrifying than his
earlier bluster, for it portends not merely an uninhibited, form-
less act of revenge but a patient, controlled, impersonal ceremony
which will culminate with the Duchess's execution.

All of this is not of course to suggest that the highly ceremonial-
ized murder of ıv ii is justified merely because it is ceremonial,
nor that Ferdinand is genuinely identified with moral order
merely because he converts an essentially private vengeance into
the appearance of public justice. Ferdinand's role is obviously
synthetic, an attempt to dignify incestuous frustrations that urge
him to retaliation. Yet by restraining his desire for immediate
vengeance, and, more important, by transforming it and his
sexual desires as well into elements of a formal process, he makes
a gesture of sublimation which, even though synthetic, suggests
a confirmation of order. It is a gesture entirely appropriate to
the nature of the Duchess's marriage, for if the crime is against
society, the punishment must in some sense proceed from society.
It is owing to this ritualization of vengeance that we apprehend
the inevitability of disaster so important in tragedy, an inevitability which arises only from our consciousness of extra-personal
forces working out the fate of the protagonist.[2]

In ıv i the ritual begins. The Duchess has been imprisoned
for an indeterminate period. Ferdinand consults Bosola about
her behaviour, seems satisfied to learn of her nobility. But when
Bosola remarks that her blood is not altogether subdued, indeed
that her very imprisonment away from Antonio 'Makes her too

passionately apprehend / Those pleasures she's kept from',
Ferdinand responds with his own brand of passion :

> Curse upon her !
> I will no longer study in the book
> Of another's heart : inform her what I told you.  (15–17)

The nature of his feelings and the difficulty with which he keeps
them subjected to the demands of ceremony are always most
apparent when some sensual reference to the Duchess's 'whore's
blood' reignites his 'wild-fire'. But he always manages to regain
control, to depersonalize the issue. When Bosola remonstrates
with him (117–21) and unfortunately mentions the Duchess's
'delicate skin', Ferdinand's reply again reveals a momentary
breakdown of his role : 'Damn her ! that body of hers . . .'. He
resolves upon further torments : so long as the sacrificial victim
lives, so long as the Duchess's blood remains unregenerate, the
latent sin within himself continues unpurged. More drastic
purgatives having been planned, he resumes his role : *'Intemperate agues make physicians cruel'* (142).
    In iv ii a new development occurs. The increasing imbalance
of Ferdinand's mind is suggested by his changing to a form of
homeopathic treatment in which the mad are to heal the mad.
He is still attempting to purge himself by proxy, but his employment of madmen symbolizes his own approaching madness. His
identification of his own sin with that of the Duchess has led him
to impute to her, not just sensuality, but all of his aberrations.
The strain of holding in balance the conflicting demands of the
synthetic role and private passion, the inevitable self-injury
involved in destroying the object of desire, and the impossibility
of genuinely purging himself by means of another – all are contri-
buting to Ferdinand's mental disintegration. As the Duchess
grows more confirmed in her personal identity (142), he begins
to lose all sense of identity in that 'wilderness' within him.
    The conclusion of the ritual is the Duchess's sacrificial death.
Bosola engages in his own form of depersonalization, assuming
the role of bellman both to conceal and to dignify his participa-
tion in what he has come to regard as an extravagant cruelty.
Ironically enough, the ceremony designed to purify Ferdinand

has served to purify Bosola, for by experiencing the Duchess's integrity of self it is he who has metamorphosed from an impersonal agent of Ferdinand's malice to a responsible individual capable of the independent action he performs in the last act of the play.

In the dialogue with Bosola over the Duchess's body, Ferdinand, rapidly nearing madness, achieves what appears to be a form of *anagnorisis*. He acknowledges both the fact and the injustice of the private act of vengeance : 'I bade thee, when I was distracted of my wits, / Go kill my dearest friend, and thou hast done't' (279–80). But the admission of injustice is in the abstract, and, qualified by the emphasis upon Bosola as efficient cause and by the claim of mental distraction, it is in effect merely a denial of personal responsibility. Appeals to justification on the grounds of ritual authority – Ferdinand as physician–priest serving society – are conspicuously absent. For evaluation from that point of view, however, we have only to wait a few lines, until Ferdinand says :

> By what authority didst thou execute
> This bloody sentence?
> *Bosola.*                              By yours –
> *Ferdinand.*                    Mine? was I her judge?
> Did any ceremonial form of law
> Doom her to not-being? (298–301)

The denial of 'any ceremonial form of law', of any communally sanctioned process by which revenge was executed, is aimed at depriving Bosola of reward, but instead deprives Ferdinand himself of that superficial ennoblement of motive which he had sought through an alliance with the forms of order. It is one of Ferdinand's last rational utterances, and it is thoroughly appropriate that as he approaches the disaster of mind which is correlative with the Duchess's death, Webster chooses to illumine the nature of Ferdinand's revenge by the same dramatic technique with which he illumined the nature of her offence : it is Webster's final use of ceremony as an 'internal scale to measure depravity'.

SOURCE : *Essays in Criticism*, XII (1962).

## NOTES

1. In some respects Webster's entire play is a comment on Shakespeare's passage, even to the point of Ferdinand's becoming, like 'appetite', a 'universal wolf' eating himself up in madness. Incidentally, there is another parallel with Shakespeare that has gone unmentioned : in IV ii Bosola, denied reward for his services to Ferdinand, says, 'I stand like one/That long hath ta'en a sweet and golden dream : / I am angry with myself, now that I wake' (323–5), which appears to be an echo of Posthumus's speech in *Cymbeline* (V iv 127–9), 'And so I am awake. Poor wretches, that depend / On greatness' favour, dream as I have done, / Wake, and find nothing'.

2. For the relationship between private action and communal order, I am indebted to Professor Robert B. Heilman's excellent book on *Othello – Magic in the Web* (Lexington, Kentucky, 1956) – and especially to his chapter, 'Othello : Action and Language', pp. 137–68.

## Irving Ribner

# FROM *JACOBEAN TRAGEDY: THE QUEST FOR MORAL ORDER* (1962)

I

When we consider John Webster's achievement as a dramatist we are struck by a general mediocrity, suddenly relieved in the middle of his career by two plays, written in quick succession, of a brilliance and power virtually unequalled in his age. *The White Devil* and *The Duchess of Malfi* were composed in 1612 and 1613, following a period of uninspired collaboration with Dekker, Heywood and others; they were followed by some further independent work and by renewed collaboration with Middleton, Heywood and Rowley, but never again, working either alone or with others, did Webster approach the aesthetic range of his two Italian tragedies. They seem to represent the artist's concentrated attempt to express a tragic vision which he imperfectly perceived in *The White Devil*, and realised fully in *The Duchess of Malfi*, after which his career could only culminate in anti-climax. He had nothing more to say.

Webster's plays often have been compared to Tourneur's, largely because both dramatists avail themselves of the neo-Senecan horror devices made popular by John Marston, but there is a difference between the two men which is far greater than any similarity. Tourneur, as we have seen, is the explicit moralist, preaching in effect an orthodox Christianity to which he is firmly committed. Webster is no less the moralist, but he does not preach. His plays are an agonized search for moral order in the uncertain and chaotic world of Jacobean scepticism by a dramatist who can no longer accept without question the postulates of order and degree so dear to the Elizabethans. In *The White Devil* Webster creates a poetic impression of this world with its inherent contradictions, but he can find in his story no pattern to relate good and evil and provide a basis for morality. In the heroic death of his heroine, her preservation even in evil of her 'integrity of life', however, he is able to excite admiration and thus to leave his audience with the impression that there is at least one certain value, if attainable only in death, in a world seemingly without value. In *The Duchess of Malfi* Webster goes on to explore the implications of this value. If death may reveal an inherent nobility in human life, such nobility is real, and it may be the basis of a moral order. In *The Duchess of Malfi* we see a new morality emerging in the final act out of evils more chilling in their horror than those of the earlier play. This search for moral order links Webster to Shakespeare in the highest range of tragedy, and to fully perceive Webster's achievement we must see his later play as the exploration of a value postulated in the earlier one and as the final resolution of the problem with which both plays are concerned.

The Italian tragedies have been celebrated for their unity of tone and temper, for their realism of characterization in spite of a glaring weakness in psychological motivation, and for the brilliance of their dramatic verse. They have been criticized for their plot construction, with its gross improbabilities, and for a concern with 'perfection of detail rather than general design'[1] which has made it difficult for most critics to find even in these greatest of Webster's plays such thematic unity as may be found, for instance, in the tragedies of Chapman or Tourneur. T. S. Eliot has called Webster 'a very great literary and dramatic genius directed toward chaos',[2] and Clifford Leech expresses a common judgment when he writes that *The Duchess of Malfi* 'is blurred in its total meaning. It is a collection of brilliant scenes, whose statements do not ultimately cohere.'[3] The final act of this play has been called an unnecessary and anti-climactic extension of what should have ended with the death of the heroine.[4]

We do no justice to Webster's achievement in these plays while, like Lucas, we regard the dramatist as a naturalistic artist, following sordid historical narratives for their own sake, the sum of his greatness being in 'atmosphere, its poetry, and two or three supreme scenes'.[5] These plays, like the greatest tragedies of their age, have an ethical and an allegorical dimen-

sion. They are symbolic works, and if their poetry is great it is
because of its perfection as the instrument by which the artist
reveals a vision of man's relation to the forces of evil in the world
and affords a basis for renewed acceptance of life which is tragic
reconciliation. The most serious error that critics of Webster have
committed has been to regard him as a dramatist lacking in
moral vision, and therefore incapable of more than a partial
view of human experience, content to limit his genius within the
bounds of a philosophically barren tradition of revenge tragedy.[6]

In *The White Devil* Webster is concerned with the deception
of appearances, the unreality of the world in which man must
live, and with the shallowness of the conventional moral order.
The play is a dramatic symbol of moral confusion, the impossibility of distinguishing appearance from reality in a world
in which evil wears always the mask of virtue and virtue the mask
of evil.[7] In this world morality seems impossible, but in *The
Duchess of Malfi* Webster reveals how it may be possible in spite
of this world. Webster's cosmic view is not the optimistic one of
Hooker, Shakespeare or Heywood. His is the decaying universe
of Chapman and Tourneur, hastening towards destruction.
Although there are references to heaven and hell in his plays,
Webster's world is 'a mist' without order or design, and with no
certainty of a divine providence directing the affairs of men. The
two plays taken together, however, do not reveal a philosophy
of negation or despair,[8] for Webster's concern is with the ability
of man to survive in such a world without direction, to maintain
his human worth in spite of all. This is a profoundly moral
concern, for morality need not be based upon faith in divine
order. Webster bases his faith upon human integrity and in the
nobility to which human life can aspire in spite of the disorder
which surrounds it.

## II

Deception and false appearance are accented both in the dramatic action and the poetic imagery of *The White Devil*. Evil wears
always the mask of good, and good disguises itself as evil, so that
at last the two are indistinguishable. This moral ambiguity is
implicit in the play's title, and it is maintained by an imagery

comprised of polar opposites : 'Sweet-meats which rot the eater
. . . Poison'd perfumes . . . Shipwrecks in calmest weather'
(III ii 80–2). False appearance is introduced in the first
speech of the play : 'Your wolf no longer seems to be a wolf /
Than when she's hungry' (I i 8–9). The garden where the
lovers meet becomes a graveyard :

> O that this fair garden
> Had with all poisoned herbs of Thessaly
> At first been planted, made a nursery
> For witchcraft; rather than a burial plot,
> For both your honours. (I ii 274–8)

The dovehouse is haunted by polecats (II i 3–5). Vittoria herself, the symbol of this confusion, is compared to the apples of
Sodom which turn to soot and ashes when they are tasted
(III ii 63–7). A recurring symbol is that of the yew tree, whose
beauty and fair height are rooted in corruption :

> Or like the black, and melancholic yew tree,
> Dost think to root thyself in dead men's graves,
> And yet to prosper? (IV iii 120–2)

Vittoria's dream of the yew tree (I ii 231 ff.) leads Bracciano
to the murders of Isabella and Camillo. Beauty is the product
of disease and decay, and this beauty is in turn the destroyer of
life, the creator of new disease in an endless cycle. Vittoria's
beauty, shining through her evil, is the symbol of this meaningless, uncertain condition of humanity.

When she is guilty of her greatest sins, she is most able to
arouse the admiration of the audience by her defiance and
heroic grandeur :

> Humbly thus,
> Thus low, to the most worthy and respected
> Lieger ambassadors, my modesty
> And womanhood I tender; but withal
> So entangled in a cursed accusation
> That my defence of force like Perseus,
> Must personate masculine virtue – to the point !

> Find me but guilty, sever head from body:
> We'll part good friends: I scorn to hold my life
> At yours or any man's entreaty, sir. (iii ii 130–9)

We do not doubt her 'modesty and womanhood' here; Webster uses the English ambassador to guide the sentiments of his audience: 'She hath a brave spirit' (iii ii 140). But while we admire Vittoria we know that she lies, and the Cardinal in pointing to her falsehood, underlines the confusion of appearance with reality for which she stands: 'Well, well such counterfeit jewels / Make true ones oft suspected' (iii ii 141–2).

Vittoria's defiance is a dramatic symbol of this moral confusion, for in the vehemence of her speech she turns her own evil back upon her judges, so that there is no difference between accusers and accused:

> You are deceived;
> For know that all your strict-combined heads,
> Which strike against this mine of diamonds,
> Shall prove but glassen hammers, they shall break, –
> These are but feigned shadows of my evils.
> Terrify babes, my lord, with painted devils,
> I am past such needless palsy, – for your names
> Of whore and murd'ress, they proceed from you,
> As if a man should spit against the wind,
> The filth returns in's face. (iii ii 142–51)

The audience has seen Vittoria's evil made explicit in action. Now it is caught up in the splendour and vehemence of her passionate denial, and it is left in a state of ambivalence. If the morality she opposes is represented by the Cardinal Monticelso, this morality is indeed a 'glassen hammer' and she a 'mine of diamonds'; she may be a whore, but the Cardinal has 'ravish'd justice, / Forc'd her to do your pleasure' (iii ii 274–5). She leaves the scene condemned but triumphant, and her final words reflect the paradox of the play: 'Through darkness diamonds spread their richest light' (iii ii 294).

Our sense of moral ambivalence is reinforced when we find the Cardinal, Vittoria's judge, as the author of the Machiavellian deception by which Francisco de Medici will accomplish

his revenge (IV i 14 ff.) In the Cardinal's book lurk all the evils
of the world, a catalogue of villainies robed in seeming virtue :

> Their number rises strangely,
> And some of them
> You'd take for honest men.
> Next are pandars.
> These are your pirates : and these following leaves
> For base rogues that undo young gentlemen
> By taking up commodities :
> For politic bankrupts :
> For fellows that are bawds to their own wives,
> Only to put off horses and slight jewels,
> Clocks, defac'd plate, and such commodities,
> At birth of their first children . . .
> These are for impudent bawds,
> That go in men's apparel : for usurers
> That share with scriveners for their good reportage :
> For lawyers that will antedate their writs :
> And some divines you might find folded there,
> But that I slip them o'er for conscience' sake.
> Here is a general catalogue of knaves.
> A man might study all the prisons o'er,
> Yet never attain this knowledge. (IV i 45–64)

Religion is the source of policy, and this policy Francisco will
use to destroy Vittoria. The Cardinal's judging of Vittoria becomes a mockery of justice, his very existence an implicit denial
of the traditional morality of which his title makes him the
symbol.

There are virtuous characters in *The White Devil*, Cornelia,
Isabella, Marcello, but real as their virtue may be, it appears to
the world cloaked in evil. Isabella's love for Bracciano must express itself in her pretence that she is the evil destroyer of their
marriage :

>                   let the fault
> Remain with my supposed jealousy, –
> And think with what a piteous and rent heart,
> I shall perform this sad ensuing part. (II i 222–5)

Her 'piteous and rent heart' will appear to the world as evil; her
brother will call her 'a foolish, mad, / And jealous woman' (II
i 264–5). In the same manner, the maternal love of Cornelia
expresses itself in her lies to protect the murderer of the very son
she mourns. Marcello sees his death as just punishment for the
evils of his family :

> There are some sins which heaven doth duly punish
> In a whole family. This it is to rise
> By all dishonest means. Let all men know
> That tree shall long time keep a steady foot
> Whose branches spread no wider than the root.
>
> (v ii 20–4)

He cannot escape the evil from which he springs. Even the young
Giovanni, attempting to restore order at the end of the play, is
closely related to the very evils he seeks to destroy, for he is the
son of Bracciano, and when he asks, 'You bloody villains, / By
what authority have you committed / This massacre?' the
answer is 'By thine . . . Yes, thy uncle, / Which is a part of thee,
enjoin'd us to 't' (v vi 283–6). Even the child shares in the
general corruption of humanity, in a world in which truth seems
impossible, where good and evil cannot be distinguished, and
where the only moral law appears to be a *nemesis* punishing sin
with new sin in a never ending cycle. Vittoria represents this disorder with its constant confusion of opposites; she is the beauty
which destroys :

> Your beauty ! O, ten thousand curses on't.
> How long have I beheld the devil in crystal ?
> Thou hast led me, like an heathen sacrifice,
> With music, and with fatal yokes of flowers
> To my eternal ruin. (IV ii 87–91)

So speaks Bracciano, reflecting the plight of man who cannot
distinguish appearance from reality, who is destroyed by evil in
his vain pursuit of what seems to be good and bears the outward
signs of beauty – music, yokes of flowers.

Bracciano's fate reminds the audience that in this world of

uncertainty and false appearance human aspirations are fruitless
and empty. Man's strivings can earn him only frustration, and
deeds come always to recoil upon the doer. The action of the
play, like that of *The Revenger's Tragedy*, is a structure of
linked ironies. While Camillo uses Flamineo, as he thinks, to win
his duchess back to him, Flamineo is, in fact, wooing her for Bracciano. The symbol of the silkworm is used to express the human
condition : 'Ha ha ha, thou entanglest thyself in thine own work
like a silkworm' (I ii 196–7). All man's efforts lead to his own
destruction, and even pleasure is its own extinction; 'But all delight doth itself soon'st devour' (I ii 204).

Francisco, lamenting the fate of his sister, cries out :

> would I had given
> Both her white hands to death, bound and lock'd fast
> In her last winding-sheet, when I gave thee
> But one. (II i 64–7)

The action will reveal that in giving her hand to Bracciano he
has, in fact, given her to death. All greatness is a vain illusion in
the world of *The White Devil*: 'Glories, like glow-worms, afar
off shine bright, / But look'd to near, have neither heat nor light'
(v i 41–2). Religion is a mask for evil. The elaborate election of
the pope is followed by a linking of opposites : 'You have ta'en
the sacrament to prosecute / Th' intended murder' (IV iii
72–3). Even the act of devotion becomes the source of hatred
and murder. The doctor knows how to 'poison a kiss' (II i 301),
and Isabella dies kissing the poisoned portrait of her husband in
a nightly ritual of love, just as Camillo has his neck broken in an
act of friendly sport and fellowship. Bracciano is strangled with
a 'true-love knot' (v iii 174), and his murderers are disguised
as holy friars, supposedly working the salvation of his soul, while
they remind him that he will 'die like a poor rogue . . . And stink /
Like a dead fly-blown dog . . . And be forgotten / Before thy
funeral sermon' (v iii 165–7). When he has been strangled, his
murderers leave with holy words upon their lips : 'for charity, /
For Christian charity, avoid the chamber' (v iii 172–3). We do
not know whether the dying Bracciano's 'Vittoria? Vittoria!'
(v iii 167) is a cry of horror or all-consuming love.

Vittoria has been as beautiful as she has been evil; the
dramatist has maintained towards her a moral ambivalence, and
when she dies with courage and defiance, preserving her 'integrity of life' to the very end, we share imaginatively in a sense
of heroism, of pride in the human condition, be it what it may.
This sense of the heroic partially counteracts the feeling of despair created by the vision of an uncertain and chaotic world
which we have beheld; it generates a pride in life itself. Delio,
speaking for the author, offers a key to both plays in the final
words of *The Duchess of Malfi*:

> *Integrity of life is fame's best friend,*
> *Which nobly, beyond death, shall crown the end.*
>                                              (V v 120–1)

Vittoria's 'integrity of life' is the source of pride, and this pride
growing out of evil is a reflection of the paradox in the play's
title, that there may be good implicit in the darkest evil. This
suggestion Webster is to develop further in *The Duchess of Malfi*,
that while we exalt the fact of life itself we escape the chaos of a
disordered world. In *The White Devil* we see an evil woman
attaining some victory by her 'integrity of life', but we do not see
the social consequences which such integrity may have, its power
to afford a basis for morality. In his next play Webster goes on
to show the power of a pride in life to destroy some of the world's
evils and thus to justify the fact of human existence in a world
seemingly without other value. By this celebration of 'integrity of
life', Webster is not glorifying the ability of man to persevere in
evil as well as good, as some have supposed. He is celebrating a
heroic pride in the human condition which can win some victory
even to an evil Vittoria, but which when embodied in a virtuous
Duchess of Malfi may have power to effect a regeneration of the
social order.

Vittoria in her defiance stands for life, as her brother,
Flamineo, stands for death. 'You are, I take it, the grave maker'
(v iv 80), his mother says to him. His role is to deliver death
directly to others as he does to Camillo and Marcello, to
instigate action which will lead to death as he does for Bracciano, and to show the others how to die when his own turn

comes. For him death is the only certainty in a world full of deception and uncertainty, the only truth of which mankind is capable:

> Prosperity doth bewitch men seeming clear,
> But seas do laugh, show white, when rocks are near.
> We cease to grieve, cease to be Fortune's slaves,
> Nay cease to die by dying.  (v vi 250–3)

Unlike Bracciano, who strives for the goodness he sees in the love of Vittoria and is led instead into desecration and death, Flamineo accepts the world as a place of horror where felicity is never more than sorrow in disguise, and he welcomes death as the final certainty which ends man's slavery to such a world. Too many commentators have equated Flamineo's view of the world with Webster's tragic vision, but Flamineo stands only for the negation from which Webster seeks to escape. Flamineo represents the death force which Webster will oppose with a force of life, sketched faintly in Vittoria and more surely in the Duchess of Malfi. In the contrast between Vittoria and Flamineo, two figures of evil, Webster foreshadows what he is more fully to develop in the later play where the Duchess will oppose the principle of life to the death world represented by her brothers, with the imagery of their speeches underlining these symbolic functions, and with Bosola moving from the one side to the other, as Flamineo now is incapable of moving.

Flamineo is a Bosola incapable of growth. In a world in which he sees morality as impossible he seeks to prosper by a deliberate cultivation of the immoral. Like Shakespeare's Iago and Edmund he stands for the negation of order and harmony in the universe, for man without links either to God or his fellow men:

> I do not look
> Who went before, nor who shall follow me;
> No, at myself I will begin and end.  (v vi 256–8)

He assumes the traditional role of the malcontent, exposing the evils of the world while he offers them as justification for his own 'Machiavellian policy'. Like Bosola, he comes upon the stage as one who has suffered through the world's evil, who has never

prospered, but who now seeks to better his position by accepting the values of a universe without direction or moral law. He
will live by 'policy', denying all human ties as he rejects his own
mother and vaunts his immorality before her :

> Pray what means have you
> To keep me from the galleys, or the gallows?
> My father prov'd himself a gentleman,
> Sold all's land, and like a fortunate fellow,
> Died ere the money was spent. You brought me up
> At Padua I confess, where I protest
> For want of means, – the university judge me, –
> I have been fain to heel my tutor's stockings
> At least seven years : conspiring with a beard
> Made me a graduate, – then to this duke's service :
> I visited the court, whence I return'd
> More courteous, more lecherous by far,
> But not a suit the richer, – and shall I,
> Having a path so open and so free
> To my preferment, still retain your milk
> In my pale forehead? no this face of mine
> I'll arm and fortify with lusty wine
> 'Gainst shame and blushing.  (1 ii 315–32)

The 'Machiavel' by Webster's day had become a conventional
stage figure, a symbol for opposition to the moral order which
cloaked itself in a mask of virtue. It stood for dissimulation. This
is the code by which Flamineo lives, but it leads him to the same
death which awaits his virtuous brother, Marcello.

There is no heroic quality in Flamineo's world. His speeches
are full of cynicism, dwelling always on the base and sordid in
human life; it is fitting that he be a pander. In his evil there is no
'integrity of life', for the 'Machiavel' to attain his ends must
practise policy, seem to be what he is not, striking always under
the guise of friendship, as when he betrays Camillo and his own
sister. He is a mirror of the very indirection and confusion of the
world he excoriates and which at last destroys him, but he never
deceives himself. He accepts the world as he sees it, and we
feel that could he have seen it otherwise, he might have lived
otherwise. He is even made to feel remorse :

> I have liv'd
> Riotously ill, like some that live in court;
> And sometimes, when my face was full of smiles,
> Have felt the maze of conscience in my breast.
>
> (v iv 118–21)

His acceptance of death, paralleling the brave defiance of his sister, lends some note of grandeur to his end also, and the audience regrets the human waste for which he stands. In the later play Webster is to exhibit in Bosola the kind of redemption which was always possible in Flamineo, but which he could not achieve. Bosola enters *The Duchess of Malfi* proclaiming the same values as Flamineo, but before his death he learns from the Duchess what Flamineo never learns, that life itself can afford a basis for morality in a chaotic world.

### III

In *The Duchess of Malfi* Webster returns to the 'mist' which is the world of *The White Devil*, but there is an immediate difference, for the later play opens with Antonio's description of the emergence of order and justice in France, and this conditions what follows, for the audience has seen at the beginning the possibility of a moral order, and nothing in the play can convince it of its impossibility. The two plays are linked by common motifs. Bosola too calls the world 'a mist' (v v 94). Vittoria in *The White Devil* dies lamenting the corruption of the court. 'O happy they that never saw the court' (v vi 261), and dying Antonio at the end of *The Duchess of Malfi* prays 'And let my son fly the courts of princes' (v iv 72). The difference is that Vittoria could not escape the evils of the world, whereas the son of Antonio will have learned how to do so.

The moral statement of *The Duchess of Malfi* is not implicit in the stock apothegms of such virtuous characters as Delio and Pescara which, as has been observed, sometimes bear but slight relation to the action and read – though, by no means, always – like later additions. It is implicit in the total imaginative impression of the play, for *The Duchess* is a unified work, with mood, action, characterization and poetry all carefully shaped

together as an assertion of the inherent dignity of man. As part of
this total thematic statement the final act is of crucial importance, for its function is to exhibit the effect upon the debased
world of the human spirit's triumph in spite of the body's
destruction. The particular effect of this tragedy is in its power
to generate a tension between our terror of a corrupt, disordered and chaotic universe and our pride in the nobility of the
human spirit which enables man to survive and triumph in
spite of such a world. In this tension is Webster's moral vision,
for the dignity of the human spirit separates man from the base-
ness of the world, and the need to preserve this dignity affords
the true basis of morality. 'The ultimate tragedy of Webster's
world', writes Travis Bogard (*The Tragic Satire of John
Webster*, p. 147), 'is not the death of any individual but the
presence of evil and decay which drags all mankind to death . . .
the tragic story is the story of a few who find courage to defy
such revelation. In their defiance there is a glory for mankind,
and in their struggle and assertion lies the brilliance of Websterian tragedy.' But this very sense of glory postulates a value
which the evils of the world cannot destroy and which makes
man superior to his world. It provides a frame of reference in
which the relation of man to the forces of evil becomes apparent,
and it leads not to a sense of despair but to one of tragic reconciliation.

When Webster's characters are considered in terms of psychological verisimilitude, glaring inconsistencies emerge. The venom
of Ferdinand is poorly motivated. We rightly wonder why the
brave soldier, Antonio, does not kill Ferdinand when he has
ample opportunity in his wife's closet; or why Bosola should
strangle the Duchess when he feels his greatest identity with her,
and why he should later suffer remorse and reverse his
allegiances. It is difficult to see why the cunning and self-assured
Cardinal should continue to trust Bosola after the death of Julia
has been revealed. None of this is explainable in terms of psychology or logical probability. The feeling of realism which
Webster creates in spite of such improbabilities is the product of
poetic illusion. His characters live in a world of imaginative
symbol,[10] and they are shaped by the specific functions they are
designed to perform as parts of the total dramatic unity.

The most important unifying element in *The Duchess of Malfi* is Bosola, a character whom critics have found particularly difficult to explain in terms of human psychology. The different roles he assumes as the play progresses may be reconciled to one another only in terms of the play's total thematic design. In the traditional pose of the malcontent he recapitulates the function of Flamineo in *The White Devil*, for he illuminates the evils of the world which will destroy the Duchess. As the instrument of the Arragonian brothers he shows this evil made explicit in action. In the death scene of the Duchess he serves a new and more complex function, for here he plays several roles, each designed to further the symbolism of the total scene. Primarily he is used to help the Duchess overcome her womanly fears and to arouse the spirit of greatness in her; he stands here for the nobility of the human spirit which he had opposed in his role as malcontent. Bosola must resolve the question posed by Cariola at the end of the first act: 'Whether the spirit of greatness or of woman/Reign most in her, I know not' (i i 504–5). 'Come, you must live' (iv i 69), says Bosola when the Duchess is almost overcome with the horror of life and looks to death for escape. When she has cursed the stars, vainly defying an impersonal nature, rather than asserting her own integrity of spirit, Bosola points out her folly: 'Look you, the stars shine still' (iv i 100). 'In this climax,' writes Lucas (*The Duchess of Malfi*, p. 187), 'Bosola's cynicism rises to the sublime, as in four monosyllables he expresses the insignificance of human agony before the impassive universe.' That the lines affirm the impassivity of the universe and the insignificance of human suffering is, of course, true, but to call them cynical is to ignore Bosola's role in the Duchess's spiritual triumph and the traditional poetic associations of shining stars. Man's awareness of the insignificance of his pain may help him to rise above it. That 'the stars shine still' is a crucial statement of the play, for it is an assertion of the permanence and indestructibility of nature. While the stars shine there is certainty, for we cannot doubt the reality of the universe and of an illuminating beauty which persists in spite of all. The stars are a symbol of hope which defeats the feeling of despair which the horrors of the play may generate. Through the office of Bosola, the Duchess is able to assert the dignity of human life and meet her death with the readiness and courage which are her triumph.[11] To know the insignificance of human pain and the certainty of an unextinguishable heavenly light is a means of escape from the horrors of the world.

To view the death scene of the Duchess in a naturalistic perspective is to render it almost ludicrous. The ghastly horrors of her torture are a symbolic portrait of the pain of the whole human condition, emphasizing as Flamineo had in *The White Devil* (v vi 252–3), that the process of living is itself a preparation for death. Before his sister in her final hours Ferdinand parades the ordinary condition of debased humanity: courtesans, bawds, ruffians and madmen. The various forms of madness represent the ordinary occupations of life:

> There's a mad lawyer, and a secular priest,
> A doctor that hath forfeited his wits
> By jealousy; an astrologian
> That in his works said such a day o'th' month
> Should be the day of doom, and failing of't
> Ran mad; an English tailor, craz'd i'th' brain
> With the study of new fashions; a gentleman usher
> Quite beside himself with care to keep in mind
> The number of his lady's salutations,
> Or 'How do you', she employed him in each morning;
> A farmer too, an excellent knave in grain,
> Mad 'cause he was hinder'd transportation,
> And let one broker that's mad loose to these,
> You'd think the devil were among them. (iv ii 45–58)

Doctor, lawyer, tailor, farmer and broker; these represent the ordinary affairs of the world, joined in a universal pageant of madness. This mad world is the world of Cariola, who will lie and beg, even plead pregnancy to spare her life; it is the world above which Bosola will help the Duchess to rise: 'when you send me next, / The business shall be comfort' (iv i 136–7).

In this symbolic portrait of a mad world decaying into death, Bosola, like Vindice in *The Revenger's Tragedy*, assumes several disguises, each indicating a different symbolic role. As the old maker of tombs he is a symbol of time and mutability, the destroyers of life, and he points to the impermanence and fragility of the human condition in words which recall those of Hamlet in the graveyard or Vindice with the skull of Gloriana:

Thou art a box of worm-seed, at best, but a salvatory of green mummy : – what's this flesh? a little crudded milk, fantastical puff paste; our bodies are weaker than those paper prisons boys use to keep flies in; more contemptible, since ours is to preserve earth-worms. Didst thou ever see a lark in a cage? such is the soul in the body : this world is like her little turf of grass, and the heaven o'er our heads, like her looking-glass, only gives us a miserable knowledge of the small compass of our prison. (IV ii 124–33)

Bosola, like Hamlet and Vindice, is here speaking the common-places *de contemptu mundi*, a system of belief which, as we have seen, emphasized the insignificance of the human body in order to make clear the contrasting eternity of the soul. The lark in its cage provides an image of striking power, stressing the ability of the soul to soar towards heaven when the fragile cage of the body is broken, just as the lark at daybreak flies straight towards the sun. The heavens remind man of the smallness of his human body in the light of eternity, just as the looking-glass in the lark's cage emphasizes the smallness of her prison. Bosola in this speech is preparing the Duchess in conventional terms for a Christian stoic acceptance of death as the liberation of the soul.[12]

Disguised as the bellman – whose traditional function was to drive away evil spirits and to invite the faithful to pray for their souls before death – Bosola stands for faith, penance, and the hope of heaven which death affords. As the executioner with his cord, he is the moment of death itself with its attendant pain. When the Duchess awakens briefly before she dies, Bosola becomes a symbol of the comfort and mercy she will merit in heaven. He tells her what she most longs to hear, that her loved ones are still alive, and because of this the last word she utters is 'Mercy' (IV ii 353).

In the final act Bosola becomes the agent through which the spirit of the Duchess is made to permeate the world. While Bosola had accepted the values of Ferdinand and the Cardinal he had been like them a symbol of death, the destroyer of life and beauty. The final act is designed to show that the way of the Arragonian brothers is that of madness and damnation, the com-

plete descent of man into beast symbolized by the lycanthropia
of Ferdinand; it shows also that the horrors for which they stand
may be defeated and rendered insignificant by a triumph of the
indestructible human spirit. This spirit forever separates man
from the beast, and it justifies human life in spite of the disorder which surrounds it. Man need not fear to live so long as
he can preserve his 'integrity of life' and die true to himself, with
courage and acceptance; and while life itself has value we have
a basis for morality. This Bosola had learned from the death of
the Duchess; now he assumes her way and carries her values into
the final act, becoming an instrument of justice which affirms a
moral order. His transformation may defy logical probability,
but it is a symbol of Webster's moral argument. When Bosola
recognizes the value of the Duchess'~ 'integrity of life', it is no
longer possible for him to live by the code which had linked him
to the Arragonian brothers. While good is possible, he must seek
for values in life, and thus he comes to stand for justice and the
restoration of order. He now can see the fate of Ferdinand not
as an arbitrary reversal of fortune in an uncertain and valueless
world, but as a punishment for sin in a world in which divine
justice operates:

> Mercy upon me, what a fatal judgement
> Hath fall'n upon this Ferdinand! (v ii 85–86)

This note of heavenly justice is in the nameless terror which comes
to haunt the Cardinal:

> When I look into the fish-ponds, in my garden,
> Methinks I see a thing, arm'd with a rake
> That seems to strike at me.  (v v 5–7)

The guilty must be punished for their sins, and in the death of
her oppressors Bosola proclaims the victory of the Duchess:

> Revenge, for the Duchess of Malfi, murdered
> By th'Arragonian brethren; for Antonio,
> Slain by this hand; for lustful Julia,
> Poison'd by this man; and lastly, for myself.
>                                   (v v 102–5)

He executes vengeance even for the destruction of his own soul, and he willingly accepts the death and damnation which in the just moral order he now envisages are his due :

> It may be pain, but no harm to me to die
> In so good a quarrel. O, this gloomy world !
> In what a shadow, or deep pit of darkness,
> Doth womanish and fearful mankind live !
> Let worthy minds ne'er stagger in distrust
> To suffer death, or shame for what is just –
> Mine is another voyage. (v v 99–105)

He dies 'in so good a quarrel', and in his death there is an affirmation of justice. The new moral order is made visible in Antonio's young son who comes upon the stage as a symbol of rebirth. The theme of an emerging justice had been carried also in the death of Julia : 'I forgive you / This equal piece of justice you have done' (v ii 281–2). It had been prepared for also in Bosola's decision to aid the cause of Antonio :

> The weakest arm is strong enough, that strikes
> With the sword of justice : – still methinks the duchess
> Haunts me. (v ii 344–6)

Bosola dies like the Duchess of Malfi, although he had lived most of his life in the service of those who would destroy her. Her death had been his regeneration :

> What would I do, were this to do again ?
> I would not change my peace of conscience
> For all the wealth of Europe : – she stirs; here's life :
> Return, fair soul, from darkness, and lead mine
> Out of this sensible hell. (iv ii 339–43)

Her 'fair soul', bright and unchanging like the shining stars, leads him out of the darkness of a world without value to an affirmation of the dignity of life for which she had stood and for which he now comes to stand. If the world is an abysmal chaos without guiding plan, in which good and evil must at last be made equal by the death which comes to all, man may still create his moral order, Webster in effect is saying, by upholding and preserving the dignity of human life. Death may destroy the body, but it cannot destroy the spirit. On one level, we may regard the play as the education of Bosola by the Duchess. He carries her values into the final act, where evil destroys itself and leaves behind only Delio, Pescara and Antonio's son, characters whose virtue is untainted. While he dwells on the blackness and pervasiveness of evil, Webster never allows us to forget the possibility of good; even in *The White Devil*, we have Isabella, Cornelia and Marcello whose virtue though sometimes hidden is always real.

The Duchess in her heroic opposition to her brothers is the symbol of life, as they are the symbols of death, and the play maintains a tension between the opposing forces of life and death, with the values of life at last triumphant. These symbolic functions of the Duchess and her brothers are carried in the poetic imagery of their lines.[18] Her only crime is 'that first good deed began i'th' world / After man's creation, the sacrament of marriage' (I i 385–6), and the generation of life to which it leads. Webster's source in William Painter's *Palace of Pleasure* had censured the Duchess for her lust, her neglect of the responsibilities of her station, and her avoidance of the rites of the church; of this censure there is no hint in Webster's play. Her courtship of Antonio is cast as a charming idyll with which we are meant to sympathize and it is contrasted to the lustful Julia's attachment to the Cardinal. The Duchess asserts her ordinary human nature :

>          This is flesh, and blood, sir;
> 'Tis not the figure cut in alabaster
> Kneels at my husband's tomb. Awake, awake, man !
> I do here put off all vain ceremony,
> And only do appear to you a young widow
> That claims you for her husband. (I i 453–8)

She stands for the life of the flesh as opposed to the cold dead statue at the tomb, and her call is one of awakening. Her right to marry Antonio is an assertion of the basic claims of life, stripped of all ceremony. As she dies her thought is only of her children :

> I pray thee, look thou giv'st my little boy
> Some syrup for his cold, and let the girl
> Say her prayers, ere she sleep.  (IV ii 203–5)

The inconsistency here, since she believes her children to be
dead, has bothered critics, but Webster abandons logic for this
striking emphasis upon his dying heroine as the creator and pre-
server of life. She has the power to 'raise one to a galliard / That
lay in a dead palsy' (II 196–7).

Her speeches are full of references to nature: birds, trees, the
heavens, symbols of life and continuity. Bosola tells her, as we
have seen, that the soul in the body is 'a lark in a cage', and she
is identified with this soul by the image with which she describes
herself:

> The robin-redbreast, and the nightingale,
> Never live long in cages.  (IV ii 13–14)

She compares herself and Antonio in their banishment to 'The
birds that live i'th' field / On the wild benefit of nature' (III
v 18–19), and she comes to see herself as such a bird fattened
only for destruction: 'With such a pity men preserve alive /
Pheasants and quails, when they are not fat enough / To be
eaten' (III v 111–13). As she and Antonio celebrate their
marriage they chorally relate their union to the life giving movement of the heavens:

> *Ant.*  And may your sweet affections, like the spheres,
>     Be still in motion.
> *Duch.*                    Quickening, and make
>     The like soft music.
> *Ant.*  That we may imitate the loving palms,
>     Best emblem of a peaceful marriage,
>     That ne'er bore fruit, divided.  (II 482–7)

Webster uses a ritual technique to emphasize that the lovers
stand for harmony, life and generation. Childbearing is a constant motif, and the speeches of Antonio and the Duchess are
full of references to children:

I have seen children oft eat sweatmeats thus.

(i i 467)

To see the little wanton ride a-cock-horse
Upon a painted stick, or hear him chatter
Like a taught starling. (i i 401–3)

The union of the bird and child images here makes clear their
thematic function.

Ferdinand, the Cardinal, and Bosola while he serves them,
stand in opposition as the destroyers of life, and the imagery of
their speeches draws upon the destructive forces of nature.
Ferdinand would

Root up her goodly forests, blast her meads,
And lay her general territory as waste,
As she hath done her honours. (II v 19–21)

He will give her 'bastard' a handkerchief 'to make soft lint for
his mother's wounds, / When I have hew'd her to pieces' (II v
28–31), and he will

boil their bastard to a cullis,
And give't his lecherous father, to renew
The sin of his back. (II v 71–3)

He stands for the desecration of parenthood, opposed to the
generation of life.

The destructive, predatory animals are called up in the
speeches of the Arragonian brothers. The Cardinal describes his
mistress, Julia, as a hawk :

I have taken you off your melancholy perch,
Bore you upon my fist, and show'd you game,
And let you fly at it. (II iv 28–30)

They are bloodhounds, vipers, a tiger. The spring in the
Cardinal's face is 'nothing but the engendering of toads' (I i
158–9). He and his brother are fed on by 'crows, pies, and cat-

terpillars' (I i 51). The law to Ferdinand is 'a foul black cob-web to a spider' (I i 178). He is 'a foul porpoise before a storm' (III iii 53) . . . 'A very salamander lives in's eye' (III iii 49). References to wolves continue to run through his lines until he emerges on the stage a wolf himself. Bosola refers to himself as a blackbird, a horse-leech; he sees man as 'eaten up of lice, and worms' (II i 55); he is called a dormouse, an undermining mole, an impudent snake.

The Cardinal stands for the guile and hypocrisy which render religion but a shallow pretence. He carries on the traditional pose of the 'Machiavel', a symbol of evil wearing the mask of a seeming virtue. The function of his liaison with Julia is in part to emphasize this. If to display the death world of the Arragonian brothers were Webster's final purpose, as has so often been supposed, the tragedy would indeed be one of total despair, and as such it could not arouse those feelings of final acceptance and reconciliation upon which great tragedy depends. But this world is not the total picture. Into it comes the Duchess of Malfi who stands for the values of life, and Webster's final statement is that life may have nobility in spite of all. The Duchess, not her brothers, stands for ordinary humanity, love and the continuity of life through children. Her brothers stand only for death and decay – emphasized also by the disease imagery with which their speeches abound – and by Bosola's striking image :

> Your brother and yourself are worthy men;
> You have a pair of hearts are hollow graves,
> Rotten, and rotting others. (IV ii 318–20)

But the play asserts the final triumph of life over death. When all of the horrors of the world have been paraded before the Duchess and she faces the inevitable end in its most horrible form, she can still proclaim that 'I am Duchess of Malfi still' (IV ii 142). The body may be subject to death and decay, but in these words the Duchess affirms the permanence of the spirit which is the really vital part of man. The line in its simple syntax echoes Bosola's 'the stars shine still' (IV i 100), and equates the permanence of the human spirit with that of nature. This is

Webster's answer to the pain of living and the fragility of the
human condition.

Antonio is more central to the design of the play than usually
has been recognized. Although deeply involved in the action, he
is also a kind of choral commentator on it, for the audience is
invited to view the play through his eyes. He stands between the
death-world of the Arragonian brothers and the world of life
represented by the Duchess. He chooses life in spite of pain and
suffering, and like all who live he must suffer and die, his death
coming by a cruel accident of fate, as death so often does. But
his choice of the values of life enables him to accept death calmly
and to conquer the lust for revenge which might have accompanied his injuries were he like Ferdinand. In spite of his
suffering he seeks at last for reconciliation. This is the first note
sounded at the opening of the final act:

> What think you of my hope of reconcilement
> To the Arragonian brethren? (v i 1–2)

There was no break between acts on the Jacobean stage, and
the word 'reconcilement', following hard upon the remorse of
Bosola which the audience has just beheld at the end of Act iv,
would give meaning to that remorse and show how it will
dramatically express itself. The initial note of 'reconcilement'
conditions all which is to follow in the final act. Antonio will go
to the Cardinal's chamber by the same means Ferdinand had
used to enter that of the Duchess, the parallel here being very
deliberate, but he will go to work good rather than evil:

> I have got
> Private access to his chamber, and intend
> To visit him, about the mid of night,
> As once his brother did our noble duchess.
> It may be that the sudden apprehension
> Of danger – for I'll go in mine own shape –
> When he shall see it fraught with love and duty,
> May draw the poison out of him, and work
> A friendly reconcilement. (v i 64–72)

This speech is crucial to an understanding of the play, for Antonio is postulating a system of values – love, duty and reconciliation – which in the world of Flamineo or the Arragonian brothers could not be possible.

It is the spirit of the Duchess which animates Antonio in the final act, just as it does Bosola, the one coming to stand for reconciliation and the other for justice. As Antonio dies he hears the names of his wife and children, and 'their very names / Kindle a little life in me' (v iv 58–9). In the echo scene the voice of the Duchess seeks to preserve his life, but Antonio has learned also from his wife that death is the inevitable end, and he accepts it calmly and peacefully. 'We are merely the stars' tennis-balls, struck and banded / Which way please them' (v iv 54–5), says Bosola. Man's pain is the product of a fickle fortune, but man may escape the bondage of fortune, as Antonio proves by the nobility of his endurance :

> Though in our miseries Fortune have a part,
> Yet in our noble suff'rings she hath none –
> Contempt of pain, that we may call our own.
>
> (v iii 56–8)

Life may be full of pain and a man a mere pawn in the hands of a capricious fate – all this Antonio recognizes in his death speech :

> In all our quest of greatness,
> Like wanton boys whose pastime is their care,
> We follow after bubbles blown in th'air.
> Pleasure of life, what is't? only the good hours
> Of an ague; merely a preparative to rest,
> To endure vexation : – I do not ask
> The process of my death. (v iv 64–70)

To pursue greatness is as futile as to pursue pleasure; there is no escaping the pain and uncertainty of life, but the important lesson which Antonio has learned from his wife is how to 'endure vexation' in preparation for his everlasting rest. Webster affirms in Antonio's death that human aspirations are nothing, that the

only good in life is the ability to endure life itself, and that man
can 'fly the courts of princes' and the abysmal evil for which they
stand, as Antonio would have his son to do (v iv 72), only by the
assertion of the human quality which separates him forever
from the beasts : his ability to accept the pain and frustration of
life and to die with courage and dignity. This is the final moral
statement to which all the parts of *The Duchess of Malfi* were
carefully designed to give poetic expression, a resolution of the
paradox implicit in *The White Devil.*

SOURCE : *Jacobean Tragedy: The Quest for Moral Order*
(1962).

NOTES

1. M. C. Bradbrook, *Themes and Conventions of Elizabethan
Tragedy* (Cambridge, 1935) pp. 186 ff.
2. *Selected Essays* (London, 1951) p. 117.
3. *John Webster* (London, 1951) p. 65. So also, Travis Bogard,
*The Tragic Satire of John Webster* (Berkeley, Calif., 1955) p. 117,
writes that Webster was 'apparently unable to discover an accept-
able system for the evaluation of good and evil', and concludes
that '*The White Devil* is a tragedy of disillusion, *The Duchess of
Malfi* a tragedy of despair' (p. 141).
4. F. L. Lucas (ed.), *The Duchess of Malfi* (London, 1958)
pp. 28–35.
5. *The Duchess of Malfi*, p. 31. Webster's weakness in structure
is stressed also by R. Ornstein, *The Moral Vision of Jacobean
Tragedy* (Madison, 1960) pp. 128–31.
6. Ian Jack, 'The Case of John Webster', *Scrutiny*, XVI (1949)
38–43, has found Webster's art deficient because 'There is no correspondence between the axioms and the life represented in the drama'.
Essentially the same point is made by Ornstein, *The Moral Vision*,
pp. 128–50, although he sees in *The Duchess of Malfi* a movement
away from 'the lack of moral discriminations in *The White Devil*
towards a more consistent moral view of life, a celebration of the
power of illusion to assure some victory for mankind in an evil
world'. That Webster is a dramatist without moral vision, capable
of only a meaningless sensationalism, has been argued also by W. R.
Edwards, 'John Webster', in *Determinations*, ed. F. R. Leavis
(London, 1934) pp. 155–78. The morality of Webster's art, on the

contrary, has been argued by Lord David Cecil, *Poets and Story-tellers* (London, 1949) pp. 27–43. Cecil tries to find Webster's morality in terms of a Calvinistic Christianity.

7. See Hereward T. Price, 'The Function of Imagery in Webster', *P.M.L.A.*, LXX (1955) 717–39; John Russell Brown (ed.), *The White Devil* (London, 1960) pp. l–lviii. It has been argued also that in *The White Devil* Vittoria achieves nobility by her ability to assume the mask of a virtue she does not possess, and that in this she is offered as contrast to the open villainy of Flamineo, the two positions balancing one another in a kind of equilibrium out of which no moral certainty can emerge. See B. J. Laymon, 'The Equilibrium of Opposites in *The White Devil*: A Reinterpretation', *P.M.L.A.*, LXXIV (1959) 336–47.

8. Thus, for Una M. Ellis-Fermor, *The Jacobean Drama* (London, 1936) pp. 172–3, Webster's chief concern is to stress the unreality of a bleak and meaningless universe: 'this negation, the quality of nothingness, this empty, boundless, indefinable grey mist is the final horror, the symbol of ignorance, of the infinite empty space in which man hovers, the material and the spiritual world both in different terms unreal.'

9. See Ian Jack, *Scrutiny*, XVI (1949) 38–43; M. E. Prior, *The Language of Tragedy* (New York, 1947) pp. 32–3.

10. See F. P. Wilson, *Elizabethan and Jacobean* (Oxford, 1945) pp. 104–6; Edwards, 'John Webster', pp. 157–8; Cecil, *Poets and Storytellers*, pp. 40–1.

11. See the fine discussion of Bosola's role in Bogard, pp. 67 ff. This very perceptive study suffers from an over-emphasis upon the satiric in Webster which tends to negate the value of the plays as tragedy. Webster, says Bogard (*The Tragic Satire of John Webster*, p. 5), 'made the satiric voice coequal with the tragic, and in doing so brought together and steadily controlled two all-but-incompatible attitudes towards human experience'. There is an inherent contradiction in Bogard's thesis, for the two aspects he sees in Webster's tragic vision are indeed incompatible. If Webster as a social satirist 'hoped his work would arouse men to a concern for their world' (pp. 118–19), he could not well have written the tragedies of negation and despair which Bogard finds. We cannot at the same time have despair and a hope for social improvement. The satiric in Webster is emphasized also by Rupert Brooke, *John Webster and Elizabethan Drama* (London, 1916), still valuable for some brilliant flashes of insight, and in Henry W. Wells, *Elizabethan and Jacobean Playwrights* (New York, 1939) p. 46.

12. So also, John Donne in *The Second Anniversary*, while he celebrates the eternity of the soul dwells upon the contrasting insignificance and physical loathsomeness of the body, 'This curded milk, this poor unlittered whelpe/My body . . . a poore Inne, /A Province pack'd up in two yards of skinne.'

13. The integral relation of imagery to action in Webster has been demonstrated ably by H. T. Price, *P.M.L.A.*, LXX (1955) 717–39. Cf. also Prior, *The Language of Tragedy*, pp. 120–35.

*Roma Gill*

# 'QUAINTLY DONE': A READING OF
# *THE WHITE DEVIL* (1966)

If we can concede that in experimental energy *The Winter's Tale* is richer than *The Tempest*, *Howard's End* than *A Passage to India*, we may extend the same judgment to *The White Devil*. Less perfect a work of art than the succeeding *The Duchess of Malfi*, the earlier play yet shows a nervous daring which is absent from the calm assurance of the later production. It is not the play that we, or the audience at the Red Bull, might have expected, knowing the Italian scandal that was its source and recognizing John Webster's name only from its occasional appearance as that of a collaborating author of pot-boilers. Webster, who had worked for Henslowe and written plays to divert the 'Citizens, and the meaner sort of People'[1] who were reputed to frequent the impresario's playhouses, ought from this employment to have acquired the skill to turn any historian's chronicling of the Corombona affair into the expected hot melodrama of alien lust. The Citizen and his Wife, cosily flattered in their self-righteousness, would have applauded. But when it was first produced the play was a flop. The dramatist generously congratulated the actors on their performance, and tried to find comfort in the thought that an English audience, and a thin one at that, could not be warmed by Italian passions when it is standing in an open theatre in an English winter.[2] This was self-delusion; even a summertime full house at the Red Bull could not have provided the 'understanding auditory' that the play demands. Contemporary spectators were probably and understandably baffled by a play with is neither revenge tragedy in the style of Kyd nor the psychological probing of motives and reactions that they later accepted from Middleton; Webster's tragedy is an unusual and unequal mixture of the two with a third component, a disturbing moral ambiguity, which is his alone. Bracciano's appreciative comment on the mechanics of Camillo's death seems to fit the play as a whole. ' 'Twas quaintly done' – done, that is, 'with ingenious art, so as to produce something artistic, curious, or elaborate'. This use of *quaintly* is obsolete; but it seems worthwhile to borrow Bracciano's authority and revive it on this occasion.

All that we know of Webster's methods of composition suggests that he was a man possessed of the dangerous tendency to focus his attention on the smaller unit instead of and sometimes at the expense of the larger. Dr. Dent's researches,[3] supporting the widely accepted theory that Webster wrote with a commonplace book at his elbow, can show how many of his lines were the product of a happy alchemy that transmuted other men's metals into 'something better, or at least something different'[4] of his own. The hazards of such a method are obvious : without strong emotional pressure to fuse them into a new whole the separate particles will remain distinct. While Massinger's borrowings have always the air of an imperfectly remembered quotation, Webster's thefts (to use Eliot's distinction) seem to have been worked on with elaborate care. Yet this implies a laborious process of concentrating on the single image or line instead of the speech, or on the speech and not the whole scene. In *The White Devil* this tendency is increased; the tragedy is disjointed and seems to have been written in episodes, not as a whole. No doubt Webster's early experience as a collaborator encouraged a natural weakness. He may have been the junior partner, writing single scenes at the instruction of a more experienced colleague who would take responsibility for the total structure. Assuming this, we can perhaps use his inexperience as a dramatic architect as one excuse for the rickety scaffolding, forever needing to be propped up with the first thing that comes to hand, which gives the play its shape. Webster, we may say, had not yet discovered in himself the inspirational vigour that drives through and unifies *The Duchess of Malfi*, and instead he resorted to the tired convention of the revenge play, never easy about its power but conscientiously introducing all its paraphernalia.

The first scene introduces an agent of revenge, the banished

Count Lodovico who promises to 'make Italian cut-works in their guts' (1 i 52) as a return for his sentence. The identity of the intended victims is left obscure. Clearly Bracciano is one of them, since Vittoria could have won Lodovico's pardon 'For one kiss to the duke' (1 i 44), but as the government of the state is in the hands of Monticelso and Francisco it seems equally likely that their guts also are threatened. The motive is inadequate anyway : Lodovico does not dispute that banishment is 'gentle penance' (1 i 36) for the 'certain murders . . . Bloody and full of horror' (1 i 31–2) that he has 'acted' in Rome. Webster must have sensed this, for he quickly gives Lodovico further reason to hate Bracciano. The Count is one of the witnesses of Isabella's death, and an audience must be alert to catch the Conjuror's explanation for his unexpected attendance on her :

> . . . by my art
> I find he did most passionately dote
> Upon your duchess. (11 ii 32–4)

This clumsiness is assisted by Lodovico's own confirmation :

> Sir I did love Bracciano's duchess dearly;
> Or rather I pursued her with hot lust,
> Though she ne'er knew on't. (1v iii 111–13)

A self-seeking lust is more consistent with what we have already gathered of Lodovico's character than an altruistic dear love; but it is less likely to turn into a desire for revenge. Now, however, Lodovico is being displaced as the agent of revenge and Francisco, with far better qualifications, steps into the role. His devotion to his sister and his consequent hatred of Bracciano have been stressed from the start and the appearance of Isabella's ghost endorses his claim to avenge her death – although the sneaking, self-conscious ghost adds to an already strong suspicion that Webster has little faith in the convention he has adopted. He does his best to give the episode a rational basis by having Francisco make a deliberate effort to summon up his sister's image :

> Let me remember my dead sister's face :
> Call for her picture : no; I'll close mine eyes,
> And in a melancholic thought I'll frame
> Her figure 'fore me.
> > *Enter* ISABELLA'S *Ghost.*
> > Now I ha't – how strong
> Imagination works ! how she can frame
> Things which are not ! methinks she stands afore me . . .
> > > (IV i 99–104)

Yet at the end Francisco is forgotten. Lodovico incriminates him in the murder of Vittoria but it is the Count himself who shows the typical avenger's pride and defiance in the last scene :

> The rack, the gallows, and the torturing wheel
> Shall be but sound sleeps to me, – here's my rest –
> I limb'd this night-piece and it was my best.
> > > (V vi 295–7)

Before we can applaud an avenger's final sangfroid we must be sure that he has done a good job well. We respect Vindice, for instance, because we are convinced of the soundness of his motives and the rottenness of his victims. We could just possibly be persuaded into thinking this of Francisco, but not of Lodovico. Even if we could forget the rioting murderer of the first scene, the lustful adorer of Isabella and the comically eager machiavel of other parts of the play, we still view him with the remnants of Vittoria's scorn clinging to him :

> 'Twas a manly blow –
> The next thou giv'st, murder some sucking infant,
> And then thou wilt be famous. (V vi 232–4)

The Stoic dignity of her end takes away any least shred of honour that his might have.

There are, it is true, suggestions for a revenge play in Webster's source. Although the historical Bracciano died a natural death after prolonged illness, Vittoria was certainly murdered by one Lodovico Orsini, a distant relation of the

Duke's who may have acted at the instigation or on behalf of the Duke of Florence. But the motive appears to have been greed for the wealth Bracciano had left to his second wife, not a pious revenge for a dead sister's honour.[5]

Perhaps this botched revenge play aspect of *The White Devil* was also in part a misguided concession to popular taste. Webster had learned that a dramatist must compromise; by choosing to write for the stage he is in duty bound to entertain his audience : *et docere et delectare*. A refusal in the manner of Ben Jonson to smudge 'The bright gloss of our intellectual'[6] may have its rewards in virginal integrity; but not many authors can be satisfied with this. In the epistle 'To the Reader' prefacing the first quarto of *The White Devil* Webster freely admits that in the writing of the play a practical consideration of its future public took precedence over the observation of theoretical prescriptions :

If it be objected this is no true dramatic poem, I shall easily confess it . . . willingly, and not ignorantly, in this kind have I faulted : for should a man present to such an auditory, the most sententious tragedy that ever was written, observing all the critical laws . . . the breath that comes from the uncapable multitude is able to poison it.

Few other concessions are made. While playing for safety in the overall pattern of the play Webster consistently defrauds expectation in all other matters, and nowhere so daringly as in his characterization.

The characters, and particularly the comic ones, of popular drama change very little over the centuries : jovial Simon Eyre and his sharp-tongued, warm-hearted wife have simply moved north from Tower Street to Coronation Street, and the science-fiction villain is cousin german to Kyd's Lorenzo in his ruthless pursuit of his own desires. The 'uncapable multitude' of all times wants its fictional figures to be immediately recognizable and understandable, constructed according to an accepted blue-print and showing none of the inconsistencies and seeming irrelevancies of real life. The superbly skeletal creatures of *The Revenger's Tragedy* could have afforded Webster a pattern for his own play; although Tourneur's tragedy as a whole calls for a poetically rich response, the separate characters are simple and unambiguous personifications. But of all the major figures in *The White Devil* only one, Camillo, elicits a response that is unfalteringly straightforward from first to last. Whether he is affecting a lordly disdain for his unconcerned wife or self-important in his cuckoldom, Camillo is a cue for ribald laughter, a clown whose ludicrous death crowns an ignoble career. Dr. Boklund has wisely cautioned against accepting any single version of the historical Corombona affair as Webster's sole source,[7] yet in none of the chronicles does the husband of Vittoria appear as the credulous oaf of the play. In this one instances it seems safe to say that Webster, intimately acquainted with standard figures of fun, drew the character from theatrical stock and married him to Vittoria instead of the real-life Peretti, a man whose youth and virility are never called in question. Peretti was murdered at Monte Cavallo and Webster, who cannot have misunderstood the place-name, gives a wry twist to history by having Camillo's neck broken as he mounted a vaulting-horse. Part of Webster's intention in this deliberate change was no doubt, as Dr. Boklund observes, 'to furnish *The White Devil* with a suitable butt for bawdy ridicule';[8] more important than this, the impotence that makes Camillo laughable provokes corresponding sympathy for his wife.

Vittoria is one of the most complex and challenging characters in the drama of this period. Many critics, of whom Clifford Leech is one, have felt compelled to afford her a kind of grudging admiration, admitting her finer qualities as it were in spite of their own moral probity :

The impression we are left with is of beauty, adroitness, a brave spirit, but Webster would not have us forget that she is the devil of his play's title.[9]

Professor Leech has here, I feel, succumbed to the ever-present temptation to fit Vittoria into a recognizable pattern. It is not, after all, difficult to acknowledge that beauty is not inevitably accompanied by virtue and that one may praise and condemn the same person for different qualities in him. But there is more to Vittoria than the admirable adultress. Certainly this is the strongest impression of her character, fixed in our minds by the

two scenes, her trial and her death, which remain longest in the
memory. But Webster photographs Vittoria from many different
angles, leaving it to the boy-player to create the whole being
from these partial views.

With mechanical exactness Vittoria performs the duties of a
good wife to her husband: 'I did nothing to displease him, I
carved to him at supper-time.' (I ii 126). We can understand
the sullen discontent: we have seen Camillo. The actor's face
must speak for Vittoria's mind in the long silence that follows
while she half-listens to Flamineo's chatter and pursues her own
thoughts. That these are of a coolly practical nature is evident
from the next line she speaks; if she is to accept Bracciano's suit,
Camillo must be safely out of the way and 'How shall's rid him
hence?' (I ii 161). These two lines and the weary humour of
her words to her husband are all Vittoria is allowed to speak
before she meets with Bracciano, when the false modesty of her
reply to his question makes it clear that she is out to improve
her social as well as her sexual fortunes.

> *Bracciano.* What value is this jewel?
> *Vittoria.*                   'Tis the ornament
>      Of a weak fortune.  (I ii 221–2)

Suddenly Vittoria becomes loquacious, narrating her 'foolish
idle dream' with an artful cunning. The dream, Dr. Bradbrook
explains,

> besides giving a picture of her as a victim rather than an aggressor,
> is vivid enough to draw off attention from its sinister purport, if the
> Elizabethan interest in the surface meaning of words is remem-
> bered.[10]

Bracciano's protective instinct is aroused, certainly, but the
shocking truth cannot be overlooked by an audience which
hears Flamineo's approving comment:

> Excellent devil.
> She hath taught him in a dream
> To make away his duchess and her husband.
>                          (I ii 256–8)

If we were to stop reading the play at the point where Vittoria
has won from the Duke his declaration that to him she shall 'Be
dukedom, health, wife, children, friends and all' (I ii 268), the
character is easy to assess. Boredom with her husband has stifled
all emotion except ambition, and she has no hesitation in snatch-
ing this opportunity to release herself from a frustrating marriage.
But further reading modifies this impression. The interruption
of Cornelia throws the scene's studied formality into chaos, and
Vittoria's assumption of amoral ease at once evaporates. The
statuesque poses collapse into a jostling for centre-stage position,
and Vittoria is pulled in three directions at once. To her mother
she owes an obedience: 'Dearest mother hear me' (I ii 278).
The Duke must not be spurned or neglected: 'Dear my lord'
(I ii 283). And a respect must be paid to the world outside the
house: 'The duchess, – ' (I ii 286). This last exclamation can
hardly be spoken in tones other than awe and fear – tones
representing a very different attitude from the calculated scorn
of 'your fell duchess' only a very little earlier (I ii 245). She is
never allowed to complete a sentence, but from the broken lines
an actor can construct another character, the opposite of the first
but no less true. A bold 'masculine virtue'[11] combines with a
woman's frailty in this Vittoria. The first speaks for her in the
trial scene (III ii), defending her against the lawyer's quillets
and the cardinal's mud-slinging, until by the end of the scene
we cannot be sure whether she is innocent or guilty. It accompanies her to the house of convertites, giving her the air of one
going into holy retreat:

> My mind shall make it honester to me
> Than the Pope's palace, and more peaceable
> Than thy soul, though thou art a cardinal.
>
> (III ii 290–2)

'Minds innocent and quiet take. . . .' Visited in this prison by
her lover, however, Vittoria's courage once again fails her when
her faithfulness is doubted, and she plays out a naturalistic scene
of feminine tantrums. After the first moment of surprise when
she realizes that Bracciano does not trust her, she bawls recrimi-
nations at him and blames him for her present situation:

What do you call this house?
Is this your palace? did not the judge style it
A house of penitent whores? who sent me to it?
Who hath the honour to advance Vittoria
To this incontinent college? is't not you?
Is't not your high preferment? Go, go brag
How many ladies you have undone, like me.
                                        (IV ii 113–19)

The anger dissolves in tears as she throws herself on the bed
while Bracciano perseveres at the tricky task of winning her
round. Tears give way to scorn and repulse; a threat to scratch
out the Duke's eyes; and then, with self-pity, reconciliation as
she is finally gathered into Bracciano's arms:

> Stop her mouth,
> With a sweet kiss, my lord.
> So now the tide's turned the vessel's come about –
> He's a sweet armful.  (IV ii 192–5)

Webster demanded a lot from his boy-actor in this scene of
intense emotion which plots every movement of a woman's
guilty mind; what is left unsaid is almost more important than
the spoken words, and the actor must supply this himself. But
the tear-stained woman who is now promised marriage, the
fulfilment of her earlier hopes in 'a duchess' title' (IV ii 221),
is a different creature from the coldly poised social climber of
her first scene. Vittoria no longer looks for the advancement the
Duke promises; she returns his love with equal love. This is confirmed on the last occasion (v iii) when we see the two together.
Again Vittoria is given few words to speak, but the simple ex-
clamations indicate the genuineness of her grief at her lover's
tortured death. The character is once again changed in the last
scene. She enters '*with a book in her hand*' (v vi s.d.) and her
brother reacts, characteristically, with disbelief: 'What, are you
at your prayers? Give o'er' (v vi 1). James Smith, who sees
Vittoria throughout the play as being consistently motivated by
a simple desire for social esteem, also interprets this entrance as
a sign of typically machiavellian hypocrisy: 'Taking advantage of
widowhood she is seeking to be rid of the past, to set herself up

at last as a great lady, even as a *dévote.*'[12] This reading makes
some sense – but not, I think, the sense that Webster intended.
The real Vittoria's piety before her death is well vouched for by
historical manuscripts and Webster was following his source
closely at this point.[13] We cannot share Flamineo's attitude now
if we rejected his scoffing at Vittoria's grief earlier (v iii 181–6).
The innocent-seeming Vittoria of the trial scene might well have
shammed piety; but the character has developed a long way
since then. We are finally reminded in this double death scene
of the split in Vittoria's personality. At first, threatened by her
brother, she is a mere woman, caught in a trap and furiously
struggling to escape. A piety is now assumed to conceal her
desperation, but it is for Flamineo's benefit, not for ours. The
'masculine virtue' reasserts itself when the situation becomes
real, and Vittoria dies with courage and resolution:

> I'll tell thee what, –
> I will not in my death shed one base tear,
> Or if look pale, for want of blood, not fear.
> (v vi 224–6)

This follows immediately on the one phrase that must guide the
actor through his portrayal of the character: 'I am too true
a woman' (v vi 223). Bored with an impotent and impoverished
husband, eager for social status, wanting to be amoral yet
admitting moral conventions, recognizing her own faults and
blaming them on others, yet capable of courageous love –
Vittoria will not fit into any neat dramatic classification. She is
too close to life for comfort.

Vittoria is one of the 'new women' on the English stage. The
Elizabethan's ideal woman seems to have died with Cordelia,
whose

> voice was ever soft,
> Gentle and low, an excellent thing in a woman.
> (*King Lear*, v iii 273–4)

and her place has been taken by a creature of suffragette
eloquence who suffers the agonies of sexual and social ambition
in a way that Shakespeare's heroines never knew. Nearest to
Vittoria is Bianca of Middleton's *Women Beware Women*.

Once her shocked virtue has accommodated itself to the Duke's passion, Bianca forgets her milky love for the humble Leantio and enjoys her success as the Duke's mistress. Like Vittoria, she comes to marry and love her seducer, and dies 'Tasting the same death in a cup of love' (v i 263). The trend was perhaps started by Kyd's Bel-Imperia. Fletcher's Evadne (*The Maid's Tragedy*) and Massinger's Donusa (*The Renegado*) are two more of the same breeding and spirit; possessed of intelligence and courage, qualities hitherto reserved mainly to the male, as well as their feminine charm, they attract admiration and fear at the same time. When such a being comes on stage she brings with her all the ambiguity of response that men can give to a woman whose head is as strong as her heart.

This reading of Vittoria's personality is admittedly a modern one, owing more to post-Freudian psychology than to Jacobean writings on the passions. Yet it is the only one that seems to embrace all sides of the character. With Isabella, too, Webster shows an instinctive understanding of the feminine mind. The character begins in the tradition of Patient Grissil, revived for English audiences in Dekker's comedy of 1603, and her meekness is exasperating as, with a would-be metaphysical image, she compares her loving arms to 'a preservative circle' of 'the precious unicorn's horn' (II i 14–15). Only a plague-crazed wretch, anyway, could put trust in that impossible remedy, and young Davenant soon found out that the test was futile; 'the Spider would go over and thorough and thorough, unconcerned.'[14] John Russell Brown reacts strongly against Isabella, feeling that the lady does protest too much, concealing a 'hidden selfishness' behind her boasted generosity. The reality, he suggests, is the character that Isabella pretends to assume, 'a foolish, mad, / And jealous woman' (II i 264–5).[15] Her hysterical violence in this role certainly 'lies like truth' when she longs

> To dig the strumpet's eyes out, let her lie
> Some twenty months a-dying, to cut off
> Her nose and lips, pull out her rotten teeth,
> Preserve her flesh like mummia, for trophies
> Of my just anger : hell to my affliction
> Is mere snow-water. (II i 246–51)

If the play had been written by a twentieth-century dramatist
it would be easy to explain how these oppositions might be
reconciled : the aggressions and the passive acceptance of injury
are both equally real, but in a civilized society the former must
either be repressed or else released only in disguise – as Isabella
releases them here. Perhaps there is a 'hidden selfishness' in
Isabella – but it is the selfishness only of a woman who wants
to keep her husband to herself. The genuineness of her misery
cannot be mistaken when she begs 'Sir let me borrow of you but
one kiss' (II i 255). The same kiss has already been coldly
refused and now, with the one word 'borrow', Isabella admits
defeat and concedes her rights in Bracciano to Vittoria.

Bracciano appears a brute in his harsh treatment of Isabella,
but at other times, whenever he appears in relation to Vittoria,
there is a quality that surprises us about the character. He is
not the royal lecher we have been led to expect from Lodovico's
hint that the Duke of Bracciano

> by close pandarism seeks to prostitute
> The honour of Vittoria Corombona. (I i 41–2)

Webster encourages these expectations for one instant as the
scene opens with all the trappings of royal lust – the coaches
and torches at midnight. No sooner are we composed to witness
a familiar seduction than our expectations are frustrated. The
courteous formality of Vittoria's greeting gives place to an
intimately personal mood where, in one line, Webster convinces
us of the true quality of Bracciano's feeling for Vittoria.

*Bracciano.* Flamineo.
*Flamineo.*                    My lord.
*Bracciano.*                              Quite lost, Flamineo.
                                                    (I ii 3)

There is a cue here for one of the silences more eloquent than
language which Webster relies on so often in this play; the rest of
the scene, indeed, depends very largely on the quality of
Bracciano's silences. In the subsequent dialogue it is Flamineo
who does the talking; flippant and cynical, he urges the Duke
onwards, either misinterpreting or attempting to pervert Brac-

ciano's passion. Flamineo's dynamic, as he later admits, is ambition; and to further his own ends he requires a blackmailing
hold over his master which only the shameful passion of lust
will allow him: 'he has to encourage the passion and at the
same time to degrade it.'[16] At one point only does he seem to
grasp Bracciano's intent. Sounding the depth of the sigh 'O
should she fail to come, – ' (i ii 38) he is instantly alerted: 'I
must not have your lordship thus unwisely amorous' (i ii 39).
We accept the genuineness of Bracciano's love because we reject
the interpretation that Flamineo puts upon it. But for final proof
of his sincerity there is the declaration he makes to Vittoria:

> I could wish time would stand still
> And never end this interview, this hour,
> But all delight doth itself soon'st devour.
> Let me into your bosom happy lady,
> Pour out instead of eloquence my vows, –
> Loose me not madam, for if you forego me
> I am lost eternally. (i ii 202–8)

The strength of the lines confirms all our earlier impressions; as
Dr. Bradbrook saw, 'There is no argument against the movement
and rhythm of such a passage.'[17]

The rhythms of Cornelia's speeches similarly admit of no
misinterpretation – and again to surprising effect. Cornelia
ought to be the fixed point that James Smith welcomed her as,
the character from whom 'we can take our moral bearings when,
amid the amount and variety of vice, they are in danger of
being obscured'.[18] Certainly Cornelia's is the voice of decalogue
morality; but in Webster's theatre this voice often sounds a wrong
note. Its first murmurings are heard when Antonelli and
Gasparo, antiphonally reminding Lodovico of his past, offer
euphuistic words of comfort that are as irritating to the audience
as to the Count:

> We see that trees bear no such pleasant fruit
> There where they grew first, as where they are new set.
> Perfumes the more they are chaf'd the more they render
> Their pleasing scents, and so affliction
> Expresseth virtue, fully. (i i 46–50)

Cornelia's first appearance on the stage has the timeliness of the Old Man's entrance in *Dr. Faustus* just when Faustus is about to commit himself to Helen and ultimate damnation. She slides into Bracciano's address to Vittoria, and her first utterance ends with the generalized jingle :

> Earthquakes leave behind,
> Where they have tyrannized, iron, or lead, or stone,
> But – woe to ruin – violent lust leaves none. (i ii 218–20)

An incurable predilection to rhyme makes her morality sound trite and superficial in this scene of deeply-felt emotion, especially when she interrupts Bracciano's honest declaration :

> *Bracciano.*                    . . . you shall to me at once
>         Be dukedom, health, wife, children, friends and all.
> *Cornelia.* Woe to light hearts – they still forerun our fall.
>                                              (i ii 267–9)

John Russell Brown is, I think, a little too anxious to discredit her. At the death of Marcello Cornelia goes mad with all the grace of Ophelia – and with some of Ophelia's lines too – as she wraps the body in its winding-sheet (v iv). Mr. Brown comments that the distracted mother is 'concerned, not with honour or virtue, but with the preservation of her son's body; her regard for virtue has not been, we may suspect, for its own sake'. The Cornelia of the lament scene, an animated tableau of considerable beauty, is not the same character who rudely interrupted the earlier episode. Her function is different now, and Webster seems to have concentrated on this rather than on any total impression the character would make – although, as with Vittoria, an actor can show a consistent and credible change here. But Mr. Brown's is a more relevant view than Mr. Smith's; to see the action as the latter sees it, through Cornelia's eyes, is to witness the regular tragedy of destructive lust, the play that Webster was refusing to write.

The absence of any character whose opinion we can rely on – or, rather, the shaking of our faith in the one we *ought* to be able to trust – is part of Webster's policy of ambiguity in this play. The audience, as often in Massinger's plays, is asked to form a jury and give its judgment on the several contrary opinions presented to its hearing. This of course is most obvious in the trial scene. Such scenes were Massinger's delight, but his more sober mind could admit only the black and white of evil and good, and he directs the court – the audience – without a shadow of hesitation. Even the arraignment of Charalois in *The Fatal Dowry* is conducted with strict justice; the accused is a man of unusual honour to whom his wife's light-hearted adultery gives ample cause for taking revenge into his own hands. But however much we have been led to sympathize with Charalois we are never allowed to question that punishment must always be left to the legal authorities :

> . . . how just soever
> Our reasons are to remedy our wrongs,
> We are yet to leave them to their will and power
> That, to that purpose, have authority.  (v ii)

The law, and by implication the social order that supports it, is shown to be a meaningless formality in *The White Devil*, trampling down human dignity and true charity. Bracciano is at first an instrument of satire. His surprise entry into the proceedings – there is 'no place assign'd' him (III ii 1) – and his superbly urbane gesture in spreading a cloak to sit on, immediately raise him in our estimation above those who stand on ceremony. Even before the cardinal starts his denunciation we have been manoeuvred on to the side of a woman whom we know to be an adulteress and, if not in fact a murderess, at least an accessory before the fact. Vittoria's splendid refusal to be accused in Latin sounds like innocence : it is not that she herself does not understand the language,

> but amongst this auditory
> Which come to hear my cause, the half or more
> May be ignorant in't. (III ii 15–17)

Monticelso defeats his own ends by the violence of his tirade, so that we almost endorse Vittoria's comment

for your names
Of whore and murd'ress they proceed from you,
As if a man should spit against the wind,
The filth returns in's face. (III ii 148–51)

Our own thoughts are spoken for us by the two ambassadors:

*French Ambassador.*                        She hath lived ill.
*English Ambassador.* True, but the cardinal's too bitter.
(III ii 106–7)

At the point where it seems that Vittoria must either lie outright
– and this, with all her evasions, she has not done yet – or betray
herself, the situation is saved by Bracciano. Monticelso asks,

Who lodg'd beneath your roof that fatal night
Your husband brake his neck? (III ii 153–4)

and the worthy Bracciano comes forward to admit that he was
there; because, he continues blandly,

I heard her husband was in debt
To you my Lord.
*Monticelso.*                        He was.
*Bracciano.*                        And 'twas strangely fear'd
That you would cozen her.
*Monticelso.*                        Who made you overseer?
*Bracciano.* Why my charity, my charity, which should flow
From every generous and noble spirit,
To orphans and to widows. (III ii 162–8)

The cardinal's lack of charity is noted; the fact that Bracciano is
not telling the whole truth (and how did he know that Vittoria
was that night a widow?) escapes through a hole driven by one
of the oldest of lawyers' tricks, the argument *ad hominem*. From
this the proceedings degenerate into a trial of strength between
Monticelso and Vittoria; the cardinal wins, as he cannot fail to
do, but it is Vittoria who is triumphant.

The scene has the effect of setting our moral natures at variance with our instinctive sympathies. Elsewhere in this play

Webster uses a still more subtle technique to disturb our composure when, through the varied characters assembled on the
stage, he presents an incident and two or more attitudes to it at
the same time. The only analogous technique is the musical one
of counter-point – as used, for example, in Britten's *War
Requiem*. The first encounter between Bracciano and Vittoria is
watched by Cornelia and Flamineo, the one with a puritan's
horror, the other with a voyeur's enjoyment. For the scene to
have its full impact we need to keep all four characters and the
attitudes they represent in full mental view – as they would be
on the stage. There is no straightforward action in this play.
'Whatever action takes place, there is always someone
observing and commenting upon it.'[19] We are prevented from being moved by Isabella's death by the presence of Bracciano,
standing between us and the dumb-show, coldly and almost
aesthetically appreciative. Cornelia's grief affects us little because
our attention is always drawn to Flamineo's reactions. For the
greater part of the play it is Flamineo's function to interpose himself between the audience and the action, always suggesting a
meaner interpretation of what is taking place. When Bracciano
and Vittoria exchange tokens, Flamineo licks his lips with the
suggestive 'That's better – she must wear his jewel lower' (I ii
228). Although we may resent the construction he put on every
word and deed, we cannot forget it. The sympathetic impression
that Vittoria makes in the house of convertites is smeared by her
brother's argument on her behalf :

> What a strange credulous man were you, my lord,
> To think the Duke of Florence would love her !
> [*aside*] Will any mercer take another's ware
> When once 'tis tous'd and sullied? (IV ii 154–7)

The merchandise image is perhaps taken from *Troilus and
Cressida* ('We turn not back the silks upon the merchant /
When we have spoiled them', II ii 69–70), and although it is
used in isolation, not as part of a poetic undercurrent, it has
some of the potency of the imagery in that play, never permitting
our response to be single and simple.

What Shakespeare achieves through poetry, Webster some-

times comes near to achieving through stagecraft. Actions and
objects take the place of words. This is a technique of modern
prose drama, seen effectively in *Hedda Gabler* where the stove
and the portrait of General Gabler, present on the stage, are
gradually invested with poetic meaning. Like Hedda's constant
retreating to her father's picture in moments of insecurity, the
ironic death of Isabella makes actual in the play an idea which
is fitfully present from beginning to end. Poison has been smoked
on to the portrait of Bracciano, and Isabella dies when she
kisses the painted lips. The union of kissing and death was pro-
phesied by Cornelia at the beginning of the play, 'Be thy act
Judas-like – betray in kissing' (i ii 298), and in subsequent
events the open and unashamed demonstration of love becomes
inextricably    linked    with    the    machiavellian's    murdering
subtlety, its complete opposite. Bracciano is poisoned with

> mercury –
>         And copperas –
>                 And quicksilver –
> With other devilish pothecary stuff (v iii 161–2)

and his last sane words to Vittoria show a loving care to protect
her which is ironic because now too late : 'Do not kiss me, for I
shall poison thee' (v iii 26).

Webster's art, as Miss Inga-Stina Ekeblad has demonstrated
in her examination of *The Duchess of Malfi*, is an 'impure' one,[20]
and *The White Devil* is a daring mixture of the old and the new
in stage techniques. The comic death-scene, parodying the
serious one it precedes, is, consciously or not, in the manner of the
*Secunda Pastorum*; the revenge structure goes back to *The
Spanish Tragedy* and the dumb-shows to *Gorboduc*. Along with
these we have a new naturalism in the presentation of Vittoria
and a skilled manipulation of the audience into unaccustomed
and uncomfortable moral positions. *The Duchess of Malfi*,
where the different techniques are more perfectly assimilated, is
the easier play to read; but the experimental stagecraft of *The
White Devil* makes this the more exciting theatrical experience.

SOURCE : *Essays and Studies*, XIX (1966).

NOTES

1. *Historia Histrionica*, cit. G. E. Bentley, *Jacobean and Caroline Stage* (Oxford, 1941–68) ii, 693.

2. See the Epistle 'To the Reader' and the final comment on the play.

3. R. W. Dent, *John Webster's Borrowing* (California, 1960).

4. In T. S. Eliot's opinion, the mark of a good poet: 'Philip Massinger', *Selected Essays*, 3rd ed. (London, 1951) p. 206.

5. The factual basis of the play has been closely examined by Gunnar Boklund in *The Sources of 'The White Devil'* (Uppsala, 1957).

6. A phrase used in Satire VIII of Marston's *The Scourge of Villainy* (London, 1598).

7. 'No document which would immediately and completely solve the problem of the origin of the play has been identified.' Boklund, op. cit. p. 133.

8. Ibid. p. 152.

9. *John Webster* (London, 1951) p. 44.

10. *Themes and Conventions of Elizabethan Tragedy* (Cambridge, 1935, 4th imp. 1960) p. 188.

11. The quality she takes on herself at the trial: 'So entangled in a cursed accusation / That my defence of force like Perseus, / Must personate masculine virtue . . .' (III ii 134–6).

12. 'The Tragedy of Blood', *Scrutiny*, VIII (1939) 278.

13. See Boklund, op. cit. pp. 69 ff.

14. Aubrey's *Brief Lives*, ed. A. Clark (Oxford, 1898) i 205.

15. In his Introduction to the Revels text (1960) pp. lii ff.

16. Smith, op. cit. 273.

17. Op. cit. p. 187.

18. Op. cit. p. 279.

19. Russell Brown, op. cit. p. xlv.

20. 'The "Impure Art" of John Webster', *Review of English Studies*, IX (1958) 253–67.

# Peter B. Murray

# FROM *A STUDY OF JOHN WEBSTER* (1969)

> Th' heaven o'er my head seems made of molten brass,
> The earth of flaming sulphur, yet I am not mad.
> (*The Duchess of Malfi*, IV ii 25–6)

*The White Devil* is negative, a searing revelation of the evil that hides under the fair surface of worldly life, and Webster felt the need to go on in his next play and explore the possibility of goodness in life. *The Duchess of Malfi* is the result, a play extending the themes and materials of the earlier play and also transcending them by evoking pity and terror for the fate of good as well as for the fate of evil. In *The White Devil* positive values were only implied through contrast with the evils exposed. In *The Duchess of Malfi* the evils are still present, but stripped of their masks and clearly false, and the positive value of true integrity and of life itself are given full development.

The world of the second play, like that of the first, is an Italianate hell, but whereas in *The White Devil* the hell was created realistically for the most part, in *The Duchess of Malfi* Webster's technique becomes more symbolic: the central part of the play, with its ghastly torments, is an epitome of hell in which the world is reduced to a dance of madmen. And at the end the devil's own child, Ferdinand, appears in his true shape as a mad wolf.

The parallels between the evil worlds of the two plays are extensive and significant.[1] Both worlds are dominated by a wrathful Duke and a dissembling Cardinal, symbolizing the union of church and state for evil in the kingdom of Satan, a union made the stronger in *The Duchess of Malfi* by virtue of the Duke and

Cardinal being brothers who are twins in quality (I i 172). In both plays the evil Cardinals dominate an evil Roman Catholic Church to banish and to imprison and destroy the heroine. And in both plays this abuse of power by churchmen is part of a larger pattern showing the perversion of religion in the kingdom of Satan. The pattern of perverted rituals in *The White Devil* finds a counterpart in the later play's repeated suggestion that the nearer to the Church one gets, the farther he is from God. This pattern is faintly suggested by the passing allusion to the legend of Winifred, the famous Welsh saint beheaded by her would-be rapist in a churchyard; by the gift of the citadel of St. Bennet to Julia, the Cardinal's concubine; and by the discovery of the mad Ferdinand, in his lycanthropy, 'in a lane / Behind Saint Mark's church, with the leg of a man / Upon his shoulder' (I i 390, V i 29–33, V ii 13–15). The pattern is strongly suggested by the pretence of Bosola, when he is about to murder the Duchess, that he is the bellman, and it is obvious in the false, dissembling pilgrimages to religious shrines, in which we see that it is literally true that the nearer the false pilgrims approach their goals, the farther they are from God. Julia makes a pretended pilgrimage to Rome in order to be available to the Cardinal (II iv 1–5). The Cardinal makes a pilgrimage to Loretto to lay aside his holy appearance and reveal the worldly reality beneath, and there he meets his sister, the Duchess :

*1. Pilg.* I have not seen a goodlier shrine than this,
    Yet I have visited many.
*2. Pilg.* The Cardinal of Arragon
    Is this day to resign his cardinal's hat;
    His sister duchess likewise is arriv'd
    To pay her vow of pilgrimage – I expect
    A noble ceremony.
*1. Pilg.*                    No question : – they come.

*Here the ceremony of the Cardinal's instalment in the habit of a soldier, performed in delivering up his cross, hat, robes and ring at the shrine, and investing him with sword, helmet, shield and spurs; then Antonio, the Duchess and their Children, having presented themselves at the shrine, are (by a*

*form of banishment in dumb-show expressed towards them by
the cardinal and the state of Ancona) banished ...*
(III iv 1–7 and s. d.)

The Duchess finds that her pilgrimage to a holy shrine only
brings her into the arms of her satanic brothers. This is the fit-
tingly ironic result of the falseness of her pilgrimage :

> *Bos.*                              Let me think :
>   I would wish your grace to feign a pilgrimage
>   To our Lady of Loretto, scarce seven leagues
>   From fair Ancona; so may you depart
>   Your country with more honour, and your flight
>   Will seem a princely progress, retaining
>   Your usual train about you.
> *Duch.*                              Sir, your direction
>   Shall lead me by the hand. . . .
> [*Car.*] I do not like this jesting with religion,
>   This feigned pilgrimage.
> *Duch.* Thou art a superstitious fool –
>   Prepare us instantly for our departure :
>   Past sorrows, let us moderately lament them,
>   For those to come, seek wisely to prevent them.
(III ii 306–22)

The Duchess thinks that to follow Bosola's advice is to act
'wisely', but the event proves otherwise. As in *The White Devil*,
we find that

> the opinion of wisdom is a foul tetter that runs all over a man's
> body : if simplicity direct us to have no evil, it directs us to a happy
> being; for the subtlest folly proceeds from the subtlest wisdom . . .
(II i 78–81)

*Self*-confident *Worldly* wisdom of cunning, 'subtle' plots and
guileful measures to obtain security are all to no avail :

> Security some men call the suburbs of hell,
> Only a dead wall between. (v ii 337–8)

In *The Duchess of Malfi*, as in the earlier play, people may be murdered in their own palaces and are never secure from the invasion of enemies even into their private chambers (III v 93–5). Ferdinand gets a false key to the Duchess's chamber, and steals in upon her at the very moment when she feels most gay and secure in love-banter with Antonio (III i 79–81, III ii 62 ff). Later this has a parallel in v ii, when Bosola invades the love-nest of Julia and the Cardinal.

In both *The White Devil* and *The Duchess of Malfi* the culmination of this exposure of the false confidence of 'security' comes in the final scene, where the idea is carried to grotesque lengths. In *The White Devil*, first Flamineo breaks into Vittoria's chamber, then Lodovico, and finally Giovanni. In *The Duchess of Malfi*, the Cardinal, 'wisely' wanting to conceal his own villainy, tells his friends not to come into the courtyard even if he calls for help, and we see that he has outwitted himself when Bosola attacks him and his friends refuse to come to his aid.

In the world of the *Duchess*, then, as in the world of *The White Devil*, appearances deceive: what appears to be near God may in reality be far from Him, and what appears to be wisdom and security may in reality be folly. Conversely, what is far from the Roman Church and appears to be folly may in reality be true holiness and wisdom: the marriage of the Duchess and Antonio, foolish by any of the standards of their world and explicitly lacking the sanction of the Church, is fruitful and spiritually true.

Through this and other patterns I shall review later, Webster directly contrasts the good in the world of the *Duchess* with the evil of the world of both that play and *The White Devil*. This second contrast, between the good in the *Duchess* and the evil in *The White Devil*, may be seen in nearly every element of the plays, from their beginnings:

*Lodovico.* Banish'd? (I i I)

*Delio.* You are welcome to your country, dear Antonio

(I i I)

to their endings; the first moralizing about evil, the second about good:

[*Gio.*] Let guilty men remember their black deeds
　　Do lean on crutches, made of slender reeds. (v vi 300–1)

[*Del.*] *Integrity of life is fame's best friend,*
　　*Which nobly, beyond death, shall crown the end.*
　　　　　　　　　　　　　　　　　(V V 120–1)

But the really significant contrasts relate to the central situations
of the plays and to the character of the heroines. Vittoria's
brother Flamineo perverts the normal relation of brother to
sister by being her pander. In contrast to Flamineo's perverse
evil, the Duchess's brother Ferdinand shows a 'most perverse'
goodness in his sadistic torture of his sister because of her love
(I i 169). The widow Vittoria is banished and killed for murder
and for remarrying by the brother and uncle of her *victims*, but
the widowed Duchess is banished and killed by her *own* brothers
merely for remarrying. Vittoria marries a man far above her in
social station, but the Duchess marries beneath her place.
Vittoria is in truth a charnel within, and dies in proud despair;
the Duchess is a teeming womb of life, and dies in Christian
humility and hope. In everything Vittoria is a white devil, fair
without and foul within; the Duchess is fair within and foul
without : because she has to conceal her marriage, she gains the
reputation of being a whore, partly due to the fact that in her
pregnancy she wears a loose-bodied gown like those worn by
Elizabethan prostitutes.[2] Indeed, the Duchess's persecutors, judging her by appearances, regard her as a whorish white devil,
ironically reversing the true relation between her appearance and
her reality (II iii 76–7, III iii 61–4).

Governing both plays is the idea that suffering tests and de-
fines a person's character, bringing out his inner strength or laying bare his weakness :

*Anto.* Perfumes the more they are chaf'd the more they render
　　Their pleasing scents, and so affliction
　　Expresseth virtue, fully, whether true,
　　Or else adulterate. (*The White Devil*, I i 48–51)

*Ant.* Man, like to *Cassia*, is prov'd best, being bruis'd.
　　　　　　　　　(*The Duchess of Malfi*, III v 75)

The seeming strength of Vittoria is in the final analysis a strength of a false kind and for a false cause. It is the courage only of despair. The strength of the Duchess of Malfi, however, is the strength of true greatness, surviving her spiritual error of using false appearances,[3] surviving a suffering so terrible it has made many critics cry 'too much!', even surviving despair to emerge purified, able to affirm life in the face of death itself.[4] It is a superbly human strength, womanish and fearful, wavering and emotional, and therefore all the more impressive.

The upright strength the Duchess is able to achieve is the 'integrity of life' Delio says is Nature's greatest gift to man (v v 18–21). I have already discussed the concept of integrity in connection with *The White Devil*, showing that it is antithetical to lack of self-knowledge, to states of despair, and to the use of false appearances to seem what one is not. Integrity is firm moral rectitude and wholeness. Coupled with love, it is the great human value that is answerable to the greatness of God, for it is this potential of human character that justifies all the suffering God permits in our world.[5]

The integrity of the Duchess is most apparent in her consistent affirmation of love and life and of their order. The opening of the play has to be seen to be fully appreciated. Ferdinand, the Cardinal, and the courtiers who surround them are turbulent, profane, quarrelsome, and disorderly, and Antonio and Delio, who stand across the stage from them through most of the scene, are made to represent order, especially in Antonio's carefully patterned formal characters of the Cardinal, Ferdinand, and the Duchess. When all the court have gone, and only Antonio and the Duchess are on stage, we have the effect of a calm after a storm, the contrast is so great.[6] Their brief courtship, with the following wedding, is a beautiful ritual creating a new social order in a disordered world.[7] Their language points to this significance:

> *Ant*. But for your brothers?
> *Duch*.                 Do not think of them,
>     All discord, without this circumference,
>     Is only to be pitied, and not fear'd :
>     Yet, should they know it, time will easily

> Scatter the tempest.
> ... a contract in a chamber,
> *Per verba de presenti* is absolute marriage : –
> Bless, heaven, this sacred Gordian, which let violence
> Never untwine.
> *Ant.* And may our sweet affections, like the spheres,
> Be still in motion.
> *Duch.*                    Quickening, and make
> The like soft music.
> *Ant.* That we may imitate the loving palms,
> Best emblems of a peaceful marriage,
> That ne'er bore fruit, divided. (I i 468–87)

Not only is their love *ritualized* to contrast it with the discord of
the Arragonian brothers, but it is also *mutual*. In the world of
the Cardinal and Ferdinand, there is flattery and selfish service,
but no love, and the only mutual act is the gulling or persecut-
ing of some third party. Antonio and the Duchess, on the other
hand, bring their loves together and join them in mutual action.
They lead each other along step by step to their love avowals,
Antonio seeming to keep in the background, as befits their difference in rank, but subtly helping to direct their progress.[8] He
makes the first advance after their opening exchanges by addressing her as 'beauteous excellence', to which she replies that she
looks young for his sake (I i 368–9). She then tells him that she
wants to make her will, and, addressing him as her steward,
makes an ambiguous proposal, to which he immediately responds
with an almost explicit suggestion that they marry :

> *Duch.* If I had a husband now, this care were quit :
> But I intend to make you overseer ; –
> What good deed shall we first remember ? say.
> *Ant.* Begin with that first good deed began i'th'world
> After man's creation, the sacrament of marriage –
> I'd have you first provide for a good husband,
> Give him all.  (I i 382–8)

From this moment on Antonio leaves the initiative to her, for she
is the great Duchess, but he continues to encourage her in his

pleasant description of the joys of fatherhood, and in his acceptance of her ring.[9]

There has been much debate among critics as to whether
Webster wants his audience to approve of this marriage. From
biblical times onward there have been voices raised against
widows who remarry, and in all societies people who marry outside their social rank have been regarded as endangering order.
Probably more Elizabethans were opposed to such marriages
than in favor of them.[10] In Painter's version of the story of the
Duchess, the marriage is presented as a mask for lust, and
although the tyranny of their enemies is also denounced, there
is no word of approval for the lovers.[11] The conventional
Elizabethan opposition to the remarriage of widows may even
be seen in two Theophrastian characters thought to have been
written by Webster himself. His 'vertuous Widdow' will not
remarry, but his 'ordinarie Widdow' does.[12]

But whatever may be the case outside of *The Duchess of Malfi*,
within the play the love and marriage of Antonio and the Duchess
is presented sympathetically. Webster knows that some of his
audience will be opposed, and he takes pains in the first act to
disarm them. First of all he discredits the opposition to the marriage by making it an expression of the character of a perverse
and violent pair of Italian devils, and second he removes the
usual bases for opposition by idealizing the love and making the
character of Antonio as noble as the blood of the Duchess.
Antonio is modeled on the ideal of Christian gentility. In the first
Act he is presented as a virtuous and strong person, respected
even by Ferdinand for his manly prowess, and wisely perceptive
about the life and the people around him. In his character of
the Duchess, Antonio makes it plain that he loves her for her
beautiful spirit and not only for her beautiful face (1 i 187–209).
Moreover, in the courtship scene he is sincerely concerned lest his
acceptance of her love should appear to be the result of worldly
ambition and not of true love (1 i 415–40). The effect of all this
is that when they marry, our chief concern is for the danger they
are in. Our reservations about the propriety of the marriage
are only great enough to prevent a sentimental response to it, so
that we demand that it should prove itself in action.

In her affirmation of love the Duchess affirms the value of life itself. Without any disrespect to her dead husband, she deliberately turns away from his tomb to embrace Antonio (I i 451–5). In mentioning her husband's tomb she may remind us of Vittoria's yew-dream, but the reminder only makes us feel the contrast between the women the more strongly: the Duchess exhorts *her* lover to let love multiply in his bosom, to *forget* about death.

The last lines of Act I ask a key question about the Duchess and her marriage:

> *Car.* Whether the spirit of greatness or of woman
> Reign most in her, I know not, but it shows
> A fearful madness; I owe her much of pity.

In Act II Webster gives us a close look at the varieties of the spirit of woman, emphasizing its weakness but finding the life-bearing center of true greatness even in the midst of its time of greatest weakness, the 'tetchiness' of pregnancy. The spirit of woman is seen at the beginning of Act II in the old woman who paints her face to hide the ugliness of nature, and the last time it appears in Act II is in a scene between the Cardinal and his mistress, Julia. The spirit of woman in these instances is physically and morally false, readily manipulated by corrupt men. Bosola thinks the Duchess is false, too, when his apricocks make her ill and her first child is born, but he is deceived by false appearances, and it is Webster's point that what Bosola thinks the Duchess to be can really be seen in Julia:

> [*Bos.*] *Though lust do mask in ne'er so strange disguise,*
> *She's oft found witty, but is never wise.* [*Exit.*]
> SCENA IV.
>                     *Enter* Cardinal *and* Julia
> *Card.* Sit: thou art my best of wishes – prithee tell me
>     What trick didst thou invent to come to Rome
>     Without thy husband.
> *Jul.*                              Why, my lord, I told him
>     I came to visit an old anchorite
>     Here, for devotion.
> *Card.*                      Thou art a witty false one: –
>     I mean to him.                          (II iii 76–7, II iv 1–6)

The Duchess's childbearing is thus set in the middle of Act II as a bright jewel against the dark foil of the false old woman and Julia. In Webster's sources, the Duchess had three children, and in his play she has three, at great cost to the unity of time, yet the point is an important one, thematically well worth making : the marriage of Antonio and the Duchess is bounteously fruitful and creative, a true source of life. In childbirth the Duchess endures 'the worst of torture, pain, and fear', which suggests a link between this suffering and that she endures later in punishment for this (II ii 67). Her suffering is not merely the endurance of affliction but an affirmation of life – here in childbirth, later on in the face of death itself.

The story of the Duchess and her childbearing is surrounded with subtle suggestions that they may have significance in connection with the Christian story of the source of life. Hopper and Lahey interpret Antonio's statement that 'She stains the time past, lights the time to come' as meaning that 'history itself became new at her birth, making all time to come different from that before'. It should be noted that this has traditionally been regarded as the significance of the Immaculate Conception of Mary's birth and its great consequence in the Incarnation of Christ. When we look around in the play, we find several allusions to the story of the Holy Family and particularly to Mary and those saints and symbols associated with her typology. Among these is the pure fountain out of which flows life and nourishment. The play opens with Antonio's comparison of a well-run court with a pure fountain nourishing its subjects (I i 5–22). As the action develops, we are made to feel that if the Duchess ruled her world, there would be 'blessed government', and when the Duchess pretends to discharge Antonio from her service, Bosola applies the metaphor of the spring directly to her, although he thinks it does *not* apply, deceived as he is by her pretence :

> You shall want him,
> For know an honest statesman to a prince
> Is like a cedar, planted by a spring :
> The spring bathes the tree's root, the grateful tree
> Rewards it with his shadow : you have not done so.
>
> (III ii 261–5)

This imagery of the fountain is supported by the passing allusion to St. Winifred, whose spring at Holywell in Wales was a famous healing shrine, and in Bosola's urging the old woman and Castruchio to seek renewal of life in the healing springs at Lucca (I i 390, II i 62). In contrast to the life-giving power of these springs are the standing pools of water associated with Ferdinand and the Cardinal (I i 49–54).

Webster goes rather out of his way to tell us the day and hour of the birth of the Duchess's first child, a boy:

What's here? a child's nativity calculated!
*The duchess was delivered of a son, 'tween the hours of twelve and one, in the night: Anno Dom. 1504,* – that's this year – *decimo nono Decembris,* – that's this night. (II iii 55–8)

This son is born in what church calendars call the month of holy infancy, immediately *after* December 18, one of the old dates on which the English celebrated the *Expectation* of Mary – usually also celebrated on March 25 as the Annunciation.[13] Later, when the Duchess, Antonio, and their three children flee to escape their persecutors, there are reminiscences of the flight of the Holy Family from the persecution of the Innocents by Herod – undoubtedly by itself a fanciful connection, as Boklund says in pointing out the similarity,[14] but perhaps more significant in connection with the other clues linked with it. The flight is to and then from the shrine of Our Lady of Loretto, which contained a relic of the Holy House at Nazareth and an image of the Virgin and child that had been rescued from infidels.[15] The Duchess justifies her use of deceit to protect her family as '*Magnanima menzogna*: a noble lie', a phrase from Tasso's *Jerusalem Liberated* II 22, where it is applied to the deceit practised by a young girl who saved Christians who had rescued an image of the Virgin from infidels.[16] Now these parallels are of course not strong enough to justify an allegorical reading, but they may help to reinforce the notion that there is value in the Duchess's love and life.

The final suffering of the Duchess is analogous to another religious archetype that affirms life – the story of Job.[17] The agony of Job as he is brought from prosperity to poverty, from health to sickness, is imaged in the experience of the Duchess. Webster even parallels the terminology and the imagery of Job in telling his story. And the character of Satan provides an analogue for Bosola, the Cardinal, and Ferdinand. Job is an honest and upright man, but Satan, an archetypal figure of envy and cynicism, believes that his virtue is all sham, that he is good only because God rewards him, and that if God will allow Job to be afflicted, He will see that Job will curse Him. Satan takes all wordly blessings from Job, but he is still true to God. Then God tells Satan to observe Job's continuing 'integritie' (2 : 3).[18] Integrity is the quality Job struggles to preserve :

God forbid that I should justifie you : till I die, I wil not remove my integritie from me. (27 : 5)

Let me bee weighed in an even ballance, that God may know mine integritie. (31 : 6)

Like the Duchess, Job yields to despair when the worst affliction comes; like her he curses the stars (3 : 9). And Bosola's answer to the Duchess's curse, 'Looke you, the stars shine still' (iv i 100), is a dramatic compression of God's final reply to Job :

Canst thou bind the sweete influences of Pleiades? or loose the bands of Orion? Canst thou bring foorth Mazzaroth in his season, or canst thou guide Arcturus with his sonnes? (38 : 31–2)

Bosola and the Arragonian brethren know that a perversely evil sickness is at work within them even when they seem to do good for others, and they can live with themselves only if they can believe that others are worse. They are Satans, 'Adversaries' who stand before the bar of Justice to accuse man and deny the possibility of true goodness so that men will despair and prove them right. If they can convince the Duchess that their injustice is God's injustice, she will despair and die into their longing, waiting arms.

The Duchess's nobility in suffering, however, makes Bosola see that his Satanic cynicism may not be justified. . . . He is now torn between trying to make her crumble and trying to save her spirit.

The net effect of Ferdinand's attempts to drive her to despair
and Bosola's ambivalent efforts is that the Duchess comes by
degrees to turn her face away from the world and toward
heaven. Ferdinand sends her an illusion of death – the wax
effigies of her husband and three children as corpses – but the
final effect is that she is helped to accept her own actual death;
he sends her a consort of madmen, symbolic of his own mad
world, but the chief result is that she is brought to an agonized
awareness of her own continuing integrity of mind.[19] Bosola's
half torturing, half religious dirge offering death as both storm
and peace (IV ii 178–95), and his cruel sermon on the imprisonment of the soul in the body move the Duchess further toward
freedom :

> *Duch.* Who am I?
> *Bos.* Thou art a box of worm-seed, at best, but a salvatory of
> green mummy : – what's this flesh? a little crudded milk,
> fantastical puff-paste; our bodies are weaker than those
> paper prisons boys use to keep flies in; more contemptible,
> since ours is to preserve earth-worms. Didst thou ever see
> a lark in a cage? such is the soul in the body : this world
> is like her little turf of grass, and the heaven o'er our
> heads, like her looking-glass, only gives us a miserable
> knowledge of the small compass of our prison.
> *Duch.* Am not I thy duchess?
> ... I am Duchess of Malfi still. (IV ii 123–42)

In this last great line the Duchess asserts her defiance of her
worldly persecutors, proudly holding her unbroken spirit before
her as a shield. But now she must still carry her integrity one
step further : she must not bow to men, but she must kneel before
God. To bring her to this final degree of mortification Webster
uses his favorite metaphor exposing false worldly appearances :

> *Glories, like glow-worms, afar off shine bright,*
> *But look'd to near, have neither heat, nor light.*
>
>                                               (IV ii 144–5)

Webster's handling of these scenes of torment is superb. When
the play is staged, our attention is drawn not to the horrors but

to the Duchess's reaction to them: she beholds horror, and we behold her. This is Webster's greatest achievement as a dramatist. His Duchess is no mere allegorical figure, a fleshless counterpart to Job. If she were, she would be on a par with the allegorical horrors themselves, simply another convention from which we turn our attention to fix it elsewhere. Our attention is fixed on the Duchess because she is so deeply and pitiably human in her anguish. Webster's treatment of her does not rise out of the meaning he intends to convey; rather, the meaning arises beautifully and naturally out of the real human experience he creates. The Duchess is not statuesque or made of steel in her lonely struggle, but frail flesh, now despairing, now hoping, now proud and defiant, now asking only to be left in peace. Native integrity of spirit leads her to make the true responses in her final crisis. With a supreme courage that has passed through the agony of despair into the hope that lies beyond, she dies with her thoughts on the lives of her children, forgetting that they are supposed to be dead (IV ii 203–5). Filled with Job's faith that the Redeemer lives, she reaches out to the hope of a life after death (IV ii 210–12). Before she is murdered, she kneels in Christian humility:

> *Duch.* Pull, and pull strongly, for your able strength
>   Must pull down heaven upon me : —
>   Yet stay; heaven-gates are not so highly arch'd
>   As princes' palaces, they that enter there
>   Must go upon their knees. — [*Kneels.*] Come violent death,
>   Serve for mandragora to make me sleep!
>   Go tell my brothers, when I am laid out,
>   They then may feed in quiet.       *They strangle her.*
>                                 (IV ii 230–7)

But her brothers cannot feed in quiet; as the writer of the *Book of Job* says, it is not the destiny of evil to find peace:

Surely he shall not feele quietnesse in his belly, hee shall not save of that which he desired. There shall none of his meat be left, therefore shall no man looke for his goods. In the fulnesse of his sufficiencie, he shall be in straits : every hand of the wicked shall come upon

him. *When* hee is about to fill his belly, *God* shall cast the fury of
his wrath upon him, and shall raine *it* upon him while he is
eating. He shall flee from the iron weapon, and the bow of steele
shall strike him through. . . . All darknesse *shalbe* hid in his secret
places : a fire not blowen shall consume him; it shall goe ill with
him that is left in his tabernacle. The heaven shall reveale his
iniquitie : and the earth shall rise up against him. (20 : 20–7)

This is the fate of Ferdinand and the Cardinal, point by point.
They are destroyed in their greatest sufficiency, and by the hand
of one of the wicked; darkness and fire consume them from
within; and heaven reveals their iniquity :

> Other sins only speak; murder shrieks out :
> The element of water moistens the earth,
> But blood flies upwards, and bedews the heavens.
> (IV ii 261–3)

They thought they were wise, but they did not know that
wisdom is not to be found in this world, since it is the knowledge
of God (*Job*, 28). The Duchess might speak of the deceits of
their false wisdom thus :

My brethren have delt deceitfully as a brooke, & as the streame of
brookes they passe away, Which are blackish by reason of the yce,
*and* wherein the snow is hid : What time they waxe warme, they
vanish : when it is hot, they are consumed out of their place.
(6 :15–17)

This metaphor to describe the way evil men come to nothing is
repeated later in the *Book of Job* : 'Drought and heate consume
the snowe waters : *so doeth* the grave those which have sinned'
(24 : 19). Webster's metaphor describing the fate of Ferdinand and
the Cardinal is similar :

> . . . These wretched eminent things
> Leave no more fame behind 'em than should one
> Fall in a frost, and leave his print in snow;
> As soon as the sun shines, it ever melts,
> Both form, and matter . . . (V v 113–17)

Because of the strength of her spirit and her Christian hope and concern for her loved ones, the *death* of the Duchess of Malfi is, paradoxically, an affirmation of *life*. A number of modern critics see something else in her death, however. To them, the fact that the Duchess dies is Webster's way of saying that her integrity was ultimately meaningless and without value, since it was unable to save her life. 'Both good and evil are appearances' in the face of death.[20] Since no amount of goodness can save a person from an evil fate, there must be no moral order outside human society, and the only value Webster cherishes is the preservation of the individual's character, whether good or evil, unbroken in the face of death.[21] The trouble with this interpretation is that it forgets that for the Christians of Webster's day, as for his Duchess, moral value and religious faith did not depend on integrity paying off in this world, because they knew that this world is the unjust kingdom of Satan. The reward for integrity comes in heaven. This point was a favorite of Elizabethan preachers like Thomas Adams :

Neither doe the crosses of this world witnesse a mans guiltinesse, nor the blessings of the world his innocence. But the good have a larger share in sufferings, then the reprobates. . . . It is the part of a Christian to suffer.[22]

Oh then doe well, though . . . great men rage, though perversenesse censures, impudence slanders, malice hinders, tyranny persecutes : there is a *Jesus*, that approves : . . . let his Spirit testifie with me, though the whole world oppose me.[23]

John Donne writes in this same vein, saying that in the 'worlds warfare', those

> . . . arm'd with seely honesty,
> With wishing prayers, and neat integritie,
> Like Indians 'gainst Spanish hosts they bee.[24]

Webster shows that the worldly life of courts and courtiers is vain, and that integrity cannot finally defeat such evil, but there is another kind of life possible, a life deriving its values from moments of love and sharing and mercy that may create happiness on earth, for however brief a time, and hope for a life hereafter that will last eternally. Donne gives a paradigm for the life and death of the Duchess of Malfi :

I can better see the stars of heaven, in the bottome of a well, then if I stood upon the highest steeple upon earth. If I twist a cable of infinite fadomes in length, if there be no ship to ride by it, nor anchor to hold by it, what use is there of it? If Mannor thrust Mannor, and title flow into title, and bags powre out into chests, if I have no anchor, (*faith in Christ*) if I have not a ship to carry to a haven, (a soule to save) what's my long cable to me? . . . if there be nothing of the next world at the end, so much peace of conscience, so much joy, so much glory, still all is but *nothing* multiplied, and that is still nothing at all. 'Tis the *end* that qualifies all; and what kinde of man I shall be at my end, upon my *death-bed,* what trembling hands, and what lost legs, what deafe eares, and what gummy eyes, I shall have then, I know; and the nearer I come to that disposition, in my life, (the more *mortified* I am) the better I am disposed to see this object, future glory. God made the Sun, and Moon, and Stars, glorious lights for man to see by; but mans infirmity requires *spectacles*; and affliction does that office. Gods meaning was, that by the sun-shine of prosperity, and by the beames of honour, and temporall blessings, a man should see farre into him; but I know not how he is come to need *spectacles*; scarce any man sees much in this matter, till affliction shew it him.[25]

Webster is of course not so purely religious as Donne, and his treatment of the death of the Duchess greatly transcends the writing of this sermon in its humanity, subtly stressing the complexity of wit and pathos in the Duchess's refusal to yield anything but her life to her murderers at the same time that she yields everything to her love for her children and to God. But the pattern Donne describes certainly has an analogue in *The Duchess of Malfi,* and even Donne's metaphor of affliction acting as spectacles to improve vision may remind one of the emphasis on the problem of seeing in the world of Webster's play. In that world men suffer because they are willfully blind, and their suffering may improve their vision. It is not so much that the world is a dark pit, as it appears to the dying Bosola, but that men seldom look at the radiance that should be their guide in life. Even in death they look to the World instead of to God:

princes' image on their tombs do not lie, as they were wont, seeming to pray up to heaven . . . they are not carved with their eyes fixed upon the stars, but as their minds were wholly bent upon the world, the selfsame way they seem to turn their faces. (IV ii 156–62)

Men turn their eyes to horoscopes and almanacs to learn their fates and guide their lives, and they seek the reputation of being speculative by reading pagan writings, meanwhile using the Bible only as a vehicle for poison (II iii; III i 60–2; III iii 21–3, 41–7; V ii 278).[26]

The language of many passages in the play may be used to show the importance of sensitive perception. There is a constant suggestion, as in *The White Devil*, that appearances are deceptive. As a consequence, people repeatedly urge each other to *see* aright. This sort of thing is epitomized in the speech of Bosola that I have quoted before:

> *Glories, like glow-worms, afar off shine bright,*
> *But look'd to near, have neither heat, nor light.*
>
> (IV ii 144–5)

In this speech the glories are those of the World. The Flesh equally blinds man's judgment:

[*Car.*] If there were propos'd me, wisdom, riches, and beauty,
　　In three several young men, which should I choose?
*Ant.* 'Tis a hard question: this was Paris' case
　　And he was blind in't, and there was great cause;
　　For how was't possible he could judge right,
　　Having three amorous goddesses in view,
　　And they stark naked? 'twas a motion
　　Were able to benight the apprehension
　　Of the severest counsellor of Europe. (III ii 34–42)

Webster presents Julia's sudden and fatal attraction to Bosola as a lust of the eyes:

*Jul.* Compare thy form, and my eyes together,
    You'll find my love no such great miracle. (v ii 167–8)

In the true love of the Duchess and Antonio, there is no blindness
caused by the radiance of the flesh. Antonio loves the Duchess
body and soul, and it is the perfection of both that is the light
that he will try to see by for all time to come (i i 187–209).
But insofar as the Duchess strays from the true path of
integrity by deceiving her brothers, she thinks of herself as doing
so blindly: 'let old wives report / I wink'd and chose a husband'
(i i 348–9). In accepting the Duchess as his wife, Antonio is
afraid he will be blinded by the glories of the World:

*Duch.*                Fie, fie, what's all this?
    One of your eyes is blood-shot – use my ring to't,
    They say 'tis very sovereign – 'twas my wedding ring,
    And I did vow never to part with it,
    But to my second husband.
*Ant.* You have parted with it now.
*Duch.* Yes, to help your eyesight.
*Ant.* You have made me stark blind.
*Duch.* How?
*Ant.* There is a saucy, and ambitious devil
    Is dancing in this circle. (i i 403–13)

Following this up, the Duchess thinks of herself as Antonio's
Fortune, proverbially blind:

[*Duch.*] I now am blind.
*Ant.*                What's your conceit in this?
*Duch.* I would have you lead your fortune by the hand,
    Unto your marriage bed. (i i 495–6)

The irony implicit in this last statement is clear later, when the
Duchess and Antonio are shortly to be destroyed. Then she says,
'Fortune seems only to have her eyesight / To behold my
tragedy' (iv ii 35–6). At the parting of the Duchess and
Antonio, Webster stresses the fact that they will never see each
other again, suggesting how important the vision of true love
has been in their lives:

[*Ant.*] . . . if I do never see thee more,
    Be a good mother to your little ones,
    And save them from the tiger : fare you well.
*Duch.* Let me look upon you once more . . .
*Bos.* . . . you must see your husband no more.

(III v 84–7, 99)

After the Duchess's death, when Antonio is trying to live by the
echo or light of her spirit, an echo tells him she is dead before
Bosola does :

*Ant.* My Duchess is asleep now,
    And her little ones, I hope sweetly : O heaven,
    Shall I never see her more ?
*Echo.*                        *Never see her more.*
*Ant.* I mark'd not one repetition of the echo
    But that : and on the sudden, a clear light
    Presented me a face folded in sorrow. (v iii 40–5)

'*Never see her more*' : this line echoes and re-echoes through
the play. Antonio *tries* to see by the clear light of the Duchess,
but other men *refuse* to look upon her and her love, and this
refusal is a sign of their false outlook on life. Instead of *seeing*
with their eyes, they would use them as weapons :

*Ferd.* O most imperfect light of human reason,
    That mak'st us so unhappy, to foresee
    What we can least prevent ! Pursue thy wishes. . . .
[*Duch.*] Will you see my husband ?
*Ferd.*                        Yes, if I could change
    Eyes with a basilisk. . . .
    Whate'er thou art, that hast enjoy'd my sister, –
    For I am sure thou hear'st me – for thine own sake
    Let me not know thee : I came hither prepar'd
    To work thy discovery, yet am now persuaded
    It would beget such violent effects
    As would damn us both : – I would not for ten millions
    I had beheld thee. . . .(III ii 77–96)

And when Ferdinand leaves his sister a little later he says to her twice, 'I will never see you more' (III ii 136, 141). He keeps his word until the Duchess is dead. When he comes to her in prison, he can be in her presence only in darkness :

> *Bos.* Your elder brother, the Lord Ferdinand,
>     Is come to visit you : and sends you word,
>     'Cause once he rashly made a solemn vow
>     Never to see you more, he comes i'th' night;
>     And prays you, gently, neither torch nor taper
>     Shine in your chamber : he will kiss your hand,
>     And reconcile himself; but, for his vow,
>     He dares not see you. . . .
> *Ferd.* Where are you ?
> *Duch.*                 Here sir : –
> *Ferd.* This darkness suits you well. (IV i 21–30)

Ferdinand thinks the darkness suits the *Duchess*, but after he murders her he knows that darkness is for *him* :

> *Ferd.* I'll go hunt the badger, by owl-light :
>     'Tis a deed of darkness. (IV ii 334–5)

He is blinded into darkness by the radiance of her dead face :

> *Bos.* Fix your eye here : –
> *Ferd.*                 Constantly. . . .
>     Cover her face : mine eyes dazzle : she died young.
>                                     (IV ii 260–4)

As before the death of the Duchess, Ferdinand blinded himself to reality by refusing to look at her, after her murder he tries to avoid his responsibility for the crime by refusing to look at Bosola :

> [*Ferd.*] Never look upon me more. . . .
>     Get thee into some unknown part o'th' world
>     That I may never see thee. (IV ii 317, 326–7)

The appropriate culmination of all this is that Ferdinand suffers 'cruel sore eyes' in his madness (v ii 64).[27]

Ferdinand and the Cardinal do not want to 'be seen in't' (1 i 225, v iv 37–8). Their villainy must be done in darkness and by the hands and eyes of other men. Bosola is to see and to kill for them :

> *Ferd.* Your inclination to shed blood rides post
> Before my occasion to use you : — I give you that
> To live i'th' court, here; and observe the duchess,
> To note all the particulars of her haviour. (1 i 250–3)

When Bosola can bear to face reality no longer, he too echoes the line *'Never see her more'*. Ferdinand tells him of the tortures he must administer to the Duchess, and he is torn with pity :

> [*Ferd.*] Your work is almost ended.
> *Bos.* Must I see her again?
> *Ferd.*                         Yes.
> *Bos.*                                         Never.
> *Ferd.*                                                         You must.
> *Bos.* Never in mine own shape,
> That's forfeited by my intelligence,
> And this last cruel lie : when you send me next,
> The business shall be comfort. (IV i 132–7)

Hereafter Bosola uses affliction as spectacles to bring the Duchess to see clearly, and in so doing he comes to see her radiance. Because he has blinded himself to her radiance less than Ferdinand has, he is rewarded with something better than dark madness. He comes to trust light enough to want to see Antonio :

> [*Bos.*] I would see that wretched thing, Antonio,
> Above all sights i'th'world.
> *Card.*                                     Do, and be happy. *Exit.*
> *Bos.* This fellow doth breed basilisks in's eyes,
> He's nothing else but murder . . . (v ii 144–7)

Because Bosola perverts justice and mercy into revenge, he does not live in the full light of the radiance of the Duchess, and so,

like Ferdinand, he ends in darkness, a literal darkness in which
he kills Antonio by mistake and in which he and the Cardinal
and Ferdinand give each other their deathblows unseen by men
standing only a few feet above them.

At death Bosola recapitulates his own experience :

> *Mal.*            Thou wretched thing of blood,
>       How came Antonio by his death ?
> *Bos.*    In a mist : I know not how –
>       Such a mistake as I have often seen
>       In a play : – O, I am gone ! –
>       We are only like dead walls, or vaulted graves,
>       That ruin'd, yields no echo : – Fare you well –
>       It may be pain, but no harm to me to die
>       In so good a quarrel. O, this gloomy world !
>       In what a shadow, or deep pit of darkness,
>       Doth womanish and fearful mankind live !
>       Let worthy minds ne'er stagger in distrust
>       To suffer death, or shame for what is just –
>       Mine is another voyage. [*Dies.*] (v v 92–105)

He begins by relating the dramatic illusion to reality, then goes
on to point the lesson of that illusion for real men. At first he
believes as he once did, that we yield no echo, but then he takes
hope. The world is a dark pit, truly Satan's kingdom, but
Bosola has seen that the light of the spirit can conquer darkness,
that courage and integrity enable human love to redeem life and
defeat the fear of death, making it imperative that man should
'ne'er stagger in distrust'.

The radiant spirit of the Duchess of Malfi cannot be killed.
Perhaps it cannot finally triumph over the darkness of the World,
but she believes that her spirit lives on in heaven, and she lights
the time to come by illuminating the characters and destinies of
the people around her. In the last few lines of the play the light
of her example is made to blaze as the sunshine to dispel the
mists that blind men and to melt evil away :

> [*Del.*] ... These wretched eminent things
>       Leave no more fame behind 'em than should one

Fall in a frost, and leave his print in snow;
As soon as the sun shines, it ever melts,
Both form, and matter : – I have ever thought
Nature doth nothing so great, for great men,
As when she's pleas'd to make them lords of truth :
*Integrity of life is fame's best friend,*
*Which nobly, beyond death, shall crown the end.*

SOURCE : *A Study of John Webster* (1969).

### NOTES

1. Parallels between similar characters have been remarked by a number of critics. See E. E. Stoll, *John Webster* (Boston, 1905) pp. 93–4, Una Ellis-Fermor, *The Jacobean Drama*, 4th ed. (London, 1958) pp. 176–8 : Flamineo–Lodovico–Bosola, Monticelso–Cardinal, Francisco–Ferdinand, Zanche–Vittoria–Julia, Isabella–Duchess, Camillo–Castruchio.

2. See F. L. Lucas's commentary on II i 67–8 in *The Complete Works of John Webster* (London, 1927) II, 146.

3. P. F. Vernon, in 'The Duchess of Malfi's Guilt', *Notes and Queries*, x (1963) 335–8, argues that the Duchess's tragic guilt is in using disguises. See also Sister B. Reinhalter, *An Interpretation of Webster's Duchess of Malfi According to the Norms of Aristotle's Poetics*, a 1939 Boston College dissertation, pp. 49–50.

4. In case I have made the reader believe that to despair once is to be damned forever, let me note that despair at the end is traditionally fatal to the soul, but that good people may suffer temporary despair. See, for example, R. Burton, *The Anatomy of Melancholy* (Oxford, 1621) ed. F. Dell and P. Jordan-Smith (New York, 1929) p. 937.

5. John Donne writes that God permits us to be afflicted so that we will be humbled and so enabled to see His glory : *Sermons*, ed. G. R. Potter and Evelyn M. Simpson (Berkeley, 1953–62) IV 170–1.

6. T. Bogard, *The Tragic Satire of John Webster* (Berkeley, 1955) p. 111, discusses this contrast.

7. James L. Calderwood, '*The Duchess of Malfi* : Styles of Ceremony', *Essays in Criticism*, XII (1962) 134–40, argues that their marriage is a perversion of ritual because it is against the norms of their society. But Webster doesn't hold that society up as a model.

The Duchess and Antonio do not attack the basis of ceremony – the desire to promote group aims – they create a group where none really exists.

8. V. F. Hopper and G. B. Lahey (eds), *The Duchess of Malfi* (New York, 1960) p. 27, note that Antonio 'covertly takes the initiative'.

9. A number of critics have felt that in 1 i 398–403 he is *disparaging* fatherhood, but note that he says he disparaged it thus when he was melancholy in his banishment : 1 i 396–7. See Hopper and Lahey, p. 30; Lucas, *Works*, 11, 21.

10. See F. W. Wadsworth, 'Webster's *Duchess of Malfi* in the Light of Some Contemporary Ideas on Marriage and Remarriage', *Philological Quarterly*, xxxv (1956) 394–407; C. Leech, 'An Addendum on Webster's Duchess', *Philological Quarterly*, xxxvii (1958) 253–6.

11. William Painter, *The Palace of Pleasure*, ed. J. Jacobs (London, 1890) iii, 3–43.

12. Lucas, *Works*, iv, 38–9.

13. *Handbook of Dates for Students of English History*, ed. C. R. Cheney (London, 1948) p. 50 : '*Expectatio beate Marie* . . . 16 Dec. *or* 18 Dec.'

14. G. Boklund, *The Duchess of Malfi: Sources, Themes, Characters* (Cambridge, Mass., 1962) p. 97.

15. See Lucas's commentary on iii ii 308–9 in *Works*, ii, 168.

16. See Lucas's commentary on iii ii 180 in *Works*, ii, 165–6.

17. A number of critics have mentioned the general parallel between the Duchess and Job. See especially Hopper and Lahey, op. cit. pp. 52 and 54–5.

18. Hereafter I shall quote from the Authorized or 'King James' Version of *The Holy Bible* (London, 1611).

19. In 'The Duchess of Malfi', *Times Literary Supplement* (13 July 1956) p. 423, Lucas says she must only see effigies of Antonio and the child with him, since a little later she thinks the other children are alive. But see iv i 58. Later, when she is under the stress of facing her murderers, it is natural for her to forget she has seen her children dead. On the masque of madmen see Inga-Stina Ekeblad, 'The "Impure Art" of John Webster', *Review of English Studies*, ix (1958) 253–67, and F. B. Fieler, 'The Eight Madmen in *The Duchess of Malfi*', *Studies in English Literature*, vii (1967) 343–50.

20. So says Bogard, p. 142. Cf. Boklund, p. 129.

21. Bogard, p. 40; C. Leech, *John Webster* (London, 1951) p. 89.

I. Ribner, *Jacobean Tragedy* (London, 1962) pp. 106, 121–2, calls this endurance itself the only value in life, but sees it as a triumph of life over death.

22. 'The Soul's Refuge', *Works* (London, 1629) p. 909. Cf. D Cecil, *Poets and Story-Tellers* (London, 1949) p. 35.

23. 'The White Devil', *Works*, p. 41.

24. 'To Sir Henry Wotton' ('Here's no more newes') ll. 10–15.

25. *Sermons*, IV, 171.

26. R. Ornstein, *The Moral Vision of Jacobean Tragedy* (Madison, 1960) pp. 134–5, observes that Webster has little use for humanism, leaving it to the foolish Camillo, the mad Ferdinand, and the warped Bosola.

27. Moody E. Prior, *The Language of Tragedy* (New York, 1947) p. 131, shows the symbolic connection between Ferdinand's killing, dazzled, and sore eyes.

## J. W. Lever

## FROM *THE TRAGEDY OF STATE* (1971)

In the sixteenth century the dispatches of the great banking house of Fugger provided the first all-European news service. During the Christmas season of 1585 the Venetian correspondent reported serious disturbances in the old university city of Padua. A band of fifty armed men, led by a certain nobleman, Lodovico Orsini, had invaded the palace of Vittoria, the Duke of Bracciano's young widow, at two o'clock on the morning of December 22nd. The gates had been opened for them; inside they shot down the lady's brother Flaminio and stabbed Vittoria to death without even allowing her time to finish her prayers. Padua was stirred at the crime, in which the hidden hand of the Duke of Florence was suspected. The students armed themselves and paraded through the streets shouting for justice. In alarm the government of Venice, which ruled the city, sent troops and cannon to attack the assassins, who had barricaded themselves in Orsini's family residence. After a struggle in which a number of the band were killed, the rest surrendered. Three were torn to pieces by the citizenry, others were taken and hanged. Lodovico Orsini himself confessed that he had performed the crime 'at the command of great personages'. He was sentenced to death by strangling; but since he claimed a nobleman's privilege, the execution was carried out in private. Moreover, a gift of fifty crowns to the executioner ensured him a speedy and relatively painless death.

Such were the happenings on which Webster based his tragedy *The White Devil*, performed early in 1612. Behind them lay a tangle of crimes and intrigues described in 109 extant accounts preserved in libraries of Italy, Austria, England and America.[1] None of these accounts exactly coincides with the story of

Webster's play; nor is it to be expected that they should, since *The White Devil* made no claim to historical accuracy. But it is generally thought that Webster drew his information mainly from the same Italian source as the Fugger correspondent in Venice. Not only the facts he used, but a number of details he altered have left their traces. For example, the fictitious Lodovico is arrested in Vittoria's palace straight after the crime, and we are not told how he died; but in the first scene of the play he remarks:

> I have seen some ready to be executed
> Give pleasant looks, and money, and grown familiar
> With the knave hangman... (I i 54–6)

This looks very much like Webster's reminiscence of Lodovico Orsini's actual conduct before his execution in Venice. In the play Vittoria is not murdered while praying; indeed we would hardly associate her with such pieties, were it not that in Act v scene vi she enters carrying a book, to be greeted by Flamineo with the words 'What, are you at your prayers?' Again, the real-life Bracciano suffered greatly from an ulcer in the leg. Nothing is said of this in the play, but in the course of his quarrel with Vittoria in Act IV she uses the striking metaphor for her love of him:

> I had a limb corrupted to an ulcer,
> But I have cut it off : and now I'll go
> Weeping to heaven on crutches. (IV ii 121–3)

As for the main motivations of the tragedy, these do not depart far from the essential facts. Bracciano was responsible for the death of his wife, sister of the Duke of Florence, – though this crime had taken place some years before his affair with Vittoria – as well as the murder of Vittoria's husband, nephew to a cardinal who soon afterwards became Pope Paul IV. With the open marriage of Bracciano and Vittoria the hostility of two powerful forces in state and church was irrevocably sealed. Bracciano died in suspicious circumstances while taking a cure on Lake Garda, and next month Vittoria and her brother were murdered in Padua, almost certainly at the instigation of the Duke of Florence.

Since this chain of murders and reprisals was a matter of historical fact, occurring in Webster's own lifetime, one need not be surprised that it served as material for drama. Nevertheless the picture of a society where such happenings could easily take place, and of eminent figures who could proceed to such crimes, hardly squared with the past as seen through the eyes of some nostalgic critics. Accordingly Webster, and not the world of his time, has been blamed for moral nihilism and morbidity. T. S. Eliot summed him up as 'a very great literary and dramatic genius directed toward chaos'.[2] Ian Jack was more explicit. Webster's drama, he objected, 'contains no convincing statement of the *positive* aspect of the doctrine of Degree. . . . It is not surprising that a mind as unbalanced as Webster's should have allowed the Machiavellian ideal to usurp the place in his thought which a more conservative poet would have reserved for Degree.'[3] Had Webster's mind been properly balanced – that is to say, suitably conservative – he would, Jack implies, have seen the Renaissance world as a radiant vision of God-given harmonies. The facts of tyranny, intrigue, hypocrisy and violence would have been neatly conceptualized into an unhealthy 'Machiavellian ideal', before being banished from the writer's antiseptic brain. Needless to say, no serious dramatist of the Jacobean age reacted in this manner. On the other hand there is some need to consider what artistic, as distinct from moral, purpose may have shaped Webster's decision to return to the Italian settings of Marston and Tourneur and to the slightly old-fashioned mode of the revenge play.

We shall best understand what is distinctive in Webster's approach if we start by noting what it has in common with this earlier kind of drama. I have to disagree with J. R. Brown, the very able editor of *The White Devil*, when he describes the play's structure as 'loose and rambling, a gothic aggregation rather than a steady exposition and development'.[4] *The White Devil* is basically well designed, building up steadily from act to act, with a minor climax in Act III and a full revenge catastrophe at the end. Acts I and II present very concisely the love intrigue of Bracciano and Vittoria, the double murder of his wife and her husband, and the arousing of the forces that will finally avenge it. Act III is centred upon the trial of Vittoria: the first, inconclusive blow struck by the revengers. In Act iv the quarrel between Bracciano and Vittoria brings out the inherent pre-cariousness of their relationship, while the revengers plan the decisive stroke that will ensure the destruction of the lovers. The last act brings the second wave of revenge, the murders of Bracciano, Vittoria and their go-between Flamineo, the deaths of the revengers, and the final restoration of order. In addition, there are some secondary elaborations, such as the installation of the new Pope, and the recurrent appearance of the six lieger ambassadors. In terms of plot-mechanics these are dispensable, but they contribute to the total thematic effect. On the other hand there is brilliant economy in presenting the double murder of Isabella and Camillo through dumb-shows, and the instigation to this crime through the narration of a dream. Viewed in terms of the revenge play tradition, *The White Devil* shows most of the familiar type-figures and relationships. The norm of authority is represented by Giovanni, the young son of Bracciano by his first wife, who in the end takes charge and punishes the wrong-doers. Bracciano occupies the position of the traditional tyrant, the unscrupulous slave of passion, committing murder and adultery and employing Flamineo as his henchman. A bad father, an unfaithful husband, his vices are offset by the presence of such virtuous characters as his son Giovanni and his wife Isabella, while his mistress Vittoria is contrasted to her mother Cornelia, and Flamineo to his brother Marcello. Ranged against them are the revengers, Francisco Duke of Florence and the Cardinal Monticelso, later to become Pope, with Lodovico and his companions as their instruments. In correspondence with the conventional masque that converted the tyrant's festivities into a scene of carnage, the revengers appear at Bracciano's mar-riage celebrations in the bizarre disguises of a Moorish warrior and two Hungarian Capuchins. After they have enacted a suit-ably horrific vengeance, the boy Giovanni restores authority, ordering that the malefactors be imprisoned and tortured.

Yet in spite of the conventional organization, the current of sympathy flows in an *opposite* direction to that of the earlier revenge drama. Bracciano, in the situation of the tyrant, is attractively virile and courageous, passionate as a lover, scorn-ful of his dangerous opponents. The advanced middle age, the

corpulence and ulcerated leg of the real-life Bracciano do not
appear in Webster's character, who gives the impression of a
man at the peak of his energies. Flamineo, his accomplice and
pander, takes over the intellectual acuteness and caustic wit
usually reserved for the revenger, and provides a satirical commentary on the vices of the great. He appears as the son of an
impoverished family made up of his sister Vittoria, brother Marcello, and their widowed mother Cornelia. There is an obvious
parallel to Vindice and his family in *The Revenge Tragedy*;
but while Vindice only pretends to solicit his sister Castiza by
way of testing her virtue, Flamineo wholeheartedly accepts his
mission as the Duke's agent, while Vittoria is entirely willing to
take Bracciano as her lover. In Tourneur's play the poor and
virtuous family unites against the self-destructive dynasty of the
tyrant; in *The White Devil* the family is divided, with Flamineo
and Vittoria juxtaposed to Marcello and Cornelia. While the
wrongdoers have colour and vitality, the innocent characters are
faded and submissive. Isabella as the deserted wife evokes a
limited degree of pity in much the same way as Shakespeare's
Octavia in *Antony and Cleopatra*, after whom she is probably
modelled.[5] Like Octavia, her alternations of mute reproach and
ostentatious self-effacement make no firm impression. Cornelia
briefly arrests attention in the first act, but she is soon silenced
by Flamineo's withering scorn. Reappearing in Act v, she is
given a contrived pathos by Webster's plagiarisms from the
speeches of the mad Ophelia in *Hamlet*; but the device is so
forced that it militates against a sympathetic response. As for
Camillo, Vittoria's husband, in life an agreeable young man, he
appears in the play as a ridiculous cuckold, a suitable butt for
Flamineo's gulling. On the other hand, the revengers, Monticelso
and Francisco, Cardinal and Grand Duke, are neither poor nor
oppressed, but specimens of the corrupt statesman inveighed
against by all the dramatists of the age. The arraignment of Vittoria is a flagrant travesty of justice, in which the Cardinal acts
as both prosecutor and judge and condemns her on palpably
flimsy evidence. The outcome is that Vittoria, sentenced as a
whore to live in a 'house of convertites', dominates the court,
and turns the charges back upon her accusers :

> It shall not be a house of convertites –
> My mind shall make it honester to me
> Than the Pope's palace, and more peaceable
> Than thy soul, though thou art a cardinal.
>
> (III ii 289–92)

Francisco is similarly defied by Bracciano when he threatens to use his military force if Vittoria is not given up:

> All thy loud cannons, and thy borrow'd Switzers,
> Thy galleys, nor thy sworn confederates,
> Durst not supplant her. (II i 61–3)

Crafty and hypocritical, the revengers are more repulsive than the wrongdoers they punish. Francisco selects his instruments of vengeance from the Cardinal's 'black book' of criminals. Compiled by intelligencers for the purposes of blackmail rather than justice, it is the only book one sees in that ecclesiastical dignitary's hands. Even the boy Giovanni, Bracciano's son but Francisco's nephew, is a questionable figure. Ostensibly the embodiment of a better order, Flamineo notes that 'He hath his uncle's villainous look already', and cryptically remarks that 'the wolf and raven / Are very pretty fools when they are young' (V iv 30, 35–6). There is no assurance that Giovanni, grown to manhood, will prove better than Francisco or any other of the 'princes' and 'great men' who make up the world of the play.

In fact it is to this omnipresent world of corruption that we must look if we are to understand the cross-currents of *The White Devil*. In form a revenge tragedy, it rejects the clear polarities of vice and virtue, oppression and revolt, which set up the moral tension of this class of drama. Innocent and virtuous characters do indeed appear and offset the wickedness of the major figures by their presence and their comments. But they have no vitality on the stage. In the world of *The White Devil*, as in the world of Jonson's *Sejanus*, their parts are condemned to be passive. Virtue is allowed, is even encouraged, to speak out; but it has no field of action; and it is in the nature of drama that the audience's sympathies are engaged by energy, not passive endurance. Still, it oversimplifies the effect if we only see this as an inversion of conventional sympathy, or respond to the parts of Bracciano, Vittoria and Flamineo with unqualified admiration. Again and again their conduct and their attitudes are set in a wider frame of reference. This is supplied not by the traditional virtues, but by the universal evil of which they form a part. When Bracciano in his jealousy vents his anger on Flamineo, he becomes identified with all the other type-despots of society.

> *Bracciano.* Do you know me?
> *Flamineo.* O my lord! methodically.
>      As in this world there are degrees of evils :
>      So in this world there are degrees of devils.
>      You're a great duke; I your poor secretary.
>      I do look now for a Spanish fig, or an Italian sallet
>      daily.... (iv ii 56–61)

In the end Flamineo and his sister recognize themselves as the victims of their rulers. Vittoria's last words are

> O happy they that never saw the court,
> Nor ever knew great man but by report.
>                              (v vi 261–2)

Flamineo's dying speech cautions those who enjoy court favour :

Let all that belong to great men remember th'old wives' tradition, to be like the lions i'th' Tower on Candlemas Day, to mourn if the sun shine, for fear of the pitiful remainder of winter to come.
                              (v vi 265–8)

This final recognition is prepared for from the first lines of the play. Guilty and innocent alike are the victims of power; it is in the light of this truth that the moral ambivalences are resolved. A clear instance may be seen in the sinuous dramatic unfolding of Act i scene ii. Bracciano's desperation in love is balanced by Flamineo's glib assurances that Vittoria will presently receive him, that her chambermaid Zanche has been 'dealt with', and that he has nothing to fear from her jealous husband. While romance is offset by cynicism, the farcical presentation of Camillo swings sympathy back to the lovers. Yet when Bracciano and Vittoria do meet, they are flanked by the sceptical presence of the two go-betweens Flamineo and Zanche; and behind these, providing yet another discordant effect, stands Cornelia, horrified by the immoral compliance of her son and daughter. She breaks up the lovers' assignation, denouncing the wickedness of her children. For once even Vittoria is overcome with guilt and leaves abruptly. But Cornelia's virtue is not the final criterion of values. When she asks, 'because we are poor, shall we be vicious?' Flamineo rounds on her with a telling account of the social circumstances that have made him what he is :

> Pray what means have you
> To keep me from the galleys, or the gallows?
> My father prov'd himself a gentleman,
> Sold all's land, and like a fortunate fellow,
> Died ere the money was spent. You brought me up
> At Padua I confess, where I protest
> For want of means, – the university judge me, –
> I have been fain to heel my tutor's stockings
> At least seven years : conspiring with a beard
> Made me a graduate, – then to this duke's service :
> I visited the court, whence I return'd, . . .
> But not a suit the richer, – and shall I,
> Having a path so open and so free
> To my preferment, still retain your milk
> In my pale forehead? (I ii 315–30)

The total effect of this scene is not to focus attention on the illicit romance, on Camillo's marital rights, on the cynicism of the go-betweens, or on Cornelia's virtue, but to place all these in the wider context of a society where declassed intellectuals find the only alternative to galleys, or gallows, in serving without scruple the desires of their rulers.

Throughout *The White Devil* the suffocating ambience of power and oppression is insisted on as the atmosphere in which all the characters move and have their being. Scene after scene reinforces the implication and sums up the theme in sententious couplets which have an impersonal choric effect. Lodovico, the arch-ruffian of the play, speaks for all when he comments :

Great men sell sheep, thus to be cut in pieces,
When first they have shorn them bare and sold their fleeces.
(1 i 62–3)

According to Flamineo,

who knows policy and her true aspect,
Shall find her ways winding and indirect. (1 ii 353–4)

The conjurer who presents Bracciano's murders in dumb-show
ends Act II with the aphorism :

Both flowers and weeds spring when the sun is warm,
And great men do great good, or else great harm.
(II ii 56–7)

And again, more pointedly, Flamineo remarks :

There's but three Furies found in spacious hell,
But in a great man's breast three thousand dwell.
(IV iii 152–3)

Through a mass of fragmentary images and conceits the iniquities
of the age fall into a kaleidoscopic pattern. Spanish reprisals in
the Netherlands are the substance of Flamineo's simile : 'When
knaves come to preferment they rise as gallowses are raised i'th'
Low Countries, one upon another's shoulders' (II i 320–2).
Monticelso the Cardinal alludes to

those tributes i'th' Low Countries paid,
Exactions upon meat, drink, garments, sleep;
Ay, even on man's perdition, his sin. (III ii 86–8)

The defeated Irish rebels selling their comrades' heads to the
English queen's officers; the forty thousand pedlars of impoverished Poland; the soldiers back from serving against the
Turk, with only enough in the way of pension to buy themselves
wooden legs and fresh plasters –

> the beggary of courtiers,
> The discontent of churchmen, want of soldiers,
> And all the creatures that hang manacled,
> Worse than strappado'd, on the lowest felly
> Of Fortune's wheel ... (III iii 92–6)

all these are the broken humanity of Renaissance Europe. Such a civilization has no tears to shed at Cornelia's pious laments, no moral indignation to waste over Bracciano's individual sins.

At the other extreme, the hollow pomps and splendours of greatness are displayed with calculated irony. Six ambassadors to the Papal court look on at the hypocritical trial of Vittoria and see her condemned as a whore. They proceed to the Pope's investiture, wearing the stately habits of their chivalric orders as Knights of the Holy Ghost, the Annunciation, the Garter dedicated to Saint George, and so on, to hear the new Pope as his first act in office decree the excommunication of Bracciano and Vittoria. Unperturbed, the ambassadors presently arrive in Padua, still wearing their emblems of sanctity and honour, to attend the wedding festivities of an excommunicated duke and a sentenced whore. Joining in the celebrations they fight at the barriers, imitating the tournaments of an obsolete chivalry, while Bracciano agonizes in his poisoned helmet. Also present at the wedding are Francisco, Lodovico and Gasparo; Francisco disguised as a glamorous Moorish warrior, the others as two Hungarian noblemen who have served against 'the enemies of Christ' and are entering 'the strict order of the Capuchins'. Outwardly simulating the nobility and sanctity of Christendom, the revengers in a fiendish parody of the last rites pronounce curses on the dying Bracciano, then murder Vittoria and Flamineo. Webster has been blamed for crowding his play with irrelevant spectacle. Much of it, as here, gives dramatic expression to the overriding theme of a corrupt society.

It is understandable therefore that *The White Devil* should be a drama without heroes. The flamboyant courage of Bracciano and Vittoria, the caustic intellect of Flamineo, evoke a measure of admiration, but this does not imply a new ethic of amoralism. *Through darkness diamonds spread their richest*

*light*: it is the depth of the surrounding darkness, not the
quality of the gems, that chiefly concerns us. Like Jonson's
*Sejanus*, Webster's satirical tragedy looks beyond individuals to
the society that has shaped them. Both plays treat revenge as the
action of greater malefactors against lesser ones, and allow virtue
no more than a passive part. Both take as their theme the de-
basement of a whole civilization. Jonson's tragic protagonist is
not Sejanus but imperial Rome. In Webster's play too there are
in the final analysis no tragic heroes or heroines. The White
Devil is not Vittoria Corombona but Renaissance Europe.

   *The Duchess of Malfi*, written about a year later, was clearly a
re-shaping of *The White Devil*. Again the story was taken from
Italian history, some seventy years before the events dramatized
in the previous play. Again Webster based the action on a ven-
detta resulting from an unconventional match, leading to the
deaths of both the revengers and their victims. The affinities are
obvious between Duke Ferdinand and the Cardinal and the
Duke of Florence and Cardinal of *The White Devil*; between
Bosola the secret agent and Flamineo the pander; between the
pair of lovers, the Duchess and Antonio, and Vittoria and
Bracciano. Further correspondences may be found in the structure, the infusion of satire and sententious comment, the appearance at the end of a child heir offering promise of a better order.
Nevertheless, *The Duchess of Malfi* is essentially different in its
perspective, its field of concern, and its tragic effect.

   Some of the reasons for this difference have been well brought
out by J. R. Brown in his edition of the play. The setting of a
small court, the concentration on immediate and topical abuses,
the story itself as 'a syndrome for contemporary issues': all show
Webster directing his attention upon England.[6] The court of
Amalfi presents in miniature the court of Whitehall, with its ad-
venturers, its feverish pulling of strings for office and promotion,
its heedless and heartless pursuit of privilege. At the time when
the play was being written, James I had dispensed with the
responsible chief minister Cecil, and placed the entire control
of the state in the hands of his young favourite Robert Carr. The
Privy Council had become a mere rubber stamp for arbitrary
personal rule. Honours were openly bought and sold; marriages
and divorces were steps to political influence. In this atmosphere

normal human relationships were stifled. The pitiful case of Lady
Arabella Stuart must surely have been present in the minds of
audiences seeing *The Duchess of Malfi*. This modest, unassuming
lady had the misfortune to have been born the king's cousin, and
therefore a possible claimant to the throne. For years she had
lived quietly at court, rejecting all attempts to involve her in the
various conspiracies against James. Then she made the mistake
of falling in love with William Seymour, who was also of royal
blood. Their secret marriage was punished by the imprisonment
of both husband and wife. Each managed to escape, and sailed
separately for Ostend, hoping to be reunited and live in peace
abroad as private persons. Seymour landed, but Lady Arabella
was captured at sea and brought back to spend the rest of her
days in prison. It is not strange that in *The Duchess of Malfi* the
affairs of England, and in particular the inner life of the victims
of state and their persecutors, shape the world of the play
beneath its Italian surface, and give to its tragic content a
more personal and sympathetic quality than in *The White
Devil*.

The difference of approach is immediately suggested in the
opening lines. *The White Devil* begins with a banishment, *The
Duchess of Malfi* with a homecoming. In the former play Lodovico rages to his fellow ruffians against fortune, the gods, courtly
reward and punishment : here, Antonio speaks to his friend Delio
of the reformed court of France, purged by its king of 'syco-
phants', of 'dissolute and infamous persons', and governed by
a council 'who dare freely / Inform him the corruption of the
times'. Instead of the imprecations of *The White Devil*, rang-
ing over the abuses of the whole Renaissance world, this play
offers the contrast of a changed society in one country, which
may set a precedent to others. The description is visually reinforced by Antonio's appearance, distinctively dressed as 'a very
formal Frenchman'. The scene opens out into a presentation of
the unregenerate court of Malfi, introducing in turn its malcontent Bosola, the Cardinal, Ferdinand, and at last the
Duchess. For over three hundred lines action is minimal, while
the audience observes these key figures, characterized by Antonio, Delio, and for a while Bosola. The Cardinal and Ferdinand,
it is learned, are

like plum-trees, that grow crooked over standing pools; they are
rich, and o'erladen with fruit, but none but crows, pies, and cater-
pillars feed on them. (1 i 49–52)

Crookedness, stagnancy and favouritism typify the great
eminences of the play, whose one action so far, the appointment
of Bosola to spy upon the Duchess, is itself tortuous and corrupt. Again, a positive contrast is struck in Antonio's ardent
praise of the Duchess, which dwells not on her beauty but on
the charm of her manner and the chastity of her conduct:

> . . . in that look,
> There speaketh so divine a continence
> As cuts off all lascivious, and vain hope.
> Her days are practis'd in such noble virtue
> That sure her nights – nay more, her very sleeps –
> Are more in heaven than other ladies' shrifts . . .
> All her particular worth grows to this sum:
> She stains the time past, lights the time to come.[7]
>
> (1 i 198–203, 208–9)

The opening scene, with its close-range focus on the principal
court characters, differs sharply from the negative panorama of
*The White Devil*. While the evils of policy are embodied in the
Duke and Cardinal, there are positive elements: the presence of
Antonio as a living reminder of possible regeneration, and the
virtuous influence of the Duchess, who 'lights the time to come'.
In this changed perspective the revenge plot operates with a different effect from that of the earlier play. In *The White Devil*
retribution fell upon two adulterous lovers whose first encounter
had precipitated a double murder. The revengers were indeed
less attractive than their victims; but all alike functioned in a
moral vacuum created by the political world to which they belonged. In *The Duchess of Malfi* the Duke and Cardinal are
motivated solely by their resentment at the innocent marriage
of a pair whose virtue is established from the start and who
offer the promise of a better way of life. Hence the sympathy of
the audience, both moral and instinctive, is ranged on the side
of the Duchess and Antonio. The play is in fact a revenge drama

only in the sense that Chapman's *Bussy D'Ambois* may be considered one : it presents the vengeance of the leaders of state and
church upon those who by their life challenge its inverted values.
For Ferdinand and the Cardinal, as for the Guise and Monsieur,
'Reward goes backward, Honour on its head'. In contrast,
Antonio the commoner and the Duchess who prefers a marriage
of love to the sterile privileges of rank and power may be taken
to represent 'man in his native noblesse'.

There would be no need to dwell on these facts were it not for
the arguments of some modern critics, whose reading of the play
contradicts the impression formed by any audience, Jacobean or
contemporary. Just as Marlowe, Shakespeare and Chapman have
been re-classified as apologists for 'order and degree', so Webster is in process of being converted from a chaotic, unbalanced
'genius' into the spokesman of a trite orthodoxy. The secret marriage of the widowed Duchess and Antonio is said to have been
wanton and irreligious, and their difference of rank to have
made it also a shocking violation of degree.[8] For confirmation a
hypothetical Jacobean opinion is invoked, unanimously agreed
on certain certainties. A sufficient answer to latter-day moralizers
might be that audiences in every age admire characters with
courage, wit and sincerity; approve of marriage for love, even
if it be the second marriage of a girl widowed at twenty; and
hate the murderous intrigues of great personages who would
turn normal human happiness into misery. Should this reply
seem too obvious to be scholarly, one might point out the
approval of Webster's contemporaries, Middleton, Rowley and
Ford, in the commendatory verses prefixed to the first edition of
*The Duchess of Malfi*. The play is described as 'this masterpiece of
tragedy'; as for the author,

> Thy epitaph only the title be –
> Write, 'Duchess', that will fetch a tear for thee,
> For who e'er saw this duchess live, and die,
> That could get off under a bleeding eye?

It has been said that the re-marriage of widows, though wide-
spread in all classes, was disapproved of; mention is made of the
strictures of Painter in the English translation of Bandello which

Webster used as his source. In fact, Painter explicitly defends re-marriage on grounds both of morality and common sense :

. . . to say the truth, they be not guided by wisdomes lore, which suffer a maiden ripe for mariage to be long vnwedded, or yong wife long to liue in widdowes state . . . a great follie it is to build the fantasies of chastitie, amid the follies of worldly pleasures.[9]

As for the violation of 'degree', Painter's characters are their own convincing apologists. They appeal over the heads of established order to God and human decency in justification of the Duchess's decision :

Is not she at libertie? To whome ought she to make accompt of hir dedes and doings, but to God alone and to hir owne conscience? . . . In this there is no cause to blame Loue of blindnesse, for all the inequalitie of our houses. . . . But from whence issue the Monarches, Princes and greater Lords, but from the naturall and common masse of earth, whereof other men doe come? what maketh these differ-ences betwene those that loue eche other, if not the sottish opinion which we conceiue of greatnesse, and preheminence : as though naturall affecfions be like to that ordained by the fantasie of men in their lawes extreme . . . I thinke we be the daily slaues of the fond and cruell fantasie of those Tyraunts, which say they haue puissance over vs; and that straining our will to their tirannie, we be still bound to the chaine like the galley slaue.[10]

There are, it is true, short pietistic insertions in Painter's story which perform an abrupt about-turn in attitude. They are to be found in all this class of *novelle* published with an eye to the new reading public.[11] The object, here as elsewhere, was to provide a sop for the more strait-laced members of the middle class. Had Painter dreamed that this moral façade would be solemnly accepted by literary scholars of the twentieth century, I feel he would have been much amused at their gullibility. As for the main drift of the narrative, it accords with the attitude of Webster's fellow writers and the response of normal theatregoers in every age.

*The Duchess of Malfi* is indeed a highly moral play; but its morality does not toady to the prejudices of an establishment.

It draws its strength from communal attitudes regardless of
historical period, and is implicit in the responses called forth by
action, characterization and imagery working in close conjunc-
tion. There is a clear difference between the dramatic effect of
the secret marriage that ends Act 1 and the assignation of
Bracciano and Vittoria in Act 1 of *The White Devil*. The
equivocal effects do not work in the same way. In *The White
Devil* the lovers are flanked by their cynical go-betweens and all
are alike condemned by Cornelia. In *The Duchess of Malfi* the
maid Cariola is out of sight, and equally out of mind, until she
comes forward at the right moment as the indispensable witness
to what is in fact a common-law contract of marriage.[12] Meanwhile the couple are alone and sympathy is not deflected by the
presence and comments of bystanders. There are no impediments
to this marriage of true minds: the Duchess's proposal en-
hances her dignity and grace; Antonio's replies show deep affection tempered by the caution natural to his situation. While the
love scene in *The White Devil* breaks up in discord, in *The
Duchess of Malfi* it is crowned by a simple ceremony. Antonio
kneels to receive the Duchess's ring as if the accolade of
knighthood were bestowed on him, and is raised to join her in
the noblesse of nature. The church – represented in this play
by the Cardinal – cannot bind faster; instead, the two direct
their prayers immediately to heaven.

> *Duchess.* Bless, heaven, this sacred Gordian, which let violence
>     Never untwine.
> *Antonio.* And may our sweet affections, like the spheres,
>     Be still in motion.
> *Duchess.*                Quickening, and make
>     The like soft music. (1 i 480–4)

Yet accompanying these affirmations of harmony there are latent
discords. The Duchess's proposal of marriage is phrased in terms
of making a will; the sheets of the nuptial bed are also winding
sheets; her kiss gives Antonio his *quietus*. Images of insanity
menace the lovers: Antonio's description of ambition anticipates
the mental torments later to be inflicted by Ferdinand:

> Ambition, madam, is a great man's madness,
> That is not kept in chains, and close-pent rooms,
> But in fair lightsome lodgings, and is girt
> With the wild noise of prattling visitants . . . (i i 420–3)

The sense of impending disaster grows not out of suggestions of
inner guilt, but from knowledge of the implacable enmity of the
outside world. In *The White Devil* the lovers are never seen at
peace with one another. Their precarious union is easily broken;
Francisco's ruse in Act iv leads to a rapid flare-up of suspicion
and mutual reproach. Bracciano, fatally poisoned, cannot bear
Vittoria's presence, and orders her away from his death-bed. In
*The Duchess of Malfi* no inner tension upsets the tranquility of
the marriage. Affection extends over the years to include both
parents and offspring. When leave-taking is forced upon her,
the Duchess, who had matched without the ministrations of the
established church, puts her trust for reunion in a higher truth:
'in the eternal church, sir, / I do hope we shall not part thus'
(iii v 71–2). The premonitions of tragedy in Act i come to
fulfilment solely through the machinations of external forces.
Fears are deepened in Act ii through events which by normal
expectation should be happy and blessed: the birth of the first
child is followed by a terrible horoscope and the kindled anger
of the Arragonian brothers. In Act iii the birth of further
children and the Duchess's revelation to Bosola that the admired
Antonio is her husband turns menace into action with the beginning of her enemies' revenge.

The malign forces are partly located in the cosmos of Webster. There is no ambivalence about the nature of human love,
but there is an unresolved doubt as to the nature of the universe
which shapes its course. As in Chapman, fortune and the stars
favour power against virtue. The Duchess and Antonio evoke
heaven to bless their match and make it fruitful; she parts from
him trusting that the eternal church will bring them together;
she dies kneeling to enter heaven's gates. But disaster is predicted
for her firstborn son; she is driven to curse the stars; after death,
her ghostly echo warns Antonio that he will never see her more;
Antonio is killed by chance when Bosola had meant to save him.
On the rational plane no causal connection can be found between

the malignancy of the cosmos and that of earthly powers. But it is in the way of the creative imagination that the evil of human tyranny should be projected out upon the universe. At the core of the drama, however, evil as well as good is embodied in the individual. In *The White Devil*, where the conspectus took in society as a whole, personal motivation was obvious and unsubtle. The legal hypocrisies of Vittoria's trial, the satirical inversion of piety and chivalry at Bracciano's murder, aroused more attention than the state of mind of the revengers. But in *The Duchess of Malfi* personality is brought into close focus. From this viewpoint again the play has marked affinities with Chapman's *Bussy D'Ambois*. Ferdinand and the Cardinal, like the Guise and Monsieur, give an individual quality to the violence and cunning of state. With both pairs the personal motive is an affront to aristocratic pride of blood. But whereas in *Bussy* the Senecan spirit of tragic fury is infused into the revenge through the choice of a jealous husband as the instrument of murder, there is no counterpart to this role in *The Duchess of Malfi*. The Duchess is faithful, and Bosola who conducts the revenge is merely a hired agent. Accordingly Webster would seem to have galvanized Ferdinand's antipathies of rank by attributing to him the jealous rage of the cuckolded husband Montsurry. The appearance of sexual anger and guilt in a brother–sister relationship results in a pattern of thought and behaviour which modern readers promptly diagnose as a case of subconscious incest. Yet it is by no means certain that this was the impression Webster wished to create. Jacobean playwrights were not at all reticent in their treatment of incest, and had he wished Webster could well have made Ferdinand's urges quite explicit. Dramatic construction and tragic effect explain his treatment more convincingly than a quest for psychological complexity beyond the capacity of the age, and in any case of little relevance to the main theme. Ferdinand's rages and remorse make their impact as a perversion of natural affection by deep-seated prejudices of rank and blood which, like the antipathies of race and class in our own society, need only factitious pretexts to erupt into savage violence. His hatred is less controlled than the Cardinal's, but both men are governed by the same murderous enmity. In Bosola's words :

Your brother and yourself are worthy men;
You have a pair of hearts are hollow graves,
Rotten, and rotting others : and your vengeance,
Like two chain'd bullets, still goes arm in arm . . .

                                              (IV ii 318–21)

*The Duchess of Malfi* takes as its main concern not a panorama
of society nor the individual subconscious, but the effects of
power upon the human heart and mind. The time-span of the
play allows for growth and development in the characters. The
Duchess herself matures from act to act; as her hair turns grey
the wit and charm of her youth change to gravity and composure. To her love of Antonio is added affectionate care for her
children and a deepening religious faith. When the time comes
for her to face her brothers' vengeance, she is immune to physical
fear and mental torture. It is in keeping with the play's central
theme that the revengers should jeer at her marriage and
assault her sanity by surrounding her with demented specimens
of their corrupt world – mad lawyer, secular priest, jealous
doctor, false astrologer, and the like – and follow this by Bosola's
attempts to undermine her belief in human dignity. The reply, 'I
am Duchess of Malfi still', is an affirmation of reason and an
assertion of the Stoic kingship of the mind, undismayed by
tyranny. Antonio's premonitions of great men's madness have
materialized, but failed in their effect upon a woman whose
greatness lies not in rank but natural nobility. With suitable
irony, the madness rebounds upon Ferdinand and is incipiently
present in the Cardinal. Ferdinand's lycanthropia – his delusion
that he is a wolf – results from the murder of his humanity and
reduces him to the level of a predatory beast. The darkness of
his deed is expressed in the shadow his own shape casts on the
ground, which in his insanity he tries to throttle. The Cardinal's
guilt likewise projects the hallucination of 'a thing, arm'd with a
rake'. Both men have poisoned the springs of reason and
natural affection, to gain only death and oblivion. The Cardinal
dies begging to be 'laid by, and never thought of'. Antonio's
honest friend Delio speaks the epitaph of these heads of church
and state :

These wretched eminent things
Leave no more fame behind 'em than should one
Fall in a frost, and leave his print in snow;
As soon as the sun shines, it ever melts,
Both form, and matter. (v v 113–17)[13]

Between the darkness of Duke and Cardinal, and the Duchess who 'lights the time to come', stands Bosola, the unwilling 'slave of power', the would-be ally of its victims. Last in the line of malcontent go-betweens reaching from Malevole to Vindice to Flamineo, he is also the most complex. Already at the beginning of the play his cynicism is changing to disgust. Having suffered seven years in the galleys for a murder suborned by the Cardinal, he is embittered, yet unable to alter his way of life. Bribed to serve again as a spy on the Duchess, he offers to return Ferdinand's gold, but soon accepts his new employment. His genuine admiration for Antonio moves the Duchess to reveal her secret marriage; yet this is a piece of information so valuable that he cannot resist the urge to disclose it and betray her. With the death of the Duchess and the end of his assignment Bosola seeks at once the reward for his crime and some opportunity to atone for it by saving Antonio. He obtains neither; but in his death he at least succeeds in killing those responsible for his own corruption. Neither villain nor hero, Bosola typifies the plight of the intellectual in the world of state, at once its agent and its victim.

The last of the great Jacobean tragedies of state, *The Duchess of Malfi* achieves a tenuous balance between facile optimism and total despair. The good perish with the bad; but human dignity is affirmed; not only in precept, but in character and action. Moreover, the choices that face man in the political world are clearly defined. The corruption of power brings with it madness, sterility and death. In juxtaposition to these, the stand of the Duchess and Antonio becomes identified with reason, fertility, and life. Whether the cosmos is governed by a beneficent heaven or the blind malevolence of the stars; whether the echo of the Duchess's voice telling Antonio he will never see her more alludes to this world or a world to come, is left an open question. But the play's ending suggests more than a merely conventional restoration of order. The young Giovanni who punished Francisco's hired murderers at the end of *The White Devil* may well grow up to become a replica of his uncle, Francisco himself. But the boy standing beside Delio in the closing scene of *The Duchess of Malfi* is Antonio's first-born son, and offers hope of bringing to pass that reformed order his father had longed for in the first scene of the play. In spite of the dread horoscope, despite the opposition of the stars, he has survived. It is arguable, indeed, that this survival was merely due to an oversight in Webster's planning; but a more positive significance cannot be entirely ruled out. A favourite Renaissance maxim declared that reason, or the wise man, overcomes the stars. The unnamed boy standing next to his father's trusted friend may perhaps be taken as a sign, however tenuous, of Webster's trust in the final triumph of reason and his ultimate belief in a better age.

SOURCE: *The Tragedy of State* (1971).

## NOTES

1. For a comprehensive account, see Gunnar Boklund, *The Sources of The White Devil* (Uppsala, 1957).

2. T. S. Eliot, *Selected Essays* (London, 1951) p. 117.

3. Ian Jack, 'The Case of John Webster', *Scrutiny*, XVI (1949) 39–40.

4. *The White Devil*, ed. J. R. Brown (London, 1960) p. xliv.

5. The parallel situations of Caesar–Antony–Octavia and Francisco–Bracciano–Isabella should be noticed. Isabella's character, her ill-judged journey to Rome, her futile hope to 'work peace' between her husband and her brother, recall Octavia. In the scene where she appears, the deliberate awkwardness of Caesar's first encounter with Antony is repeated at the meeting of Francisco with Bracciano:

*Caesar*: Welcome to Rome.
*Antony*: Thank you.
*Caesar*: Sit.
*Antony*: Sit, sir.

(*Antony and Cleopatra,* II ii 28–31)

> *Enter* Bracciano *and* Flamineo.
>
> *Francisco* : You are welcome, will you sit?
>
> > (*The White Devil*, II i 20)

Caesar's accusations of Antony are also paralleled in Monticelso's rebuke of Bracciano, delivered on behalf of Francisco.

> *Caesar* :   Let's grant it is not
> Amiss to tumble on the bed, of Ptolemy,
> To give a kingdom for a mirth, to sit
> And keep the turn of tippling with a slave . . .
> > (*Antony and Cleopatra*, I iv 16–19)

> *Monticelso* :   It is a wonder to your noble friends,
> That you . . .
> Neglect your awful throne, for the soft down
> Of an insatiate bed. O my lord,
> The drunkard after all his lavish cups
> Is dry . . .
> > (*The White Devil*, II i 26–7, 31–4)

Note how Webster's metaphor of the drunkard takes up the direct reference to drunkenness in Caesar's speech.

6. *The Duchess of Malfi*, ed. J. R. Brown (London, 1964) p. xxxix. See also G. P. V. Akrigg, *Jacobean Pageant* (London, 1962) p. 227.

7. Antonio is of course biased in the Duchess's favour; but at this point in the play no one knows that he is in love with her, and his words have an effect of choral objectivity.

8. The case was put tentatively by Clifford Leech, *John Webster* (London, 1951) pp. 68–77, who pointed out that the remarriage of widows, though quite lawful, was viewed with scepticism or disapproval. Chapman's comedy *The Widow's Tears*, and Jeremy Taylor's strictures in *Holy Living*, were cited. (This of course has nothing to do with arguments based on 'order and degree', and depends on attitudes to the individual : stepmothers too are unpopular figures, though Phaedra was a tragic heroine.) Leech nevertheless observed that, as compared with the Cardinal and Ferdinand, 'the Duchess does seem virtue itself', and that 'her revolt against the nature of things seems justified' (pp. 78–9). Inga-Stina Ekeblad repeated Leech's negative arguments, and mentioned Painter's account purporting to show the Duchess as 'an *exemplum horrendum* to all women contemplating a second marriage', in 'The "Impure

Art" of John Webster', *Review of English Studies,* ix (1958) 260
(reprinted in *Elizabethan Drama: Modern Essays in Criticism,* ed.
R. J. Kaufmann (New York, 1961) pp. 257–8). Finally in James L.
Calderwood's article *'The Duchess of Malfi* : Styles of Ceremony',
*Essays in Criticism,* xii (1962) 133–47, opinion hardens into dogma.
The Duchess is punished for her 'uninhibited passion', her 'violation
of Degree', and her 'disrespect for external realities'.

9. William Painter, *The Palace of Pleasure* (1567) ii, nov. xxii,
reprinted in *The Duchess of Malfi,* ed. Brown, p. 179.

10. *The Duchess of Malfi,* ed. Brown, pp. 182–4.

11. On this practice see J. W. Saunders, 'The Façade of Morality',
in *That Soueraine Light: Essays in Honor of Edmund Spenser
1552–92,* ed. William R. Mueller and D. C. Allen (Baltimore,
1952) pp. 6–7, and Paul Siegel, 'Christianity and the Religion of
Love', *Shakespeare Quarterly,* xii (1961) 371–2.

12. Marriage in the presence of a witness was valid by canon law
and English common law when consent was expressed *per verba de
praesenti,* 'in words of the present' ; see E. Schanzer, 'The Marriage-
Contracts in *Measure for Measure',* *Shakespeare Survey,* xiii
(1960) 81–9. In Catholic countries such marriages were forbidden
in the mid-sixteenth century by the Council of Trent, but its juris-
diction was not of course recognized by the Church of England,
and Protestant audiences would see nothing inherently sinful in the
Duchess's marriage to Antonio. Her remark,

> How can the church bind faster?
> We now are man and wife, and 'tis the church
> That must but echo this (i i 491–3)

would be a normal English comment. The marriage should have been
later solemnized; whether or not this took place we are not told in
the play; but when Ferdinand calls her children bastards according
to 'our national law', the Duchess replies 'You violate a sacrament
o' th' church' (iv i 39).

13. Cf. *Sejanus,* v 893–7 :

> Forbear, you things,
> That stand upon the pinnacles of state,
> To boast your slippery height. When you do fall,
> You pash yourselves in pieces, ne'er to rise,
> And he that lends you pity is not wise.

*Ralph Berry*

# FROM *THE ART OF JOHN WEBSTER* (1972)

## I CHARACTER

. . . The idea that Shakespeare presents a defined 'character' is, of course, totally misleading. He does nothing of the sort. He has left us primarily a set of stage directions, hints for productions. His text does not delineate character, but suggests depth possibilities. The words are a *Gestalt*, filled severally by the producer, actor, and spectator. The simplest instance will suffice. One's whole reading of the 'character' of Henry V turns on the line : 'May I, with right and conscience, make this war?' There is no means of locating the nebulous 'character' from which this stems. Are the lines spoken with the brisk, eager zest of a young man impatient to have the last obstacles removed before he can have his war? Or do they illuminate the *Realpolitik* of a prince knowing well that policy can use legality and morality? Or do they reveal the agonized hesitation of a ruler almost crushed by the weight of the dread responsibility that is his? All these, and more possibilities are contained in the text; and perhaps in the man; it is not, in our time, possible to refer to 'character' as an entity capable of absolute definition.

If we apply these ideas to Webster we find a similar blurring of outline. Partly this can be traced to an avoidance of a final statement that indubitably sums up a character. Final statements there always are, but they may be unconvincing (is Bosola's faith in his 'own good nature' justified?) or enigmatic ('let me / Be laid by, and never thought of'). Certainly we have, especially in *The Duchess of Malfi*, 'characters' that serve as constructional devices, useful guidelines to the audience; but they are beginnings, not ends. But the blurring of outline is accomplished very considerably through the use of imagery, which sets up a suggestive undertow to the surface of the speaker's words and actions.

Vittoria is an excellent instance of this method. How are we to regard her? Is she everything that Monticelso claims, or is her magnificent performance on the brink of death a true index to her character? Our emotions are deeply engaged; we sway first one way, then the other. This balance is described thus by M. C. Bradbrook: 'There is, as it were, a subordinate side of Vittoria which is innocent. Actually, she is guilty, but there is a strong undercurrent of suggestion in the opposite direction. It never comes to the surface clearly but it is there. Her character is a "reconciliation of opposites".'[1]

And yet, on precisely the same evidence, I should arrive at the opposite conclusion. I should say: Vittoria is innocent, but the imagery damns her as guilty. This may at first appear an extraordinary statement. Vittoria, it may be urged, is 'obviously' guilty. I ask, of what? On the evidence given in the play, no jury would convict her of anything but the attempted murder of Flamineo (and a good defence counsel would get her off, on the plea of self-defence). Vittoria did not kill Camillo or Isabella; Bracciano did, through his agents. She may have incited him, but the text is ambiguous; nothing is proved; the actress can play it either way. She may have had foreknowledge of the murder; Francisco advises Monticelso to drop the charge. She may have committed adultery with Bracciano; Monticelso cannot prove it, circumstantial evidence notwithstanding. She marries Bracciano afterwards; that is neither a sin nor a crime.

Against each of the charges brought against Vittoria, we must on the evidence of the text bring in a verdict of 'not proven'. But the imagery damns her. The title apart, she is a disease; a wolf; a hawk; a devil under a fair skin. Examples are manifold. The conclusion is clear: Webster knows that she is guilty, and constantly fixes her guilt in the imagery. As a man of the theatre, he keeps her guilt as an undercurrent, and does everything possible on the surface to secure for her our sympathies. Precisely the same method is employed towards the other malefactors. Our sympathies may be engaged, but the imagery constantly asserts their evil.

The full mastery of the Websterian character-presentation is

revealed in *The Duchess of Malfi*. He builds up a character-
*Gestalt* carefully. First comes a charcoal sketch, the Act 1
'character', then the overlaying of the personage's words and
actions, together with the colouring of imagery and the slighter
(but no less important) 'character' observations of other
personages. Thus, in Act 1 we have Antonio's 'ethereal' miniature
of the Duchess, stressing her continence and holiness:

> But for their sister, the right noble duchess –
> You never fix'd your eye on three fair medals,
> Cast in one figure, of so different temper:
> For her discourse, it is so full of rapture
> You only will begin then to be sorry
> When she doth end her speech: and wish, in wonder,
> She held it less vain-glory to talk much,
> Than you penance to hear her: whilst she speaks,
> She throws upon a man so sweet a look,
> That it were able raise one to a galliard
> That lay in a dead palsy, and to dote
> On that sweet countenance: but in that look,
> There speaketh so divine a continence
> As cuts off all lascivious, and vain hope.
> Her days are practis'd in such noble virtue
> That sure her nights – nay more, her very sleeps –
> Are more in heaven than other ladies' shrifts.
> Let all sweet ladies break their flatt'ring glasses,
> And dress themselves in her. (1 i 187–205)

Over this is superimposed the perfectly obvious evidence of her
sensuality: explicit in her relations with Antonio, and 'filtered'
by Ferdinand: 'Grown a notorious strumpet' (ii v 4), 'con-
veyances for lust' (ii v 10), 'If thou do wish thy lecher may
grow old / In thy embracements' (iii ii 100–1), etc.: and
Bosola:

> and this restraint
> (Like English mastiffs, that grow fierce with tying)
> Makes her too passionately apprehend
> Those pleasures she's kept from. (iv i 12–15)

The 'divine' Duchess takes a brusque line with the Church when it suits her. Of her private wedding ceremony she asks:

> What can the church force more?
> . . . How can the church bind faster?
>                                    (I i 488, 491)[2]

And her decision to make a 'feigned pilgrimage' to Ancona meets with Cariola's disapproval and a violent reaction: 'Thou art a superstitious fool' (III ii 319). Again, while the 'character' stresses her femininity, the Duchess uses several images of war that suggest the masculine and dauntless side of her nature. For instance,

> and even now,
> Even in this hate, as men in some great battles,
> By apprehending danger, have achiev'd
> Almost impossible actions – I have heard soldiers say so –
> So I, through frights, and threat'nings, will assay
> This dangerous venture. (I i 343–8)

Also III ii 155–7; III v 105–6; III v 142; and IV i 90. Small wonder that Bosola, in the elegiac survey of her life that precedes her execution, can say:

> A long war disturb'd your mind,
> Here your perfect peace is sign'd. (IV ii 184–5)

Nothing stated in Antonio's 'character' of the Duchess is necessarily untrue, yet everything in it has been sharply modified. The interplay of light and shade can imply a statement, or its reverse.

It is, moreover, true of the Duchess as of the other personages that 'The very existence of the baroque figure . . . is bound to the other motives in the picture. Even the single portrait head is inextricably woven into the movement of the background, be it only the movement of light and dark.'[3] The image motifs affect all the characters, with differences of emphasis. Thus, Ferdinand's animal images merely intensify the theme of human animality, which (as Bosola asserts in his meditation, Act II, scene i) includes the whole of humanity: Cariola's comment on the 'madness' of the Duchess extends to the mad-deaf-blind images that run throughout the play: the images of contract, payment, reward, and punishment that run through *The White Devil* affect all the major characters. No Websterian figure is isolable.

This blurring of outline can be traced to other factors. There is, in Webster, a wild oscillation between extremes of behaviour within the same person. Flamineo, who likes to think of himself as a materialist bent only upon self-advancement, twice abandons his course for a wayward impulse of generosity and honour. He is ready to fight Lodovico for calling his sister a whore (III iii 111–24): he inexplicably defies his lord, Bracciano, when that same fatal word is again flung at him (IV ii 44–56). It is, to put it mildly, inconsistent to act as pander to one's sister, and then be ready to fight with anyone who will apply the appropriate term to that sister; but it is the inconsistency of life, not that of careless dramaturgy. Again, when Bracciano is dead, and can do no more to advance Flamineo, the latter comes out with a quite astounding observation:

> I cannot conjure; but if prayers or oaths
> Will get to th'speech of him, though forty devils
> Wait on him in his livery of flames,
> I'll speak to him, and shake him by the hand,
> Though I be blasted. (v iii 208–12)

He surprises us; he surprises himself. Of this sort of behavioural spasm, Brooke well observes that 'you see the instincts at work jerking and actuating them, and emotions pouring out irregularly, unconsciously, in floods or spurts and jets, driven outward from within, as you sometimes do in real people'.[4]

Behaviour leads us to the heart of the enigma, identity itself. The problem of identity becomes, with Webster, acute. His characters probe themselves for identity. 'Who am I?' asks the Duchess (IV ii 123). 'I have a strange thing in me, to th'which / I cannot give a name, without it be / Compassion' wonders Flamineo. And the account they give of themselves is unsatis-

factory. We cannot believe that Ferdinand's policy is to gain 'An
infinite mass of treasure' from the Duchess's death (IV ii 285);
we believe that he has grossly deceived himself. A suspicion
remains at the end of *The Duchess of Malfi* that Bosola's faith in
his 'own good nature' may be misplaced. The same may be said
of Shakespeare: does Othello satisfy us at the last when he
asserts that he is 'not easily jealous'? He *thinks* he is not. But
with Webster the gap between statement and acceptance opens
wider.

## II  THEMES

The ends–means equation must dominate a discussion of Webster's art. The first necessity of baroque is that the audience
should be gripped, excited, moved. But major art rests on
foundations that remain valid after the turbulence of the immediate emotions has died. And these foundations must include
the content – I do not mean, the subject matter – of the drama.
That can afford an answer to the question: what are the positive
concerns of the playwright? What, even more simply, are his
plays about?

The obvious answer is that the *sententiae* constitute the moral
concerns of the plays. These are the points where the action
halts, the text leaps into inverted commas, and a moral general-
ization is enunciated on the situation of the characters. Naturally,
most of the action is completely opposed to the drift of the
*sententiae*, and Ian Jack sees in this the fundamental flaw of
Webster:

. . . this background of moral doctrine has nothing to do with the
action of the plays: so far from growing out of the action, it has all
the marks of having been superimposed by the poet in a cooler, less
creative mood than that in which the Duchess and Flamineo had
their birth. There is no correspondence between the axioms and
the life represented in the drama. This dissociation is the fundamental flaw in Webster.[5]

The dissociation is certainly a fundamental fact of Webster; but
it prefers no charge against the playwright. It is obviously true

that 'There is no correspondence between the axioms and the life represented in the drama'. This is on a par with writing: 'There is no correspondence between Clytemnestra's action in killing Agamemnon and the views expressed by the chorus.' For this is what the *sententiae* amount to. They fulfil, in diffused form, the function of the chorus; and the practice of Euripides (especially) and Sophocles had demonstrated that the choric viewpoint, though an important one, is not final and definitive. And the drama consists essentially of the gap between the choric morality and the actions of the principal characters. Webster himself, *in propria persona*, had lamented that he could not include in his play 'the sententious Chorus . . . the passionate and weighty Nuntius',[6] but found the true correlative of the chorus. His *sententiae* outline a body of conventional moral wisdom, to which his characters refer, but to which they cannot adhere. Such a situation is not much unlike life itself. It is curious that Webster should be censured for a most original dramatic procedure: that is, the development of the old chorus not into a self-contained unit of expression (Enobarbus, Thersites) but as a part of the character's mind. As a depiction of a disintegrating world order, this procedure deserves some recognition in the twentieth century.

The *sententiae* do not, in themselves, tell us what the plays are about. A broad indication, of a sort, is supplied by the plots. The plots of Webster's three plays, taken alone, afford inadequate but not misleading statements of his intentions. *The White Devil* is essentially a pattern of evil-doers and of retribution; *The Duchess of Malfi* reveals humanity, rather than evil-doers, gripped by a malevolent or indifferent fate; *The Devil's Law-Case* is a story of wrong unpunished. Such are the stories, and such the essences of his three plays. But to demonstrate fully the playwright's design one must look elsewhere.

The concerns of Webster are located in the imagery of his plays. The imagery is the basic content of his work; it reveals the primary symbols through which Webster's imagination expresses itself. It is not solely a matter of verbal imagery; as we have seen, the interconnections of action, character, and words make all partial analyses highly provisional. But a study must be based on the words of the text. These texts are massive growths of imagery; it would be misleading to speak of a 'pattern of imagery' as a sort of necklace of verbal brilliants that rest on the otherwise unadorned body of the play. On the contrary, *The White Devil* and *The Duchess of Malfi* would have virtually no text left were one to remove the imagery. The motifs that can be discerned here offer the best indications of Webster's concerns.

The method for establishing image themes, as developed by Caroline Spurgeon, Wilson Knight, and Wolfgang Clemen, lends itself to varying emphases but in essence remains constant. Two stages are necessary : first, a descriptive analysis, by subject matter, of the play's images; second, a reclassification of the images that brings together images from various groups into one thematic category. The second stage of the analysis concentrates on the images that seem to play a special and functional part in the movement of the play. Usually the analyst can obtain certain clues, apart from his own judgement, in locating these special images. One is likely to find, on a comparison with other plays by contemporary dramatists, or with other plays by the same dramatist, that certain motifs leap into prominence. Thus Caroline Spurgeon found a major significance in some ten images of clothing in *Macbeth*. Webster, however, usually makes his thematic points through a considerable weight of iterative imagery. They give the impression (which is supported by his own admission of being a slow worker) of being deployed in accordance with a conscious intellectual design.

A primary classification of Webster's images reveals his fascination with certain areas of subject matter. Images of animals and disease figure very largely in all three of his plays. *The White Devil* and *The Duchess of Malfi* draw heavily, in addition, on images that embody the opposition of appearance and reality. Passing from images, defined strictly, to words significantly repeated in the two tragedies, one finds many references to devils and to witches; and in the Machiavellian group, to 'great men', 'princes', 'politic', and 'policy'. These are the data which a secondary classification must interpret. All of these images and words are subsumed in a single theme, that of evil. Evidently, this theme is embodied in the actions of the leading characters. His plays are saturated with a consciousness of human evil.

There is a further area of subject matter, treated in all three plays, which points towards the other grand theme that dominates the imagination of Webster. It is the Law. Numerically far fewer than those embodying the theme of evil, images of the Law occur at critical points in *The White Devil* and *The Duchess of Malfi*. (The Law is, of course, the substance of the plot itself in *The Devil's Law-Case*, and the dialogue there contains a multitude of literal references in addition to certain metaphors.) The idea of the Law is supported by a number of verbal counters that present aspects of the same concept: justice, revenge, service, payment, reward. Moreover, an important aspect of the Law – retribution – is present in the many images of storm in the two tragedies. Finally, we can note that the trial scene is the theatrical centre of *The White Devil* and *The Devil's Law-Case,* and a miniature trial (the dialogue of Ferdinand and Bosola) is correspondingly placed (IV ii) in *The Duchess of Malfi*. The images of the Law, together with its associated terms, stand for the mechanisms whereby man governs himself – and by which the universe governs him. They constitute one of the two major themes that dominate Webster's imagination. While other themes of importance exist in his plays – most notably the theme of knowledge in *The Duchess of Malfi* – only these themes figure largely in all three plays.

The relationship between evil and the Law is the intellectual tension that grips *The White Devil*, *The Duchess of Malfi* and *The Devil's Law-Case*. The resolution of that tension is the main concern of each play; for while human evil may be a constant, the Law is not. It is presented in turn as a simple retributive mechanism that punishes wrongdoers, as the ineluctable fate that awaits a sinful humanity, and as a moral and ethical code of human conduct – a central, albeit unfulfilled, ideal.

SOURCE: *The Art of John Webster* (1972).

NOTES

1. M. C. Bradbrook, *Themes and Conventions of Elizabethan Tragedy* (Cambridge, 1935) p. 187.

2. Concerning the 'guilt' of the Duchess in remarrying, the matter has been debated by F. W. Wadsworth, 'Webster's *Duchess of Malfi* in the Light of Some Contemporary Ideas on Marriage and Remarriage', *Philological Quarterly,* xxxv (1956) 394–407, and by Clifford Leech, 'An Addendum on Webster's Duchess', *Philological Quarterly,* xxxvii (1958) 253–6. The point, surely, is that it can be debated. The issue is debatable, and is meant to be so experienced by the audience.

3. H. Woelfflin, *Principles of Art History* (London, 1932) p. 169.

4. Rupert Brooke, *John Webster and the Elizabethan Drama* (London, 1916) p. 123.

5. Ian Jack, 'The Case of John Webster', *Scrutiny,* xvi (1949) 39.

6. Webster's 'To the Reader' of *The White Devil.*

# PART THREE

# Reviews of Productions from 1919 to 1971

# Anon.

## 'A PLAY . . . PREPOSTEROUSLY INCOHERENT' – *THE DUCHESS OF MALFI* (1919)

'The Phoenix', an offshoot of the Stage Society, has opened its first season by the production, at the Lyric Theatre, Hammersmith, of Webster's *Duchess of Malfi*. The Society is to be congratulated upon its audacity, and upon the success of its audacity.

Most lovers of Elizabethan plays have had an intense curiosity to see this particular play performed. The reader is apt to skip 'several sorts of Madmen'; he ignores the stage directions, which inexorably pile corpse upon corpse on the stage; he mentally shirks the realization that the scenes which follow the climax of the Duchess's death must take about an hour to play. His 'selective attention' has been wholly concerned with the strange character of Bosola; the charm of the Duchess herself, especially as it is shown in the scene in which she proposes to Antonio; and last, has delighted in the thousand beauties of the verse. How will it be when the play is acted, when all the persons take flesh and we must listen at immense length to an impartial rendering of the whole naïve, fantastic jumble of blood and rhetoric? The experiment has been tried. In the first place, perhaps a modern audience is chiefly struck by the abominable construction of the piece. As what we call a 'play' it is preposterously incoherent and comically full of bloodshed. 'What is this talk fit for a charnel-house?' But though hardly for a moment does Webster allow us to forget that he was a sexton and not a dramatist, he also never lets us doubt that he was a poet.

But, alas! in the present production, this was where the actors came in. They did their best for Webster as a dramatist, which he was not; but as the inspired and ingenious poet that he was, they assassinated him. They tried all through the play to be naturalistic. They left out the whole of the famous Dirge. They interrupted the rolling periods of the dying speeches made by each of the eight persons who are murdered on the stage, by realistic splutters and gurgles. They tried to individualize every 'item' in the massacre by each dying in a different attitude. Having exhausted every other possible posture, the Duke Ferdinand was reduced to expiring upside down, his head on the ground and his feet over the back of an armchair. All the actors, without exception, 'broke up' their lines till they were unrecognizable as blank verse.

> *Duke Ferdinand* (*enters staggering, draws aside curtain, and sees corpse of* Duchess).
>     Cover her face.
> (Bosola *does so with spare overcoat.* Duke *takes quick turn round stage.*)
> *Duke* (*to audience*). Mine eyes dazzle.
>     (Duke *pulls up socks and tidies his hair.*)
> *Duke* (*to* Bosola). She died young –

a rendering which annihilated one of the most wonderful blankverse lines ever written. The fact is that it was a mistake to take the plot so seriously. Next time the Phoenix produces an Elizabethan play, could not the attitude of the actors be changed? Could they not say to themselves : 'We will banish from our minds the idea that this is a play at all. We will pretend that it is a series of tableaux in which recitations are to be given. First will come real sympathetic declamation of the poetry, second will come clothes and stage groups. Our action and postures shall be formal. We will try to remember that the Townley Mystery plays lie behind us and Johnson's *Irene* before, and we will leave *vraisemblance* to take care of itself.'

As to the clothes and the background, at this performance they were excellent. The stage was formal and did not change. It was draped in black. High up was a gallery with brilliant pink balustrades. Against the black archways which formed exits and entrances the Cardinal's pinky-scarlet robes, Antonio's flame-colour, and Julia's cloth-of-gold and grass-green were perfectly gorgeous. Mr. Tom Heselwood and Mr. Norman Wilkinson are to be congratulated. Though we may criticize the acting and the play, the net effect of the performance was both moving and beautiful.

We do trust that the Phoenix will not be afraid if indignant subscribers write and tell them that *The Duchess of Malfi* is a bad play. So it is. But that was a fact that their performance could alone tell us with certainty. Their discovery is just as interesting as, and perhaps more curious than, if they had discovered that it was a dramatic as well as a poetic masterpiece. They are rendering a real service to every student of English literature, and we owe them our grateful support. For as they themselves say in their leaflet: 'These neglected plays were written for the Theatre, and it is in the Theatre that they may best be studied and enjoyed.'

SOURCE: *The Spectator* (29 November 1919).

# E. M. Forster

# THE WHITE DEVIL AT CAMBRIDGE (1920)

The Marlowe Dramatic Society has just given some performances of the less known of Webster's two great masterpieces, and one came away full of admiration and in revolt against the unfortunate traditions of acting in London. The actors here were undergraduates; the world they depicted was the Inghilterra Italianata of the Elizabethan imagination. But, unlike London actors, they found nothing odd about such a world, remote though it must be from their experiences. Lusts, quaint devices for death, intrigues, hasty fratricide, rapid repentances – they generally accepted them and so made them credible to the audience. And even when they did not accept them, but moved through the welter and the beauty unrealising, they were never apologetic, never shocked; they did not imply, like their professional *confrères*: 'Here is a queer old play, but with the help of my elocution-mistress and my gymnastic-master I will do the best

for it that I can. Here are some round sentiments expressed in
metre, such as :

> Thou hast led me, like an heathen sacrifice,
> With music, and with fatal yokes of flowers
> To my eternal ruin

or :

> My soul, like to a ship in a black storm,
> Is driven I know not whither

for which I must ask the kindly sympathy of the audience. I will
pour out my breast when I say them, I will gasp and grin, and
then they will be recognised as poetry and condoned as such.'
The actors at Cambridge never apologised. As a rule they understood their strange world, and even when they did not they were
not upset; at the worst they were impassive, and at the best they
were very fine indeed.

The character of Flamineo, copious, restless, embittered, is
perhaps the most interesting in the play. Like Bosola, in *The
Duchess of Malfi*, he is mainly a villain, but partly a chorus.
When he has leisure for a little and can stand back from the
horrors that he has helped to cause, he catches glimpses of the
Tartarean darkness over which Webster's imagination brooded,
and he sees in it not only worms and blood, but tiny grotesques,
such as King Pepin selling apples. These tiny grotesques are
essential. If they are omitted, Flamineo becomes colourless; if
they are magnified, he becomes a buffoon. Their proportion was
perfect on this occasion, and in the dying speech, when the world
is soaked with gore and invaded by night, the actor could say
the lines :

> I have caught
> An everlasting cold. I have lost my voice
> Most irrecoverably

and yet could add to the universal terror.

The centre of the terror should have been the White Devil
herself, Corombona, harlot and murderess, the sincerity of
whose sense of guilt (as Hazlitt points out) triumphs over the
hypocrisy and officialdom of her accusers. She should be a pest,

a whirlwind, and a flame, and, present or absent, shake the
stage. The actor who was robed for this tremendous part could
not rise to it, and showed no signs of having seen what she
should not. The Moorish confidante was far more vital and,
seductive yet humorous, gave a vivid impression of low class sin.
But though Vittoria failed to command, she never distracted,
she did no harm to the play; she was far preferable to the self-
consciousness and exaggerations that would have confronted us
on a West-End stage. She looked well, spoke distinctly, and
moved quietly; she was an outline instead of a sumptuous
Renaissance masterpiece, but there was nothing in her figure
that marred the general design. One contrasts her on this point
with the Cardinal. The Cardinal's acting was far more competent and finished; he knew what to do with his hands, robe,
etc., and his efficiency served him well in his big speech at the
trial scene, where he becomes for a moment the pivot of the
action. Yet he struck the only jarring note : the taint of profes-
sionalism and of insubordination against the general effect was
creeping in. He belonged to that gloomy pyramid whose apex
is the Actor-Manager, whereas Vittoria, despite her omissions,
belonged to the drama.

The rendering of the difficult part of Bracciano was admirable;
indeed, it had a touch of the heroic about it. His magnificent
figure and distinguished face went with dignified movements,
passionate speech. He was a great and unscrupulous gentleman,
and yet no stick; he really loved, and really died. His last
moments, when the poisoned helmet has eaten into his skull and
mind, were terrifying, and into his final cry of 'Vittoria!
Vittoria!' he put something of the agony of a child who is
struggling against a nightmare. Indeed, all the deaths were impressive, contrary to one's expectation. One had been told that
Webster is ludicrous on the modern stage because of his corpses,
but the performance disproved this. The producer (who, like
the actors, remains anonymous) deserves the highest praise, for
he has not won his success at the expense of the author. He has
cut out the ghosts, to be sure, but the ghosts are unusually
intractable in *The White Devil*; one of them actually smashes a
flower-pot. And he has also cut some of the anecdotes and
dreams. But the gloomy yet fantastic atmosphere was preserved,

and the queerest incidents (e.g., the necromantic vision of the poisoned picture and the procession of the Cardinal's dinner-dishes into the Conclave) seemed natural and appropriate. The stage management, the scenery, were all that one could have wished and the incidental music finely conceived. It was one of the best Elizabethan performances that we are likely to see for a long time.

SOURCE : *The New Statesman* (20 March 1920).

*Anon.*

# 'A STYLISED MASQUE OF RHYTHMIC MOVEMENT' – *THE DUCHESS OF MALFI* (1935)

Elizabethan stock is looking up. First *'Tis Pity* at the Arts Theatre Club and now *The Duchess of Malfi* at the Embassy – a very much better play, far more satisfyingly presented. This is a vivid adventure at Hampstead, not to be missed by anybody who has realised Webster's lurid genius only from the Mermaid edition hitherto. But the question remains, can modern players, who must, for their stomachs' sake, specialise in the anaemics of our present tradition, hope to compass the full-blooded fury of Webster, or even Ford? This charnel-house atmosphere to a modern audience is all too dangerously quaint, and when the number of bodies on the stage exceeds two, the titters begin, titters which not even Webster's packed bitterness can silence. Blame the audience or blame the players, the result is the same – a slackening of the dramatic tension which assuredly is there, a sensation of good-humoured curiosity rather than the emotional exaltation which is so fine a poet's due. Mr. John Fernald has seen the difficulty, and hedged. The dead-hand scene is produced in a pleasant amber light and the pallor of human flesh is hidden by a glove. No danger of laughter here, but no chance of the

shiver which Webster intends. The gibbering of the madmen at
the hapless Duchess resolves itself – quite rightly perhaps – into
a stylised masque of rhythmic movement, which is extremely
interesting but no more. One is tempted at moments to cry out
for no more Elizabethan plays outside the study, but there are
generous compensations after all. In John Laurie's hands the
epileptic frenzy of Ferdinand becomes genuinely terrible and
his ranting has a ghastly perverse sincerity. Miss Joyce Bland
with the Duchess has the problem of beginning a part in a
suppressed heat of passion and working beyond it to the icy
dignity of utter despair. In the early love scene she fails. Her
personality is ascetic rather than voluptuous. But she shows
magnificent strength and tenderness in the later scenes, and
altogether gives a lovely performance. The chief disappointment
is Bosola. Here is a character of an immense passionate complexity yet Roy Graham's villainy is thin-blooded and intellectual
with only the most perfunctory sign of inward conflict.

SOURCE : *The New Statesman* (19 January 1935).

## Anon.

## 'A CLASSIC WHICH TIME HAS TAMED' – *THE DUCHESS OF MALFI* (1945)

Of the several revivals in recent years of Webster's 'tragedy of
blood' – each an unavailing attempt to reanimate a classic
which time has tamed – this is the most resolute.

Mr. John Gielgud and his producer, Mr. George Rylands,
indeed the whole of their company, have meant business. Not
much more in the way of staging and acting could well be done
to put us into the frame of mind of the original public for whom
Burbage played Ferdinand. And the reward of all this care and
accomplishment last night was that the audience, though

naturally it could not discard its thwarting modernity, followed all that happened on the stage with a respectful curiosity which rose at times to emotional sympathy and never once descended to misplaced tittering.

Those who know the play and the almost insuperable problems which it sets the present-day producer will not regard such praise as faint. That we do not smile at the heap of corpses on which the final curtain falls implies that the actors have fixed attention with Ferdinand's soul-stricken ravings, with the Cardinal's unequal struggle against implacable fate, and with Bosola's strangely intense remorse – thus flouting Johnson's opinion that the genius of the play comes in and goes out with the Duchess.

It is true, however, that while the Duchess lives in the person of Miss Peggy Ashcroft, the players' adventure seems less perilous than it afterwards becomes. Her wooing of the steward is delightful in its ease and certainty of touch, and her indiscreet gossipings with her husband, her maid, and the open-eared Bosola have the authentic sparkle that happiness assumed as a matter of right may confer. Nor does she fail when she is called upon to communicate the horror of the tortures and to reveal the resistant spirit of the doomed woman. The tortures, 'the mortification by degrees', are perhaps more decorative than horrible. To be anything else would require an apparatus of grisliness which no modern producer can effectively employ, resolute though he may be.

Mr. Gielgud plays Duke Ferdinand less as a Renaissance monster of deadly hate and fiendish cruelty coveting his sister's wealth than as a petulant pervert, a reading to which the text apparently lends itself. But the supreme attraction of the revival is Mr. Cecil Trouncer's superbly vital study of Bosola as a murderer of fortune prematurely aged in the galleys, who appears to look deeply into wickedness with the paradoxical desire of seeing good blossom there. Beside this completely observed character the Cardinal of Mr. Leon Quartermaine and the hero of Mr. Leslie Banks are but sketches, though these sketches do not lack accomplishment.

SOURCE: *The Times* (19 April 1945).

*Stephen Potter*

# THE WHITE DEVIL AT THE
# DUCHESS THEATRE (1947)

The best theatrical spectacles in London are still being provided
by the Great Revivals – but what productions they are! Now,
before memories of Cecil Trouncer as Bosola have faded, there
is a chance to see Robert Helpmann as Flamineo in the *Duchess
of Malfi*'s great twin, *The White Devil*.

The chief praise goes to the producer, Mr. Benthall. Although scenes and characters have been cut, he has given us a
vivid impression of the play. A vision of Webster, revealing by
flashes of lightning, the drama of a playwright who was himself the thunderstorm and tempest of the Jacobean stage.

Webster is produced in terms of Webster. Even the cuts intensify the obscurities of the casually strung plot. Dim figures
converge from nowhere, with the grandeur and the ferocious
good looks of fallen angels, to carry monstrous loads of guilt till
they are themselves murdered. The sadism and sensuality, the
blood and the disembowellings, which might so well be made to
look ridiculous if presented with the amiable equivocation of a
timid producer, seem credibly horrible when we see them presented with something of Webster's own exultation.

The beauty and mystery of the ordinary meant nothing to the
dramatists of Webster's time, nor did its triviality and boredom.
Indeed, even the average Jacobean dramatist is strongest just
where our best are now weakest – at moments of crisis and passion. Humour and moral truths are equally perfunctory, but *The
White Devil*, where the characters are doomed from the moment
they enter, is one long dying speech, and the richest, therefore,
in high poetry.

The great words are admirably delivered, particularly by Miss
Rawlings, who with her return to the stage seems to have shed
a certain English and limiting intensity, to be swept along by
the volleying passions of her part. Mr. Helpmann's voice is not
quite so impressive as his movement, which has the kind of

absolute control one imagines to have been part of the secret of the power of Irving. Nothing could be more eloquent than his slow walk, waiting to pounce; or the horrified contemplation of his right hand, after he has struck the face of the dead duke. The rest of the cast, with the help of Mr. Paul Sheriff's magnificent costumes, fitted the scheme most aptly, particulary Mr. Hugh Griffith as the Cardinal, and the graceful and dignified Mr. Roderick Lovell as Duke Bracciano.

SOURCE : *The New Statesman* (15 March 1947).

## *Jack Landau*

## ELIZABETHAN ART IN A MICKEY SPILLANE SETTING (1955)

...*The White Devil* is the initial individual playwriting effort by Webster and dates from 1610. This was some nine years after *Hamlet* and twenty-one years after *The Spanish Tragedy*, and Webster was carrying on the fine tradition of revenge tragedy, blood-and-thunder drama. Though he is generally considered the greatest writer working during the 'last flowering' of Elizabethan drama, Webster's reputation relies mainly on textbook summaries and T. S. Eliot's 'Notes to *The Waste Land*', which borrows three times from the play. There is an illusion of familiarity about the work. (It is also possible that a lot of people seem to remember *The White Devil* as being something by Hemingway filmed in Africa.) The greatness of the play, however, is not in its position in the history of English drama but in its overpowering theatricality and style, qualities which the work shares with many of its contemporaries – including *Hamlet*, *Macbeth* and *The Changeling*. Like these, it is crowded with characters of a bold, imaginative stamp – newspaper headline figures of the day. The language they speak subtly and imaginatively works toward a unified effect. The music of poetic drama contributes to the action. This, added to an acute sense of the dramatic situation under the pressure of events, gives a rightness and inevitableness to everything that happens.

Revenge is the end. The ingredients are murder, adultery, perjury, rape, the madman's laughter and the widow's tears. The vitality – Rupert Brooke named it 'the foul and indestructible vitality' – of these people intrigued Webster. They live in what might be called an Elizabethan Mickey Spillane world. Webster himself refers to his characters as 'glorious villains', and the lives they lead as 'vain'.

The real interest in *The White Devil* is not Webster's implied moral tone but the dramatic conception of particular scenes. The play is a mine of electric situations, and the greatest problem in producing it is how to contain so many of them in one evening. Critical tradition labels the trial scene as one of the great moments of the English stage. It clearly is; it crackles with bitter irony. The situation involves a corrupt and sanctimonious judge – indeed, a 'bought' court versus the most fabulous beauty of the day; and the charge is adultery and conspiracy to murder. There also is the murder of the Duke, who is poisoned and then, on his deathbed, strangled by hired killers disguised as priests performing the final sacrament. There is a mother, near hysteria over the corpse of a son murdered by his brother, in her last rational moment defending the brother–murderer. There are ghosts and visions and nightmares, and suddenly there is the simple question of an orphan child, 'What do the dead do, uncle? do they eat, / Hear music? . . .' It is a nightmare world like any gangster world. While it lasts, it is fascinating and illuminating to behold.

This nightmare world of *The White Devil* can be looked at in different ways. It can be a Renaissance explosion – vistas of gorgeous fabrics, stone and metal, an orgy of blood-colored hangings, the murders behind the arras. It can be a bare, unyielding world in which these 'glorious villains' stand out, each with a hard cutting edge, a world in which the nightmare is a vision with words – words that involve our imaginations in ways no simple visions can.

The literary value of *The White Devil* is very great, and, from an academic point of view, the play is very penetrating (Webster's imagery – how many graduate theses?). But it was written for the stage, and that's where its greatest impact is. The first production problem was editing the text. I cut the play as carefully and yet as boldly as I could. The uncut play would have run about four and a half hours, much too long for practical considerations, and I also sought to bring it into an intelligible unity. This meant eliminating part of a sub-plot, apparently designed for a spectacular scene in which the corrupt cardinal is elected pope. Other excisions were of a minor order and apparently troubled no one, including a fair sprinkling of Webster scholars in the audience. Most of these were as surprised as the non-scholars at the Webster punch. . . . The decision to be simple, spare, relentlessly concerned with the action of the play and the intelligibility of the words, made all technical and mechanical considerations alarmingly unimportant. . . .

By way of historical note, *The White Devil* was not published until 1612. The original Globe production had not been a success because, according to Webster, 'it was acted, in so dull a time of winter, presented in so open and black a theatre, that it wanted (that which is the only grace and setting out of a tragedy) a full and understanding auditory . . .'. Somewhere the shadow of John Webster must be as happy as we are that the first professional American production of his play had just that at the Phoenix in New York last March.

SOURCE : *Theatre Arts* (August 1955).

## Kenneth Tynan

## A SEA OF COLD SWEAT (1960)

With a rattle of skeletons and a fanfare of maniacal screams, the Stratford-on-Avon company has opened its first London season. *The Duchess of Malfi* (Aldwych) is a play for which exaggerated claims have sometimes been made; as a traumatic experience,

branding the mind with panic, it is not to be compared with
Alfred Hitchcock's grisly masterpiece, *Psycho*, and G. H. Lewes
was right, though turbid in utterance, when he condemned 'the
irredeemable mediocrity of its dramatic evolution of human passion'.

Webster is not concerned with humanity. He is the poet of
bile and brainstorm, the sweet singer of apoplexy; ideally, one
feels, he would have had all his characters drowned in a sea of
cold sweat. His muse drew nourishment from Bedlam, and
might, a few centuries later, have done the same from Belsen.
I picture him plagued with hypochondria, probably homo-
sexual, and consumed by feelings of persecution – an intensely
neurotic mind, in short, at large in the richest, most teeming
vocabulary that any age ever offered to a writer.

One imagines his contemporaries dismissing him as 'that
charnel-house poet', much as we nowadays dub Beckett the
dramatist of the dustbin. And although we cannot call him the
inventor of the sick joke (a field in which Kyd, Marlowe and
Shakespeare were all ahead of him), he certainly rolled back
the frontiers of the new genre – as witness the scene in which
Duke Ferdinand extends a hand for his sister to shake, omitting
to warn her that it has lately been severed from a corpse. In the
whole of Webster's work, scarcely an act is committed that is not
motivated by greed, revenge or sexual rapacity.

Yet his characters die superbly, asserting their selfhood to the
last breath – even the least of them, such as the Duchess's maid,
who expires with a sudden, plaintive cry of : 'I am quick with
child!' Webster's people are most themselves when the knife,
noose or potion is nearest; you might say that his plays come
alive the closer they get to death. *The Duchess of Malfi* is an
intricate tale of the vengeance sought and obtained by two
brothers – one ducal and incestuous, the other ecclesiastical and
more normally lecherous – on their widowed sister, who has
offended by marrying beneath her.

The present production, by Donald McWhinnie, is a forth-
right, noisy affair, played all out for melodrama; effective
enough in its way, but far from the subtle, imaginative interpretation of which I for one went in hopes. Peggy Ashcroft's
Duchess is more ripely moving than her Haymarket performance

of fifteen years ago; but I wished, as I listened to Eric Porter's strangled ranting, that Gielgud were still playing Ferdinand, still imparting the same thrill of finality to the line : 'I will never see thee more.' As Bosola, the private eye with a nose for corruption, Patrick Wymark is properly earthy, if a bit too obviously sly, and Max Adrian plays the Cardinal with enough relish to get anyone drummed out of the Vatican. There are no blatant weaknesses in the cast, and nothing is lacking in the production, save finesse and originality.

SOURCE : *The Observer* (18 December 1960).

# *Benedict Nightingale*

## GAUDY MONSTER (1969)

Up goes the curtain on *The White Devil* at the National, and there, looming from floor to flies, is a wall. It's the kind of wall, rough-hewn from honey-coloured stone, that one might find outside some crumbling Mediterranean villa; but with an insulting difference. This wall has been grossly magnified. Each rectangle is several feet across. It is a wall as it might be perceived by insects or small reptiles : toads, perhaps, or grasshoppers or drones. Individual members of the audience must decide which shrunken *persona* fits them best, and how much or how little they have in common with the various parasites that actually live in the crevices. After all, can *we* claim so much broader horizons, so much deeper a perspective on life than Webster's characters, stuck in their tiny ecology? Might there not even nowadays be ideas, mysteries, analogous to the villa which may or may not exist behind the wall? Frank Dunlop, who directs, hasn't perhaps gone so far as to invoke Plato in his programme note; but he has managed to dig up a relevant, suggestive sentence from Rupert Brooke, of all unlikely substitutes. The characters are 'writhing grubs in an immense night, and that night is without stars or moon'. Their lives are spent recklessly pursuing their various appetites, for power, fame and, especially, sex; beyond which they can only perceive a fearfully finite death.

The designer is Piero Gherardi, well known for his work with Fellini. It's his wall and his costumes that the characters flaunt after they've crept out into the sun. Their bodies consist of lace or down – even the soldiers wear a sort of felt, evoking moths – and, for wings, they have elaborate ruffs. The metaphor lasts the length of the play, as does a special emphasis on sensual contact, insect rubbing insect. 'Nay lower, you shall wear my jewel lower', breathes Derek Godfrey's softly stalking Bracciano as his arms slide down the sinuous, undulating body of Geraldine McEwan's Vittoria; a moment faintly echoed later when Gasparo, kneeling before her, carefully searches her abdomen with his dagger. She dies of cunnilingus, or so it seems; and Edward Woodward's sly, confident Flamineo, who has writhed happily on top of the two lovers, clasping them as they embraced, dies beside her, of fellatio.

All this baroque sexuality seems to me entirely appropriate, consistent with Webster's garish poetry and with his conception of human nature as (mostly) either lecherous or prurient. But there are times when Dunlop goes too far. There may be no reason to object to his strong hints of incestuous attraction between Flamineo and Vittoria, but surely John Moffatt's Cardinal exceeds the demands of text and sub-text alike. Prosecutor in the court scene, a tense, rapt, white-faced figure, he lingers over words like 'whore' and 'Gomorrah', and, fascinated, frustrated, can scarcely control his wandering hands. Earlier he has fingered Bracciano's little son with poorly concealed longing. Now he jerks abruptly and repeatedly towards Vittoria's breasts, galvanised by their electricity. Later still, he's elected Pope, dons a tall, cream, conical hat and manages to look like an erect penis, thus externalising what's been barely covert all along.

Webster's brand of flamboyant perversity isn't easy to handle. Venture too deeply into caricature, push the moral nightmare too far, and you may end with lewd, camp pantomime. This risk hasn't always been avoided; yet there's enough in Dunlop's production to suggest that the National is back in form after its last, disastrous year. Webster's gaudy monster of a play does come to life as a recognisable whole, and it does also produce some superbly theatrical moments : two mimed murders, for instance, executed with grisly, erotic languor. Here, and elsewhere, we're witnessing the abstruse sexual rituals of a destructive sub-species, but one which honest men won't disavow.

SOURCE : *The New Statesman* (21 November 1969).

## Ronald Bryden

# MALFI AS MADHOUSE (1971)

We all know people who, rather than betray any uncertainty of taste, live with as little furniture and decoration as possible, making an aesthetic out of showing no taste at all. I'm beginning to wonder whether this isn't the trouble with the Royal Court's approach to its classical revivals. Peter Gill's production of *The Duchess of Malfi* has all the negative virtues. It's bare, spare, chastely free of flamboyance, exaggeration or 'style' for its own sake. What's missing is any indication of what's meant to be left.

Gill has taken his cue from the scene where the Duchess's tormentors fill her dungeon with lunatics. He's staged the whole play as if in a madhouse : in a bare, institutional void where dejected figures slump in dingy uniforms against a naked brick wall. William Dudley's costumes are all cut from the same monotonous ochre-yellow : a sallower version of the chalk-grey in which Peter Brook's madmen sleepwalked through the *Marat-Sade*. The cast, heaped like apathetic puppets, are summoned one by one to play out their scenes, like entranced voodoo devotees galvanically possessed by their gods.

Well, yes : an interesting idea, but not one to sustain a whole evening. The only justification for Gill's approach would be if it cleared the stage for pure, superlative acting, freeing the audience to concentrate on it as they could in Brook's *Midsummer Night's Dream* or Pinter's *Exiles*. There's not enough in this *Duchess* to redeem the cost in austerity. Its blanket verdict of madness on its principals is used to bypass motivation.

Oliver Cotton's Duke is simply an assemblage of meaningless tics, snarls and arm-flingings. Malcolm Tierney's Cardinal looks well, but manifests neither the towering pride nor incestuous[1] lust which would account for his cruelty. Victor Henry's Bosola suggests that perhaps the idea behind the production was that nothing could account for these people, anyway: that they are random, existential marionettes, jerked by the strings of passion. If so, his performance exposes the dangers of the approach at their fullest. It is virtually blank, an expressionless face signalling total emptiness within.

What's left? Here and there the short scenes between Judy Parfitt's Duchess and Desmond Gill's Antonio display the skilled, subtle naturalism which transfigured the director's Lawrence trilogy. Their wooing is beautifully tender, their parting between their children pathetic and haunted. But the play allows only snatches of such naturalism. It scatters them through a text whose unity is the sick, manic grandeur and sombre floridity of its language. A director may rightly regard these qualities as morbid, and show this in his handling of the play. He can't just leave them out and hope to bring Webster's *Duchess* to life. Its taste may be as horrendous as that of a Victorian funeral. Corrected and chastened, it has no taste at all.

SOURCE: *The Observer* (24 January 1971).

NOTE

1. [Bryden seems to be confusing the Cardinal with Ferdinand.]

*Ronald Bryden*

# BLOOD SOAKED CIRCUS (1971)

I suppose that you could define a pessimist as a man who thinks John Webster's *Duchess of Malfi* a great play; an optimist as one who believes it actable. Clifford Williams's revival of it for the Royal Shakespeare Company at Stratford, their first since the memorable production with Peggy Ashcroft which launched their Aldwych tenancy a decade ago, gives the impression that he approached it as an optimist, but left it a sadder, wiser man.

Either you believe *The Duchess* a profound and truthful statement about the human condition, that evil reigns inexorably and inexplicably at the heart of things. Or else you consider that it can be given a human explanation, traceable through the tangle of ordinary men's mixed motives. In the first case, you can't try to act Webster's tragedy, you can only perform it, turning it into an abstract ballet or poem about cruelty, blood and darkness. This is how most recent productions have tackled it, making its characters puppets who jerk through a dance of death choreographed by the same inscrutable forces that piled bodies like rag dolls in the mass graves of Auschwitz.

It's good to see an attempt to turn it once more into a play for actors : to account for its motorway pile-up of corpses and dismembered limbs in terms of character, as a result of analysable human emotions and errors. The first step towards preventing a recurrence of Auschwitz is to recognise it as the work of men, not devils or metaphysical abstractions. But it has to be said that Williams's attempt is only half successful. He makes admirable sense of the play's good characters, which is to say its victims. Its villains elude him and his cast. The harder they work to present them as people, the less plausible their efforts become.

Probably this is because we've lost the ambivalent Renaissance attitude to greatness as both good and evil, magnificent and dangerous. The great have more blood than ordinary folk, therefore are likelier to spill it. Something of this comes over in Williams's opening image of the Duchess and her brothers, a knot of closely grouped figures in cascading scarlet against the

gloom of a discreet, subfusc court. They are poles in an over-
charged circuit of power whose rupture is bound to produce
lightning. Whatever they feel for one another will be magnified
by their greatness, raised to madness by sheer intensity of being.

So that the Duchess's attempt to find ordinary humanity by
marrying her steward is filled with ambiguities by Webster. The
eye Antonio casts on his mistress is bloodshot; the anger with
which he shields her from her brother's spies in childbirth brings
on a nosebleed. He is over-sanguine, ambitious of sharing her
greatness. In Richard Pasco's performance, these effusions of
blood are simply omens of misfortune. He shrinks from the
Duchess's proposal of marriage with a modesty which verges on
fear, forcing her to lead his nerveless hand to her bosom.

Similarly, Webster's Duchess is never greater than when
laying her state aside and baring her neck for her stranglers.
'I am Duchess of Malfi still' : it is part of her pride to go on her
knees to enter the low door of heaven. Judi Dench gives the
play's most famous line a new, wondering reading, turning it
almost into a question. Is she still the Duchess, and if so must
she not shed what remains of her greatness to perfect the
ordinary mortality she sought by dying?

All the same theirs are the production's most satisfying performances, hanging together as strong, coherent characterisa-
tions. Pasco's Antonio, troubled, uneasy and loving, manages the
difficult task of conveying virtue with charm and no ounce of
complacency. He's one of the few actors who can bring to
ordinariness the scale of heroism. And Judi Dench's Duchess is
one of her finest achievements, adding a commanding decisive-
ness to the glow of young matronhood she gave her Hermione
in *The Winter's Tale*. The glory of her talent is lucidity.
Emotion shines through her acting as directly as meaning
through her delivery of the lines. As she listens to Bosola
craftily praising her steward, tears come to her eyes as naturally
as dew.

The difficulty is applying this kind of acting to her torturers.
Michael Williams tries to suggest an inner history of incestuous
passion for his sister in Ferdinand's jealousy, but the result is
to diminish the horror of his collapse into madness. Geoffrey
Hutchings's bluff opportunist evades the issue of Bosola's

motives. Emrys James's Cardinal is better; but it succeeds by making no attempt at explanation. It's a technically stylish portrayal of conventional villainy, cold, ferret-faced but empty.

Perhaps the production comes closest to success when it abandons realism for waxwork dumbshows of heaped bodies and collapsed limbs, and the shadowy dungeon image of Farrah's sets. Webster's tragedy doesn't really attempt to understand evil. It only celebrates it, like the Chamber of Horrors at Tussaud's, as something to confront and bear with the Duchess, therapeutic only as nightmare. As an optimist, I'm grateful for the acting of Pasco and Judi Dench, some of the best we've seen at Stratford this season; but I have to admit that the performance-groups who treat the play simply as a circus of evil are right.

SOURCE : *The Observer* (18 July 1971).

# SELECT BIBLIOGRAPHY

EDITIONS

The best modern-spelling editions are by Elizabeth M. Brennan in the New Mermaids series (*The White Devil*, London, 1966; *The Duchess of Malfi*, London, 1964) and John Russell Brown in the Revels Plays (*The White Devil*, London, 1960; *The Duchess of Malfi*, London, 1964). The standard edition of Webster is F. L. Lucas, *The Complete Works of John Webster*, 4 vols (London, 1927).

BOOKS AND ARTICLES

Gunnar Boklund, *The Sources of The White Devil* (Uppsala, 1957).

Gunnar Boklund, '*The Duchess of Malfi*: Sources, Themes, Characters (Cambridge, Mass., 1962).

M. C. Bradbrook, 'Two Notes upon Webster', *Modern Language Review*, XLII (1947) 281–94.

Elizabeth M. Brennan, 'The Relationship between Brother and Sister in the Plays of John Webster', *Modern Language Review*, LVIII (1963) 488–94.

C. W. Davies, 'The Structure of *The Duchess of Malfi*: An Approach', *English*, XII (1958) 89–93.

W. A. Edwards, 'John Webster', *Scrutiny*, II (1933) 12–23.

Inga-Stina Ekeblad, 'The "Impure Art" of John Webster', *Review of English Studies*, IX (1958) 253–67.

T. S. Eliot, '*The Duchess of Malfi* at the Lyric: and Poetic Drama', *Art and Letters*, III (1920) 36–9.

T. S. Eliot, '*The Duchess of Malfy*', *The Listener*, XXVI (18 December 1941) 825–6.

William Empson, 'Mine Eyes Dazzle', *Essays in Criticism*, XIV (1964) 80–6.

Charles R. Forker, 'Love, Death, and Fame: The Grotesque Tragedy of John Webster', *Anglia*, LXXXXI (1973) 194–218.

Louis D. Giannetti, 'A Contemporary View of *The Duchess of Malfi*', *Comparative Drama*, III (1969–70) 297–307.

D. C. Gunby, *Webster: The White Devil* (London, 1971).

G. K. Hunter and S. K. Hunter (eds), *John Webster: A Critical Anthology* (Harmondsworth, 1969).

Clifford Leech, *John Webster: A Critical Study* (London, 1951).

Clifford Leech, *Webster: The Duchess of Malfi* (London, 1963).

Brian Morris (ed.), *John Webster: A Critical Symposium* (London, 1970).

J. R. Mulryne, '*The White Devil* and *The Duchess of Malfi*', *Stratford-upon-Avon Studies I: Jacobean Theatre* (London, 1960) pp. 201–25.

Robert Ornstein, *The Moral Vision of Jacobean Tragedy* (Madison, 1960).

Hereward T. Price, 'The Function of Imagery in Webster', *P.M.L.A.*, LXX (1955) 717–39.

Moody E. Prior, *The Language of Tragedy* (New York, 1947).

Christopher Ricks, 'The Trouble with Harry', *Times Literary Supplement* (26 July 1974) 790–1.

George Rylands and Charles Williams, 'Introduction' to *The Duchess of Malfi* (London, 1945) pp. v–xxii.

James Smith, 'The Tragedy of Blood', *Scrutiny*, VIII (1939) 265–80.

P. F. Vernon, 'The Duchess of Malfi's Guilt', *Notes and Queries*, X (1963) 335–8.

## BIBLIOGRAPHIC ADDENDUM 1984

Nicholas Brooke, *Horrid Laughter in Jacobean Tragedy* (London, 1979).

Anders Dallby, *The Anatomy of Evil: A Study of John Webster's 'The White Devil'* (Lund, 1974).

Jacqueline Pearson, *Tragedy and Tragicomedy in the Plays of John Webster* (Manchester, 1980).

Joyce E. Peterson, *Curs'd Example: 'The Duchess of Malfi' and Commercial Tragedy* (London, 1978).

# NOTES ON CONTRIBUTORS

RALPH BERRY. Professor of English at the University of Manitoba; author of *Shakespeare's Comedies: Explorations in Form.*

TRAVIS BOGARD. Professor of English at the University of California at Berkeley; co-editor of *Modern Drama: Essays in Criticism* and author of *Contour in Time: The Plays of Eugene O'Neill.*

FREDSON BOWERS. Professor of English at the University of Virginia; distinguished bibliographer and textual critic. His works include *Principles of Bibliographical Description* and major editions of Dekker and Marlowe.

JOHN RUSSELL BROWN. Professor of English at the University of Sussex and Associate Director of the National Theatre; has published numerous books on Shakespearean and modern drama.

RONALD BRYDEN. Formerly theatre critic of *The Observer*; has published a collection of reviews and essays entitled *The Unfinished Hero.*

JAMES L. CALDERWOOD. Associate Professor of English at the University of California at Irvine; author of *Shakespearean Metadrama* and numerous articles on Shakespeare.

LORD DAVID CECIL. Goldsmiths' Professor of English Literature at Oxford until 1969; has published numerous works of criticism and biography, the most recent being *The Cecils of Hatfield House.*

UNA ELLIS-FERMOR (1894–1958). Was Professor of English at Bedford College, London; her publications include works of drama criticism, editions of plays by Marlowe and Greville, and translations of plays by Ibsen.

E. M. FORSTER (1879–1970). Major novelist, essayist, short-story writer, and critic. He began a lifelong connection with Cambridge when he went up to King's College as an undergraduate in 1897.

NORTHROP FRYE. Professor of English at the University of Toronto; has published books and essays on Shakespeare, Milton, and Blake, and studies of Romanticism and the social context of literature.

ROMA GILL. Senior Lecturer in English at the University of Sheffield. She has published various essays on Elizabethan and Jacobean poets and dramatists, but is particularly concerned with the editing of Marlowe.

IAN JACK. Lecturer in English at the University of Cambridge. His works include *Augustan Satire, Keats and the Mirror of Art*, vol. X in *The Oxford History of English Literature*, and an edition of Browning's poems.

JACK LANDAU (d. 1966). American theatre producer; co-director of the American Shakespeare Festival Theatre from 1956 to 1962. He produced *The Duchess of Malfi* at the Phoenix Theatre, New York, in 1957, and *The White Devil* at the Circle in 1965.

J. W. LEVER. Professor of English at Simon Fraser University; author of *The Elizabethan Love Sonnet* and editor of *Measure for Measure* and *The Rape of Lucrece*.

F. L. LUCAS (1894–1967). Was Reader in English at the University of Cambridge; a prolific author of poetry, plays, short stories, translations from French and Classical literature, as well as literary and dramatic criticism.

HERBERT J. MULLER. Professor of English at the University of Indiana. Besides *Modern Fiction* and *The Spirit of Tragedy* he has published many books on political, historical, and sociological subjects.

PETER B. MURRAY. Professor of English at Macalester College, Minnesota; author of *A Study of Cyril Tourneur* and *Thomas Kyd*.

BENEDICT NIGHTINGALE. Journalist and drama critic; author of *Charities*, a study of charitable institutions in Britain.

STEPHEN POTTER (1900–69). Was Lecturer in English at London University until 1938, then writer–producer for the B.B.C., literary journalist and reviewer, and professional author; best known for such works as *Gamesmanship* and *One-Upmanship*, though he also wrote *D. H. Lawrence: A First Study*, and edited the Nonesuch *Coleridge*.

IRVING RIBNER. Professor of English at the State University of New York at Stony Brook; has published several books on Shakespeare and edited plays by Marlowe, Shakespeare, and Tourneur.

KENNETH TYNAN. Drama critic, author, and journalist; has edited Farquhar's *The Recruiting Officer* and published collections of theatre criticism in *He that Plays the King*, *Curtains*, and *Tynan Right and Left*.

# INDEX

Adams, T. 179
Adrian, Max (as Cardinal) 237
Aesop 54
Akrigg, G. P. V. 211 n.
Alexander, William 85
AMBASSADORS 33, 122, 160, 193, 199
ANTONELLI 157, 168
ANTONIO 14–15, 31, 38–40, 42, 50, 55–6, 62–3, 67–8, 106–10, 114, 129–30, 134–7, 140–2, 165, 167–74, 181–3, 185–6, 188 n., 200–3, 205–6, 208–10, 211 n., 212 n., 215–16, 224–5, 240, 242
*Appius and Virginia* 44
Archer, William 19–20, 22, 27 n., 45–9
*Arden of Faversham* 85
Aristotle 103
Ascham, Roger 50
Ashcroft, Dame Peggy (as Duchess) 231, 236–7, 241
Aubrey, John (*Brief Lives*) 163

Bandello, Matteo 32, 51, 203
Banks, Leslie (as Antonio) 231
Bateson, F. W. 27 n.
Beaumont, Francis 23, 54, 86
Beckett, Samuel 236
Benthall, Michael 232
Bentley, G. E. 163 n.
Berry, Ralph 26, 213–22
Bland, Joyce (as Duchess) 230
Bogard, Travis 12, 25, 69–71, 130, 142 n., 143 n., 187 n., 188 n.
Boklund, Gunnar 150, 163 n., 174, 188 n., 210 n.

Borgia 42
BOSOLA 15, 20, 40–3, 46–53, 55–6, 62–3, 67, 69, 72, 80–1, 104–5, 114–16, 117 n., 127, 129–41, 165–7, 172–6, 180–1, 183–6, 187 n., 189 n., 200–2, 206–9, 213, 215–18, 221, 224–5, 227, 230–2, 237, 240, 242–3
Bowers, Fredson 26, 62–5
Boyer, C. V. 51–3
BRACCIANO 13–14, 31, 37, 55–6, 67, 78–80, 86–91, 94–7, 99, 121, 124–7, 146–9, 151–3, 156–62, 190–200, 205–7, 210 n., 214, 217, 228, 233, 238
Bradbrook, M. C. 24, 28 n., 102 n., 142 n., 151, 157, 214, 221 n.
Britten, Benjamin (*War Requiem*) 161
Brook, Peter 239
Brooke, Rupert 13–14, 21, 53–7, 143 n., 217, 222 n., 234, 237–8
Brown, John Russell 26, 28 n., 84–102, 143 n., 155, 158, 163 n., 192, 200, 210 n., 211 n.
Bryden, Ronald 27 n., 239–43
Burbage, Richard (as Ferdinand) 47, 230
Burckhardt, Jakob 50
Burton, Robert (*The Anatomy of Melancholy*) 187 n.

Caesar 41–2
Calderwood, James L. 25–6, 103–17, 187 n., 212 n.
Calvinism 25, 66, 143 n.

CAMILLO 14, 86, 88, 91, 121,
125–6, 128, 146, 150–1,
187 n., 189 n., 193–4, 196–7,
214
CARDINAL (*The Duchess of Malfi*)
20, 39, 47, 50–2, 55, 63, 67–8,
80–1, 105, 110–13, 130, 133–4,
136, 138–40, 164–7, 169–70, 172,
174–5, 178, 185–6, 187 n.,
200–3, 205, 207–9, 211 n., 213,
225, 231, 237, 240
CARIOLA 15, 23, 46, 50, 107,
110, 131–2, 166, 172, 181, 205,
216–17, 236
Carr, Robert 200
Castiglione, Baldassare 79
CASTRUCHIO 174, 187 n.
Catiline 41–2
Cecil, Lord David 25, 66–8,
143 n., 189 n.
Cecil, Robert, Earl of Salisbury
200
Chapman, George 47, 84–5,
119–20, 203, 206; *Bussy D'Ambois*
203, 207; the Guise 203, 207;
Monsieur 203, 207; Montsurry
207; *The Widow's Tears* 211 n.
*Characters* (by T. Overbury,
additions by Webster) 171
CHILDREN (of Duchess) 14–15,
31, 46, 48 n., 50, 68, 129, 133,
136, 138, 141, 165, 172–4, 176,
183, 188 n., 206, 210, 212 n.,
240
Christ 72, 173, 179–80, 199
Clemen, Wolfgang 220
Coleridge, Samuel Taylor 82
CORNELIA 67, 87–9, 96–7, 99,
123–4, 126, 136, 152, 157–8,
161–2, 193–4, 197–8, 205
Cotton, Oliver (as Ferdinand)
240

Davenant, William 155
Dekker, Thomas 35, 47, 86,
118, 155; Simon Eyre (*The
Shoemakers' Holiday*) 149

DELIO 15, 50, 69, 126, 129, 136,
167–9, 186, 201, 208, 210
Dench, Judi (as Duchess) 242–3
Dent, R. W. 146, 163 n.
*Devil's Law-Case, The* 219, 221
Donne, John 21–4, 179–80,
187 n.; *The Second Anniversary*
144 n.; *Sermons* 180, 187 n.;
'To Sir Henry Wotton' 179
DUCHESS OF MALFI 14–16, 23,
26, 31–3, 35–8, 40, 44, 46,
50–3, 56, 62–3, 66–8, 72–3, 77,
82, 104–16, 126–7, 129–41,
165–80, 182–6, 187 n., 188 n.,
200–9, 211 n., 212 n., 215–18,
222 n., 224–5, 230–1, 236, 240–2
Dudley, William 239
Dunlop, Frank 237–8
Dyce, Alexander 16, 37–8

Edwards, W. A. 24, 28 n.,
103–4, 142 n., 143 n.
Ekeblad, Inga-Stina 162, 188 n.,
211 n.
Eliot, T. S. 20–4, 27 n., 28 n.,
119, 146, 163 n., 192, 210 n.,
233; *The Waste Land* 233;
*Whispers of Immortality* 24
Ellis-Fermor, Una M. 58–61,
143 n., 187 n.
Emslie, McDonald 103
Euripides 219; *Alcestis* 72;
Phaedra 211 n.
*Exiles* (James Joyce) 239

FERDINAND 13, 15, 18–19, 26,
28 n., 37, 39, 43, 47, 49, 51–2,
59–61, 63, 67–8, 81–2, 104–7,
110–16, 117 n., 130, 132–4,
138–40, 164–5, 167–71, 174–6,
178, 183–6, 187 n., 189 n.,
200–3, 205, 207–9, 211 n.,
212 n., 215–16, 218, 221, 225,
230–1, 236–7, 240
Fernald, John 229
Fieler, F. B. 188 n.
Fitzgeffrey, Henry 13, 30

FLAMINEO 13, 28 n., 41–2, 56, 59, 64–5, 67, 77–80, 84–92, 94–5, 97–101, 125–9, 131–2, 141, 143 n., 151, 153–4, 156–7, 161, 167–8, 187 n., 190–1, 193–200, 209, 211 n., 214, 217–18, 227, 232, 238
Fletcher, John 23, 54, 62, 86; *The Maid's Tragedy* 155; Evadne 155
Ford, John 62, 203, 229; *'Tis Pity She's a Whore* 229
Forster, E. M. 27, 28 n., 226–9; *Howard's End* 145; *A Passage to India* 145
FRANCISCO 13, 28 n., 55, 59–60, 65, 80, 86–8, 94–6, 100, 102 n., 122–5, 147–8, 187 n., 193–5, 199–200, 206, 210, 210 n., 214
Frye, Northrop 72–3
Fugger 190–1

Galileo 32
Galsworthy, John 22
GASPARO 31, 36, 157, 199, 238
Gherardi, Piero 238
Gielgud, Sir John (as Ferdinand) 230–1, 237
Gill, Desmond (as Antonio) 240
Gill, Peter 239
Gill, Roma 26, 145–63
GIOVANNI 27, 44, 59–60, 61 n., 65, 78, 84, 87, 101, 124, 167–8, 193, 195, 210
God 25, 66, 68, 70, 82, 127, 165, 167, 169, 175–6, 178, 180–1, 192, 204
Godfrey, Derek (as Bracciano) 238
*Gorboduc* 162
Gosse, Edmund 11, 19
Goulart, Simon 32
Graham, Roy (as Bosola) 230
Griffith, Hugh (as Monticelso) 233

Hardy, Thomas 72; Tess 72

Hazlitt, William 11, 16, 35–7, 227
Heilman, Robert B. 117 n.
Helpmann, Robert (as Flamineo) 232–3
Hemingway, Ernest 233
Henry, Victor (as Bosola) 240
Henslowe, Philip 145
Herod 174
Heselwood, Tom 225
Heywood, Thomas 47, 118, 120; *A Woman Killed with Kindness* 85
Hitchcock, Alfred 236; *Psycho* 236
H. M. (*Blackwood's Magazine*) 11, 16–17, 34–5
Hooker, Richard 120
Hopper, V. F. 173, 188 n.,
Horne, R. H. 18
Hunter, G. K. 27 n.
Hunter, S. K. 27 n.
Hutchings, Geoffrey (as Bosola) 242–3

Ibsen, Henrik 19; *Hedda Gabler* 162; Judge Brack 28 n.
Irving, Henry 233
ISABELLA 14, 67, 88, 95–7, 99, 121, 123–5, 136, 147–8, 155–6, 161–2, 187 n., 193–4, 210 n., 214
Iscariot, Judas 42, 162

Jack, Ian 11, 24–5, 76–83, 103–4, 142 n., 192, 210 n., 218, 222 n.
James I 26, 200–1
James, Emrys (as Cardinal) 243
James, Henry 76
*Job* 177–8; Job 174–5, 177, 188 n.
Johnson, Samuel 225, 231; *Irene* 225
Jonson, Ben 17, 47, 86, 149; *Sejanus* 195, 200, 212 n.; Sejanus 200
JULIA 14, 50, 130, 134–6, 138–9, 165, 167, 172–3, 181–2, 187 n., 225

Kingsley, Charles   17–18, 39–40
Knight, G. Wilson   28 n., 220
Kyd, Thomas   22, 62–5, 145,
   236; *The Spanish Tragedy*   162,
   233; Bel-Imperia   155;
   Lorenzo   149; Pedringano   64

Lahey, G. B.   173, 188 n.
Lamb, Charles   16, 19, 22, 33,
   37, 49, 80
Landau, Jack   27, 233–5
La Rochefoucauld, François duc
   de   58
Laurie, John (as Ferdinand)   230
Layman, B. J.   143 n.
Lee, Vernon   49
Leech, Clifford   104–5, 119, 150,
   188 n., 211 n., 222 n.
Lever, J. W.   20, 26, 190–212
Lewes, G. H.   18, 236
LODOVICO   13, 31, 36, 59, 65,
   80, 86–8, 101, 102 n., 147–8,
   156–7, 167, 187 n., 190–1, 193,
   197–9, 201, 217
Lorrique (Henry Chettle's
   *Hoffman*)   62, 64
Lovell, Roderick (as Bracciano)
   233
Lucas, F. L.   21, 28 n., 57–8,
   104, 119, 131, 142 n., 187 n.,
   188 n.

Macaulay, Thomas Babbington
   49
McEwan, Geraldine (as Vittoria)
   238
McWhinnie, Donald   236
MADMEN   19, 26, 33, 40, 45, 68,
   115, 132, 164, 176, 188 n., 208,
   224, 230, 239
MALATESTE   53, 186
*Marat–Sade* (Peter Weiss)   239
MARCELLO   67, 87, 89, 96, 99,
   123–4, 126, 128, 136, 158,
   193–4
Marlowe, Christopher   62–5,
   203, 236; *Dr Faustus*   158

Marston, John   62, 86, 118, 192;
   *The Fawn*   86; *The Insatiate
   Countess*   84; *The Malcontent*   53,
   86; Malevole   209; *The Scourge
   of Villainy*   163 n.
Mary, Virgin   173–4
Massinger, Philip   17, 62, 146,
   159, 163 n.; *The Fatal Dowry*
   159; Charalois   159; *The
   Renegado*   155; Donusa   155
Medici   41
Middleton, Thomas   22, 118, 145,
   203; *The Changeling* (with
   Rowley)   233; *Women Beware
   Women*   84; Bianca   154–5
Moffatt, John (as Monticelso)   238
MONTICELSO   37, 80, 86–7, 100,
   102 n., 122–3, 147, 152, 159–60,
   187 n., 193–5, 198, 200, 211 n.,
   214, 228–9, 233, 235, 238
Muller, Herbert J.   71
Mulryne, J. R.   27 n.
Murray, Peter B.   25, 164–89

Napoleon   41–2
Nightingale, Benedict   237–9

OLD WOMAN   172–4
Ornstein, Robert   142 n., 189 n.

Painter, William (*The Palace of
   Pleasure*)   136, 171, 188 n.,
   203–4, 211 n.
Parfitt, Judy (as Duchess)   240
Pasco, Richard (as Antonio)
   242–3
PESCARA   129, 136
PILGRIMS   165
Pinter, Harold   239
Plato   237
Poe, Edgar Allan   26
Poel, William   19–20, 27 n.,
   48–51
Porter, Eric (as Ferdinand)   237
Potter, Stephen   27, 232–3
Price, Hereward T.   102 n.,
   143 n., 144 n.

Prior, Moody E.   143 n., 144 n.,
   189 n.
Prometheus   56

Quartermaine, Leon (as Cardinal)
   231

Racine, Jean (*Athalie*)   72
Rawlings, Margaret (as Vittoria)
   232
Reinhalter, Sister B.   187 n.
Reynolds, J. (*The Triumph of God's
   Revenge*)   40
Ribner, Irving   25, 118–44,
   189 n.
Rowley, William   118, 203
Rylands, George   230

Saintsbury, George   18
Salingar, L. G.   24, 27 n., 29 n.
Satan   164–5, 175, 179, 186
Saunders, J. W.   212 n.
Schanzer, E.   212 n.
*Secunda Pastorum, The*   162
Seneca   72, 77–8, 118, 207;
   *Octavia*   72
Seymour, William   201
Shakespeare, William   11–12,
   16–17, 22, 36, 39, 41, 47, 52, 54,
   57, 60–1, 63, 69, 80, 82, 84,
   103, 117 n., 119–20, 161, 203,
   213, 218, 236; *Antony and
   Cleopatra*   85, 194, 210 n.;
   Antony   210 n.; Caesar   210 n.;
   Enobarbus   219; Octavia   194,
   210 n.; *Coriolanus*   61 n.;
   Marcus   61 n.; *Cymbeline*   72,
   117 n.; Iachimo   84; *Hamlet*
   53, 60, 63, 65, 83 n., 103, 194,
   233; Hamlet   70–1, 86, 133;
   Ophelia   102 n., 158, 194;
   *Henry IV*   85; *Henry V*   213;
   *King John*   85; *King Lear*   14,
   39, 41, 61 n., 83 n.; Cordelia
   154; Edmund   80, 127; Fool
   60; Lear   60; *Macbeth*   60,

83 n., 85, 220, 233; *Measure for
   Measure*   81; Duke Vincentio
   81; *A Midsummer Night's Dream*
   239; *Othello*   39, 41, 117 n.;
   Iago   80, 82, 84, 127; Othello
   218; *Richard II*   85; *Richard III*
   39, 80; *The Tempest*   145;
   *Troilus and Cressida*   109, 161;
   Thersites   219; *The Winter's
   Tale*   61 n., 145, 242; Hermione
   72, 242; Mamillius   61 n.
Sharpham, Edward   86; *Cupid's
   Whirligig*   86; *The Fleer*   86
Shaw, George Bernard   19, 27 n.
Sheppard, Samuel (*Epigrams
   Theological, Philosophical, and
   Romantick*)   13
Sheriff, Paul   233
Siegel, Paul   212 n.
Smith, James   102 n., 153–4,
   157–8
Sophocles   219;
   Agamemnon   219;
   Clytemnestra   219
Spillane, Mickey   233–4
Spurgeon, Caroline   220
Stevenson, Robert Louis   51
Stoll, E. E.   53 n., 65 n., 187 n.
Stuart, Lady Arabella   201
Swinburne, A. C.   16, 22, 41–3,
   45, 64
Symonds, John Addington   19, 21,
   43–5

Taine, Hippolyte   28 n.
Tasso, Torquato   32, 174;
   *Jerusalem Liberated*   174
Tate, Nahum   14, 28; *Injur'd
   Love: or, The Cruel Husband*   14
Taylor, Jeremy (*Holy Living*)
   211 n.
Theobald, Lewis   14–15, 28,
   31–2; *The Fatal Secret*   14, 31–2
Theophrastus   103, 171
Tierney, Malcolm (as Cardinal)
   240
Tillyard, E. M. W.   76

Tourneur, Cyril   22, 27 n., 28 n.,
   43, 45, 62, 71, 86, 118–20, 192;
   *The Revenger's Tragedy*   65, 125,
   149–50, 194; Castiza   194;
   Vindice   132–3, 148, 194, 209
Trouncer, Cecil (as Bosola)   231–2
Tussaud, Madame   18, 27 n., 243
Tynan, Kenneth   235–7

Vega, Lope de   32
Vernon, P. F.   187 n.
VITTORIA   13–14, 16, 26, 33–4,
   36–7, 39, 44, 55–6, 59, 64–5, 67,
   78–80, 84–99, 101, 113, 121–7,
   129, 143 n., 147–8, 150–62,
   167–9, 172, 187 n., 190–7, 199–
   200, 205–7, 214, 227–8, 238
Wadsworth, F. W.   188 n.,
   222 n.

Watson, William   11, 17–18
Wells, Henry W.   143 n.
Wendell, Barrett   21, 28 n.
Wilkinson, Norman   225
Williams, Clifford   241
Williams, Michael (as Ferdinand)
   242
Wilson, F. P.   143 n.
Winifred, St   165, 174
Woelfflin, H.   222 n.
Woodward, Edward (as Flamineo)
   238
Wordsworth, William   34
Wright, Abraham   13, 31
Wymark, Patrick (as Bosola)   237

ZANCHE   79, 88–9, 97, 187 n.,
   196–7, 228